THE COMMUNICATION
OF
IDEAS

RELIGION AND CIVILIZATION SERIES

RELIGION AND THE WORLD ORDER

WORLD ORDER: ITS INTELLECTUAL AND CULTURAL FOUNDATIONS

FOUNDATIONS OF DEMOCRACY

WELLSPRINGS OF THE AMERICAN SPIRIT

F. Ernest Johnson, *Editor*

GROUP RELATIONS AND GROUP ANTAGONISMS

CIVILIZATION AND GROUP RELATIONSHIPS

UNITY AND DIFFERENCE IN AMERICAN LIFE

R. M. MacIver, *Editor*

LABOR'S RELATION TO CHURCH AND COMMUNITY

Liston Pope, *Editor*

GENERAL EDITORIAL BOARD

Louis Finkelstein

F. Ernest Johnson   R. M. MacIver

George N. Shuster

RELIGION AND CIVILIZATION SERIES

THE COMMUNICATION
OF
IDEAS

A series of addresses

EDITED BY

Lyman Bryson

COOPER SQUARE PUBLISHERS, INC.

New York   1964

HM258
.I5
1964

FOREWORD

From November, 1946, through February, 1947, the Institute for Religious and Social Studies, a graduate school conducted with the cooperation of Catholic, Jewish and Protestant scholars, at the Jewish Theological Seminary of America in New York City, presented a course on "The Problems of the Communication of Ideas." This volume is based principally on the lectures in that series which was moderated by the editor.

TABLE OF CONTENTS

I. Problems of Communication   *Lyman Bryson*   1

II. Some Cultural Approaches to Communication Problems
         Margaret Mead   9

III. Classic Theories of Communication   *Whitney J. Oates*   27

IV. The Structure and Function of Communication in Society
         Harold D. Lasswell   37

V. Speech and Personality   *Wendell Johnson*   53

VI. The Psychologist's Contribution to the Communication
    of Ideas   *Irving Lorge*   79

VII. Mass Communication, Popular Taste and Organized
    Social Action   *Paul F. Lazarsfeld and
         Robert K. Merton*   95

VIII. Communication and the Arts   *Lennox Grey*   119

IX. Communication in Practical Affairs   *Leo Nejelski*   143

X. Science and Writing   *James Mitchell Clarke*   155

XI. Radio   *Charles A. Siepmann*   177

XII. Problems of Freedom   *Robert D. Leigh*   197

XIII. A Case History in Cross-National Communications
         Margaret Mead   209

XIV. Leadership, Science, and Policy   *Joseph M. Goldsen*   231

XV. Attention Structure and Social Structure
         Harold D. Lasswell   243

XVI. Popular Art   *Lyman Bryson*   277

CONTRIBUTORS TO "THE COMMUNICATION OF IDEAS"   287

INDEX   289

I

PROBLEMS OF COMMUNICATION

BY

LYMAN BRYSON

Communications is a term that covers a vast and varied field of human action. The mere uttered sounds, the audible symbols that make some difference in the environment of a listener and thus, as we say, convey a meaning, are in themselves difficult phenomena. When these audible symbols are represented by visual symbols such as the characters of a written language, complications arise. They are both psychological and sociological and they are hard to understand. In spite of that, of course, we go on in naïve self-assurance doing what is necessary to live in community; we communicate. By the invention of printing, the complications were multiplied and now we have what we call mass media to enrich our lives and burden us with new problems; talking pictures, cheap print, and broadcasting.

In this series of essays, first delivered in part as lectures, the authorities summoned to the task have undertaken to describe social or psychological behavior in terms of the factors of communication involved and they have asked some searching questions. The table of contents shows that the problems tackled by different contributors are widely different and it will show also that there is no systematic outline of a theory of communications. We tried to put things in logical relation but we had to keep within our various limits of competence and the noticeable disproportions in our arrangement of observation and hypothesis will chiefly go to show that nearly every thoughtful student of human behavior today, no matter what he calls his field, is likely to find that something which he will have to call "communication" obtrudes itself in the complex. Communication makes community possible and community is both the location of our interest and the basic concept of our present thinking.

Our concern with communication is in some ways an educational reversion; we are going back to an interest in language which once made up, almost entirely, the subject matter of formal education and the critical content of culture. Education was mostly in Latin and Greek. These two ancient languages and literatures made the gentlemen and the gentlemen made the country and if we think that this was mere snobbishness and waste of time we ought to be reminded of the material and intellectual achievements of the nineteenth century. It is true, of course, that European literature is full of rebellion against the process of teaching languages and languages alone but literature always has been, and one suspects always will be, full of rebellion against the schools. The geniuses are generally rebels.

Charles Darwin records that he was bored because there was nothing but Latin and Greek in his school and others were doubtless as unhappy as he. But, if we can judge by what happened afterwards, this linguistic obsession did not prevent a great many able men from growing up. A preoccupation with languages would not do as education for today, but it still may be true that we have missed something very important by turning away from languages and that our present interest in "communication" is a result of our unconscious realization of that mistake. This is made the more likely by recollecting that, in those days, the best teachers as well as the worst used languages as a vehicle. A good teacher can make the formal beauties and wisdom of a dead language into great educational experience.

Our return to communication is more than this. It is also a recognition, in new fields, of the dominant intellectual tendency of our time, which is to think more of processes and less of things. Community is made up of things and processes both. But the process of communication, that web of signals and expectations and understandings that makes living together possible, has not had much attention as a factor in everyday reality, nor have we considered sufficiently the extent to which the process controls the institutions and the other things that are more easily observed. Moreover, the process of communication, in its private manifestations, within the single mind, is a controlling factor in personality. Social living is impossible unless people can exchange and share meanings and, as Wendell Johnson shows in his chapter in this book, the organization of a single personality is also impossible unless the person can play his part in communicating.

The process is central to our personal integration and our social existence and that explains why our own culturally acquired form of communication should seem to us so natural. We make all kinds of suppositions about the way "human beings" will naturally exchange meanings. The chapters by Margaret Mead, covering both primitive and complicated situations, show how naïve these suppositions may be. By looking at the speech manners and the responses of the Arapesh in New Guinea and the analogous behavior of visiting British lecturers in the United States, with some detachment, we can better understand our own.

It is our good fortune that the renewed concern with the process of talking and writing and making signs to each other should coincide with the really new developments in the methods of describing social behavior, the new kinds of anthropology and sociology and psychology that are giving us some scientific and relativistic knowledge of ourselves as human beings. These new methods and insights have made us more cautious in saying that we "understand" any single language but have also helped us to understand much more of language in general. We can see that symbolic systems do shape and determine and color thought; that makes us go slow in translating from one system to another. But it makes it possible for us to see that symbol habits, like all other habits, are components of personalities, and also the bonds that unite some persons in communal groups, shutting out others, controlling social relationships.

This knowledge of unity and difference among persons caused by, or at least expressed in, language habits is desperately needed now in a world that has been made physically one, thrown together in a physical juxtaposition, without preceding sympathy or even tolerance. We are one world in the sense that a huddle of ship-wrecked people may be in one boat. There has not been, up to now, much assurance that the boat will have a navigation system or a navigator; we are all one in the sense that anybody who rocks the boat may destroy us all. How much of the trouble among nations and political systems could be reduced by better knowledge of communication, we do not know. We can at least apply the new insights to see better what is going on.

There is small comfort, however, in easily conceived schemes of cultural exchange, of communication between "peoples," or between the elite of one country with either the elite or the people of another. It is true, as will be said in these discussions, that we now have, for the first time in history, the machines for conveying thought to wide mass audiences from single diffusion points. If there were a prophet now, he could get a much greater hearing than any prophet ever got before in his own time *provided,* of course, that the psychological as well as the mechanical obstacles between him and his hearers or readers could be surmounted.

I know a poet who believes that there is now a chance for the poets of one country to speak to the people of others and break across the barriers with friendliness. It would be too rude perhaps to remark that there are no poets now who speak to any large numbers of people with friendly messages even inside their own cultures. Why should we count on their succeeding better with the peasants of Yugoslavia or the ryots of Pakistan than they do with the store-keepers of Dakota? The truth is that there is little historical reason for thinking that cultural exchange will do the work that needs to be done unless we can find new ways of exchanging and new things to hand across. The cultural exchanges between Germans and French, in books, pictures, music, philosophies and science, were incessant and copious for two hundred years. So also were the wars between their governments. Unless cultural exchange can somehow manage to keep peoples peacefully disposed toward each other, what-ever their governments want to do, cultural exchange will not be communication for world community.

However, to find out how to do these things is a proper quest for our time and it may be one contribution to the solution of our most urgent problem, immediate peace. In the meantime, it seems likely that it is also urgent not to frustrate what little progress is promised in this quest by allowing vast expectations to be built up, especially in the American public mind. Our people have ruined other great ideas by expecting too much and selling out too soon.

In this urgent problem and in long term questions that will be urgent from time to time in the future, we need to remember that communication between persons of different cultures is not so complete as between persons in the same culture. The failures in the real exchange of meanings between people of different cultures are likely to be understood as differences in intention instead of only differences in symbolic habit.

Between me and my neighbor (my real neighbor, I mean, the man who lives in my actual physical surroundings, not my spiritual brother elsewhere) between me and this man there is something like real communication. The web of habits which is most of me and the pattern of expectations that is his notion of my personality fit together fairly well because there have been many opportunities for us to get used to each other. If we try, however, to communicate more general ideas, if, for example, my neighbor writes a book about our neighborhood, I am likely to see that he and I have different ideas, and different meanings for our common symbols. How much more likely it is that I shall read, in an English book about a Devon village for example, all kinds of strange meanings—even though it is written in my language—meanings that would not be understood either by the author, or by the people he describes who would also, probably, differ much among themselves. Every communication is different for every receiver even in the same neighborly context. No one can estimate the variations of understanding that there may be among receivers of the same message conveyed in the same vehicle when the receivers are separated in either space or time.

If this is true as regards the literature and the journalism and the private messages that come in *my* language, what happens when messages are "translated" from one language to another? Communication for pragmatic purposes is possible in many difficult circumstances, of course, even by wiggling the fingers, and that fact obscures the much more important fact that it is very easy to misunderstand in the most favorable circumstances. We actually have no dependable apparatus for transcultural communication that we can be sure will stay friendly. This is the obvious aspect of one of the most staggering problems of our time: to turn to good purposes the machinery that now carries meanings from single points to all the world.

The great communities of our day, great in size and complexity and extent and power; the cities like New York and London; the countries like Russia and the United States; these hold together because a certain degree of communication is possible. They would fall apart if it failed. It may well have been failure in communication that made the ancient empires disintegrate. At least we can say that orders were not communicated and the information, including threats, that would have held the outer satraps to the throne were often too long delayed to do their work. Communication not only keeps California in the United States as it flows westward but, by flowing eastward, communication also gives to the whole world something that is, for better and for worse, an essential component of the American ethos. It is something new in the world for a single diffusion point like Hollywood to project some aspects of a whole civilization to the rest of the world; that is obvious. It is not so often noted that it is also something new for a country three thousand miles wide to exist as a single highly homogeneous organization. Both are achievements of communication. They make in combination an excellent example of the dual significance of all the modern inventions. Inventions can be either good or evil and are both good and evil most of the time.

They are both good and evil in the fact that you can make one community out of millions of people and wide miles of territory with the tools of communication, the symbols and the machines, but when you invent a system whereby millions listen to one voice, you get the millions together at the price of silencing a good many voices. This is a result of technological change that is often decried. Some critics appear to think that it is the result of some machination, profit making or power hungry. In fact, it is inevitable. Several of the authors in this volume touch on the point. Margaret Mead and Charles Siepmann and Robert Leigh all regard frankly the fact that mass communication has this inescapable character: it is a relation between a single point of diffusion and a great mass of audience.

It is not mass communication when a mass of people communicate with another great mass of people by multitudes of private messages, or even by a multiplicity of messages shouted in public. The characteristic and frightening thing about our technologically conditioned situation of today is that a few voices speak to millions not once but incessantly. The one motion picture, made by a small group, dominated perhaps by a still smaller group, is seen by millions. The one magazine, expressing the selective judgment, if not the propaganda purposes, of a small group of editors and owners, is read by millions. The one broadcaster may talk to millions.

These are the concentrations of control that are so much questioned; they are the substantial elements of any possible system of mass communication. If one man speaks to millions, not once but often, then many men are not going to be heard. However, unless one man speaks to millions, and speaks often, there is no community of ideas in a vast mass of one hundred and fifty million people. The benefits of mass communication are the common feelings and ready sympathy and quick responses of the masses that could not possibly merge and act in unison if there were no single message for them. The mass production of the minor gadgets of comfortable living is probably an unmixed good; a good many people each have a toothbrush and a newspaper and a pair of shoes because mass production makes those things cheap. The mass production of ideas raises other questions. Some of them are discussed in this book.

In this book we have a comparative study of communication habits in different cultures, and a discussion of the roots of our ideas in the ancient thinkers and in our present sociological systematic ideas. We are shown how modern psychologists observe and measure the phenomena of transferred ideas and the vehicles of transfer. We learn a good deal about what men do with words and ideas and what they could do. We get back to the subject of controlling our technological opportunities with considerable enlightenment from several different points of view. All this, we hope, is groundwork for communications research and for philosophy and statesmanship of communication in the future.

II

SOME CULTURAL APPROACHES TO COMMUNICATION PROBLEMS

BY

MARGARET MEAD

The cultural approach to any problem is by definition so wide and all embracing that each separate discussion which invokes it must, of necessity, limit itself. In this paper, I shall, arbitrarily and for purposes of this discussion only, treat communication as those activities in which one or more persons purposefully communicate with a group of other persons. In this way all the simple interrelationships of every day life, as a mother calls her child, or a husband a wife, a dog is whistled to heel, or a horse urged on to a gallop, will be excluded. So also will the simple message, the notched stick or the knotted bit of bark which is sent from one individual New Guinea native or American Indian to another, or the drum beat in which a single household in Manus calls the father home from the lagoon fishing grounds. All of these are of course communication, and the whole mesh of human social life might logically, and perhaps, in other contexts, fruitfully, be treated as a system of human communications. But the considerations advanced in this article will be addressed to the problems which are facing us today, specifically in mass communications, when the words or images fashioned professionally by one group of people are sent out to influence, persuade, or merely inform many times the number of those responsible for creating the original communication. Within this expanding field of activity, we may distinguish three smaller questions (1) the way in which communication systems are related to given cultural values, (2) the particular ethical problems of responsibility raised by our current use of communication systems, and (3)

9

problems of communication when cultural boundaries have to be transcended.

Some Primitive Contrasts

In any consideration of the way in which formal communications fit into the values of a given culture records of primitive societies provide useful contrasts. Our knowledge of these small societies, in which the whole culture must be carried in the memories and habits of a few hundred persons, is much more detailed and exact than our knowledge of our own or other great civilizations. Furthermore, the great civilizations of which we do have any first hand knowledge are becoming more and more part of one great world culture, where comparable techniques of communication are—to a degree—producing increasing uniformities. Primitive societies which for many centuries have been isolated by land and water barriers and by their own ignorance of transportation, developed sharper contrasts, each to each. They provide ready-made examples from which it is possible to glimpse the diversity of ways in which the communicator and his audience have been institutionalized.

I shall discuss here three cultures in which I have worked [1] where the attitudes are exceedingly different; all three, however, come from the same part of the world, the Southwest Pacific. Other orders of contrast could be developed by examining material from other great areas of the world, North and South America, or Africa.

Among the Arapesh [2] people of New Guinea, communication is

[1] The sacrifice of the widest amount of available contrast by restricting illustration to one area of the world seems justified because, when an anthropologist attempts to organize field results around a new problem, this can be done much better against a background of intimate knowledge of the culture.

[2] For accounts of this culture see:
Margaret Mead, *Sex and Temperament in Three Primitive Societies*, William Morrow and Company, New York, 1935.
Margaret Mead, editor, *Cooperation and Competition among Primitive Peoples*, McGraw-Hill, New York, 1937, Chapter I, "The Arapesh of New Guinea."
Margaret Mead, "The Mountain Arapesh," Part I, "An Importing Culture," *Anthropological Papers of the American Museum of Natural History*, 36, 1938, pp. 141–349.
Ibid., Part II, "Supernaturalism," 37, 1940, pp. 319–451.
Ibid., Part III, "Socio-Economic Life," 40, 1947, pp. 171–231.
Ibid., Part IV, "Diary of Events in Alitoa," 40, 1947, pp. 233–419.
R. F. Fortune, "Arapesh," *Publications of the American Ethnological Society*, 19, 1942, J. J. Augustin, New York.

seen primarily as a matter of arousing the emotions of the audience. This small group of two to three thousand mountain people, who do not even have a name for the whole group who speak their language, live in steeply mountainous country, with hamlets perched precariously on razor back ridges, and stiff climbs intervening between one man's garden and another. Food is scarce and land is poor, and the people spend a great deal of time moving about from garden to garden, sago patch to sago patch, or hunting in small groups in the deep bush. Any unexpected event is likely to find them widely scattered, and a system of calls, with linguistic peculiarities, and slit-gong beats are used to attract the attention of those at a distance, and to convey a little imperfect information. Among the Arapesh the clue to the relationship between any communicator and the group is given by the behavior of a man or woman with a headache, or some other slight ailment, a burn from a fire stick thrown by an exasperated husband or wife, a scratch got out hunting. Such suffering individuals wind their foreheads or other affected parts in bark or scarify them slightly or daub them with paint and then parade up and down the village, invoking sympathy. The situation in which the wound was obtained, or the headache contracted, is irrelevant, but each individual turns his own personal state into a matter for group emotional involvement. So ready is this response that even the narration of some hurt, a finger crushed long ago in an accident in some other land, brings out a chorus of expressive vocalizations from any group of listeners. The communicator indicates a state of feeling, the group responds with a state of feeling, and a minimum of information is conveyed.

When, among the Arapesh, some event of importance occurs, a birth or a death, a quarrel of proportions, the visit of a government patrol, or a recruiting European, or the passage through the village of a traveling party of strangers who bring trade and the possibility of sorcery into each community they visit, there are shouts and drum beats from hilltop to hilltop. But all that the signals convey is that something has happened about which the listeners had better become excited. A furious drumming on one hilltop starts off a series of shouted queries in a relay system from hilltops nearer to each other, or a child or a woman is dispatched to find out what has happened. The listeners immediately set about guessing what all the excitement can be about, speculating rapidly as to who may be dead, or traveling, whose wife may have been abducted, or whose wife sorcerized. A dozen explanations may be introduced and, according as they appear plausible, the movements of all the listeners will be altered or not. If no one can think of a plausible reason for the commotion, most of the listeners are likely to set off in the direction of the sounds.

There is some slight attempt to differentiate drum beats, but so contrary is specificity to the cultural emphasis of the Arapesh, that the distinctions are always getting blurred. The point of communication is to excite interest and bring together human beings who will then respond, on the spot, with emotion, to whatever event has occurred. They will also, once gathered, bury the dead, set out to find the sorcerer, or reluctantly line up to fulfil the requests of the visiting government official. But all specificity of information about the event, and of behavior appropriate to the event, follows after the emotional response has gathered them together.

So, when a group of people are working on a house, some individual, not necessarily the owner of the house to be, will come and shout out to a group that rattan is needed. His voice emphasizes the need for people to listen and the need for somebody to do something about it. Sooner or later, someone will go and get some rattan, but the initial request, in most cases, does not directly set such a purposeful series of acts in motion.

Interestingly also, when people tell stories about past events, they tend to impute to the moment when the drum beat was heard from a distant hilltop, a full knowledge of what they learned only after they had responded to the drum beat. So, a narrator will say, "when he was returning from a journey inland and still far away he heard the gongs being beaten and he *knew* that his brother had taken his wife," although he finds out only after he has reached his own village, his steps quickened in response to the sound.

This treatment of communication in which a state of readiness of excitement, a mixture of fear, dread, anxiety and pleasant expectation, is aroused before any information is given or any action sought, is obviously always a possible theme in any complex communication system, and one which is sometimes involved in our culture. Walter

Winchell's strong punctuation of his broadcast with the word *Flash,* any radio program in which a strong signal is used first to awaken the audience, has this element in it. Some of the possible implications of such a theme become evident when it is seen writ large in the culture of a people; such as the extraordinary lack of precision which characterizes Arapesh thinking, their short attention span, their tendency to substitute emotional congruity for any sort of logical construct when each communicator seeks to evoke first undifferentiated emotional response, and only then to sharpen and specify events and action sequences.

Among the lagoon dwelling Manus [3] people of the Southern Coast of the Admiralty Islands, there is a very different emphasis. The Manus are a hard headed, puritanical, trading people, interested in material things, in economic activity, in continuously purposive behavior. Where the Arapesh seldom count to a hundred and then with units of a low degree of abstraction, the Manus count into the hundred thousands. Where the Arapesh set a day for a ceremony, and as likely as not the ceremony takes place a day earlier, or a week later, the Manus announce their plans weeks in advance and carry them out. Where the Arapesh set up traps and snares in the bush and then wait until game falls into them, often even depending upon a dream to direct their footsteps back in the direction of the trap, the Manus make their principal catches of fish each month in a timed relationship to the tide. Action is stimulated in Manus, not by creating an atmosphere of warm interdependent responsiveness, but by setting up exact instigating situations—a prepayment, a loan, an advance—to which other individuals respond, under penalty of supernatural punishment from their own exacting ghostly guardians, and the potentially hostile ghostly guardians of other people. Exact, effective, properly timed

[3] For accounts of this culture see:

Margaret Mead, *Growing Up in New Guinea,* William Morrow and Company, New York, 1930.

Margaret Mead, *Cooperation and Competition among Primitive Peoples,* McGraw-Hill, New York, 1937, Chapter VII, "The Manus of the Admiralty Islands," pp. 210–239.

Margaret Mead, "Kinship in the Admiralties," *Anthropological Papers of the American Museum of Natural History,* 34, 1934, pp. 183–358.

R. F. Fortune, "Manus Religion," American Philosophical Society, Philadelphia, 1935.

action, which is physically and ethically appropriate, is what the Manus are interested in.

In such a culture, communications take a very different shape. There are a series of drum signals, which include formal openings which set the stage, not in terms of excitement but of content, so that a certain pattern of beats means: "I am about to announce the date at which I will give a feast." Then, an intellectual readiness to listen for a piece of relevant information being established, the drummer goes on to beat out the number of days before his feast, accurately, carefully, and the listeners count and take note. Each houseowner has a special pattern of beats which is his signature, the same beat that his household use to call him home. Between villages, careful tallies and other accurate mnemonic devices are used to convey the same sort of information.

The other characteristic form of communication in Manus is oratory, used in most cases angrily, as a stimulant to economic activity. Some of this is purely ceremonial hostility, the accompaniment of some large scale economic transaction of display and exchange, but some of it is argumentative and situational. Men inveigh against their debtors and battle bitterly over details in the calculations. This sort of behavior in which actual items of the number of dog's teeth or jars of coconut oil are at stake confuses the clarity with which the Manus habitually operate. And it is significant that as soon as my pencil and notebook entered the scene, people began to try to substitute my records for this angry, confusing welter of accusation and refutation, which they had lacked the techniques to prevent. The Manus prefer action in a well defined context, under the spur of past careful definition reinforced by guilt, with anger introduced as stimulus in ways which will not compromise the accuracy of the operations. This attempt to keep thought and action clear of immediate emotion, but reinforced by unpleasant emotions, of anger and fear of the reproaches of their own consciences and supernatural punishments from their ghosts, runs through the formal communications of the society.

Bali [4] which is not a primitive society because writing is known, but

[4] Gregory Bateson, "Bali: A Value System of a Steady State." To be published in *Social Structure: Studies Presented to A. R. Radcliffe Brown*. Clarendon Press, England, 1948.

is a society with a culture exceedingly different from our own and perhaps comparable in political and economic organization to the early middle ages in Europe, presents a quite different picture. The Balinese live in closely knit village communities, in which the citizens are bound together by a very great number of shared tasks, both ceremonial and economic. Each such community has its own traditional law which was respected by the Balinese feudal rulers in the past, and by their Dutch successors in the colonial period. Citizens, whose names are arranged in a series of rotas, share in the work necessary to maintain the elaborate irrigation system, keep up the roads, repair the numerous temples, provide the materials for offerings and prepare them for the gods, maintain forces of watchmen, town criers, messengers between the village and extra village authorities.

An intricate calendar of several systems of weeks which turns on itself like the cogs in several different sized wheels, governs the recurring series of ceremonial events, and systems of trance and possession give the necessary slight pushes to the calendrical system to provide for emergencies, stimulate a sluggish community, or slow down an excessively active one. Residence in a given village, location in a given place in the status system, as to caste, age, sex, and marital status, the day of the week, position on a rota of citizens, and occasional formal instigation of action by a diviner or seer, provide the framework within which each individual acts. There is no oratory, no exhortation, no preaching. A day or so before the ceremony in a village like Bajoeng Gede, the man whose turn it is to be town crier will go through the streets, announcing the coming feast, and specifying what each household is to contribute, *e.g.,* "rice, a large measure, betel pepper leaves five, grated coconut, a level container full." He may further specify what those who are on duty that month will give, *e.g.,* "two woven square packets, eight bundles of white cooked rice meal,

J. Belo, "A Study of Customs Pertaining to Twins in Bali," *Tijdschrift voor Ind. Tall., Land., en Volkenkunde,* 75, 1935, 4, pp. 483–549.

Margaret Mead, "Administrative Contributions to Democratic Character Formation at the Adolescent Level," in *Personality in Nature, Society and Culture,* Henry A. Murray and Clyde K. Kluckhohn, Chapter 37, Part III. Alfred A. Knopf, New York, 1948.

Gregory Bateson and Margaret Mead, "Balinese Character," *Special Publications II,* New York Academy of Sciences, 1942.

eight bundles of cooked black rice meal, five small containers of rice, eight items of red sugar meal, and one hundred units of pork." He will announce which groups in the population, as the full male citizens, full female citizens, the boys' group, the girls' group, are to appear at the temple at what time and for what services.

The people do not have the burden of remembering from day to day what is to be done, for remembering is the assigned duty of special officials, most of whom take turns over the years. It is assumed that all that is needed is information about the correct behavior which will then, in most cases, be forthcoming. For those who fail to make their appropriate contribution, in work or offering materials, or fail to accept their share when the offerings are redivided among the participants—for in Bali there is small distinction between obligation and privilege—there are small fines, well within the resources of every citizen. If the fine is not paid, it mounts, and if the citizen is seen as unwilling to pay the fine, it mounts at a tremendous rate and the individual is virtually cut off from the community until it is paid. But neither to the man who fails to perform a single duty, nor to the man who refuses to pay his fine, nor even to those who have violated some fundamental tenet of the caste or religious system, is anger shown. The system is impersonal, unyielding and unequivocal. Those who run up against the laws of one community may, in most cases, leave it, but their choice is between a no man's land of vagrancy, beggardom and thievery and casual labor, and again becoming members of another community that has and enforces a different but equally stringent set of laws.

In this system the communicator, whether he be rajah, Dutch official, or village council (which contains all the full citizens of the village), acts as if the audience were already in a state of suspended, unemotional attention, and only in need of a small precise triggering word to set them off into appropriate activity. The stimuli are as simple as red and green lights in a well regulated, traffic situation, where no policeman is needed to reinforce the effortless, uninvolved stopping and starting of groups of cars, driven by men who accept the traffic signals as part of the world. Communications, even from the gods, when, through the mouth of a possessed person, instructions are given to renovate a temple, repay some old village obligation, combine two clubs, or regularize an irregular marriage, have all the impersonality of the voice which tells the telephoning American, "When you hear the signal, the time will be . . . ," or "United States Weather Bureau report for New York and vicinity, eight o'clock temperature forty-two degrees, . . ." The voice that tells the time does not include in its note an urgency about trains to catch or children to get off to school, roasts to come out of the oven, or cows to be milked. People dial the correct number to find out what time it is so that they may act appropriately. Such a system, carried to the lengths to which Balinese culture carry it, in which there is a very deep personal commitment to maintaining a continuity and a steady state, can be maintained with a lack of either expressed emotion or expressed effortfulness. The communicator states a position; the people, conditioned throughout their development to find safety and reassurance in following well established routines in company with others, respond.

Description of the cultural setting of communication, such as these three from Arapesh, Manus and Bali, could be multiplied to sharpen appreciation of the variety of themes and their implications which are involved in our own communications system. They serve to point up the very great number of ways in which communicator and communicator's intent, audience and audience's responses, may be institutionalized in different cultural systems, and also in different facets of the same cultural system. In our own society, it is possible to distinguish the communication methods which rely on arousing emotion first and slipping in suggestions for action only after the individual members of the audience are suffused with feeling, those which are concerned with giving accurate information which will lead to indicated action, those which are concerned merely with giving information upon which individuals may act.

The Problem of Responsibility in Communications

The great contemporary concern with communication problems must be laid not only to the enormous advance in technology and the resulting shrinking of the world into one potential communication system, with all the attendant difficulties of communication across cultural boundaries, but also to the increase in social awareness on the one hand, and the disintegration of the institutionalized centers of responsibility on the other. It is true that, through the centuries, expanding movements and nations have used various methods of propaganda [5] to advance their causes, to convert the unconverted, bring in line the recalcitrant, reconcile the conquered to their lot and the conquerors to their conquering role. It is also true that secular and religious hierarchies have consciously used these methods to advance their avowed and unavowed ends. But the addition of modern technological methods, by which the ownership of one radio station may decide the fate of a local revolution, and a single film or a single voice may reach the whole of the listening and watching world, has changed the order of magnitude of the whole problem.

At the same time development of social science is making it possible for communications to change their character. Instead of the inspired voice of a natural leader, whose zestful "We shall defend our Island, whatever the cost may be. We shall fight on the beaches, we shall fight on the landing ground, we shall fight in the fields and the streets, we shall fight in the hills; we shall never surrender. . . ." galvanizing people to action, the appeals can be, to a degree, calculated and planned. Instead of the politician's hunch as to how some program is going over, polls and surveys can be used to bring back accurate information to the source of the propaganda and introduce a corrective. Theories of human nature which are no longer the inexplicit emphases of a coherent culture, but instead the partly rationalized, partly culturally limited formulations of psychological research, can be used as the basis of planned campaigns.[6]

The thinking peoples of the world have been made conscious, during the past quarter of a century, of the power of organized and con-

---

[5] Margaret Mead, "Our Educational Emphasis in Primitive Perspective," in *Education and the Cultural Process,* editor, Charles S. Johnson. Papers presented at Symposium commemorating the 75th Anniversary of the founding of Fisk University, April–May, 1941. Reprinted from the *American Journal of Sociology,* 48, May, 1943, 6, pp. 5–12.

[6] Ernest Kris, "Some Problems of War Propaganda," *Psychoanalytic Quarterly,* 12, 3, pp. 381–399 (for a discussion of the way in which Nazi propaganda methods drew upon Le Bon's psychology of the crowd).

trolled communication, glimpsing that power both from the point of view of the victim or "target" and of the victimizer, he who wields the powerful weapon. Dissection of the methods of the enemy, the conscious cultivation of an immunity against appeals to one's own emotion, desperate attempts to devise methods appropriate to a democracy, while we envied totalitarian propagandic controls, have all contributed to the growth of this consciousness in the United States.

But consciousness of the potential power of communication has peculiar implications in the United States, in a country where no institution, neither Church nor State, has any monopoly of the organs of communication. The American, during the past twenty-five years, has seen systems of propagandic control develop in other countries, and even when propagandic moves of extreme importance have actually been promoted within the United States, they have usually been phrased as inspired by Berlin or Tokyo, London or Moscow, rather than as the expression of American attitudes.

The local American emphasis has thus been on resisting high powered communication pressures, and this has been congruent, not only with the Americans' fear of playing the sucker role *vis-à-vis* other nations, more skilled in international necromancy, but also with the great importance of advertising in the United States. Those European peoples which have felt the impact of modern totalitarian communications had as a background for the experience a past in which Church and State traditionally controlled and manipulated the symbols which could move men to feel and to act. The American on the other hand has experienced instead the manipulation of the same sorts of symbols, of patriotism, religious belief and human strivings after perfection and happiness, by individuals and groups who occupied a very different and far less responsible place in the social hierarchy.

In our American system of communications, any interest, wishing to "sell" its products or message to the public, is able to use the full battery of available communication techniques, radio and film, press and poster. It is characteristic of this system that the symbols used to arouse emotion, evoke attention, and produce action, have come into the hands of those who feel no responsibility toward them. In a society like Bali there is simply no possibility that such a symbol as "The Village," also spoken of as "Mr. Village" and as "God Village," could be used by a casual vendor or rabble rouser. The symbols which evoke responses are used by those whose various positions in the society commit them to a responsible use. But in the United States, most of the value symbols of American tradition are ready to the hand of the manufacturer of the most trivial debased product, or the public relations counsel of the most wildcat and subversive organizations.

The American is used to experiencing the whole symbolic system of his society, in a series of fragmented and contradictory contexts. These beget in him a continually heightened threshold to any sort of appeal (with a recurrent nostalgia for a lost innocence in which his tears could flow simply or his heart swell with uncomplicated emotion) and a casual, non-evaluative attitude toward the power wielded through any communication system. As he straightens his tie and decides not to buy the tie which is being recommended over the radio, or in the street card ad, he gets a sense of immunity which makes him overlook the extent to which he is continually absorbing the ad behind the ad, the deutero [7] contexts of the material which he feels he is resisting.

We may examine the types of learning which result from the various uses of symbols in the United States in terms of: Whose symbol is used? What is the order of relationship between the symbol-possessing group and the group which is using the symbol? What is the nature of the product or message for which the symbol is being used? Who benefits by its use?

As examples of various types of symbol usage, let us consider the use of the symbol of Florence Nightingale, devoted ministrant to suffering and dying humanity. In the first position, a maker of white broadcloth might put out an advertisement which said, "In the great tradition of Florence Nightingale, American nurses are to be found

---

[7] For a discussion of the concept of deutero learning see: Gregory Bateson, "Social Planning and the Concept of 'Deutero-Learning'," *Science, Philosophy and Religion, 2nd Symposium,* Conference on Science, Philosophy and Religion, New York, 1942, pp. 81–97.

ministering to the suffering. And, needing the very best, in order to fulfil their devoted mission, they use *Blank's* broadcloth for their uniforms, because it wears—through sickness and death." The reader of this advertisement learns that Florence Nightingale is a name to conjure with, that she was admired and respected, and that *Blank's* broadcloth are using her to enhance *their* prestige. To this degree the value of Florence Nightingale's name is increased. But at the same time the reader or listener may also add a footnote, "Trying to tie their old broadcloth on to Florence Nightingale's kite," and the sense of a synthetic, temporary quality of all symbol associations is strengthened in his mind.

In the second case, the advocates of a dishonest correspondence course in nursing might use the name of Florence Nightingale in a plea to individuals to rise and follow the lamp once carried aloft by the great Nurse, and prepare themselves, in only twenty lessons, money down in advance, to follow in her footsteps. Here, to the extent that the listener realized that the correspondence course was phony, Florence Nightingale's name would also be shrouded with some of the same feeling of the phonyness, bedraggled and depreciated.

In the third case, a nurses' association might decide to put themselves back of a public education program in chest x-rays for tuberculosis control, and develop a poster in which they placed their great symbol, Florence Nightingale, beside an appeal for support for the local anti-tuberculosis committee. The reader and listeners here recognize that Florence Nightingale is a great and valuable symbol, because those to whom she is a value symbol have themselves used her name to advance some newer and younger cause. This last type is of course characteristic of the historical use of symbols in society. Even when groups which represented religious or political subversion from the point of view of those in power have appropriated to themselves the sacred symbols of those against whom they were fighting, such moves have been made seriously and responsibly by those who believed that their subversion and their heresy were neither subversion nor heresy but political justice and religious truth. Symbols which change hands between orthodox and heterodox, between conservative and liberal, do not suffer by the change as long as each group of users acts responsibly. Instead such exchange is an invaluable ingredient of continuity and consistency within a changing society.

But the advertising agency, the public relations counsel, as institutionalized in our culture, has no responsibility of this sort. An advertising agency, whatever the personal sense of conscientious rectitude of its staff, has one set of functions to perform, to sell the product successfully while keeping within the law. With sufficient sophistication, a refusal to spoil the market, either for the same product in the future, or for other products, might be included within its functions. But our society has no higher jurisdiction to which such agencies owe allegiance. The regulations formulated by patriotic societies to protect the flag have to be respected, or you get into trouble. Religious symbols can be used only if you are sure the churches will not get in your hair. Claims must be muted to the sensitivities of the Pure Food and Drug Administration. If you expect to keep the contract a long time, do not overplay a line which may go sour. If you do not want trouble from your other clients, or other agencies, do not take too obvious a crack at other products or organizations or causes. It is upon such disjointed rules of thumb that the day by day manipulation of the responsiveness, the moral potential of the American people, depends.

The National Nutrition Program, administered under Federal auspices during the war, was one interesting attempt to deal with this contemporary situation. Agreements were worked out by which advertisers were permitted to use the name of the National Nutrition Program, if, and only if, they acceded to certain conditions, the final ethical sanction for which came from the best scientific knowledge of nutritionists. Advertisers were not permitted to misquote, quote in part, or add to, the gist of the Nutrition theme which had been agreed upon, nor could they use it in association with products of no nutritional value. In spite of the many small expediencies which clouded the issues, this was a genuine attempt to supply an ethical sanction, rooted in science and administered by government, to a whole mass of communications on the subject of food and its uses. On a very simple level, this program represented one possible direction in which a country like the United States might move to give ethical form to the almost wholly unregulated mass of communications which now serve the interests of such a variety of groups—one way in which control can be vested in those to whom the symbol belongs.

A continuation of the present state of irresponsibility is exceedingly dangerous because it provides a situation within which steps backward rather than steps forward are so likely to occur. One possible response to the confused state of our symbolic system and the dulling of our responsiveness is an artificial simplification, a demand for the return of control to central authorities who will see to it that there is no more of the haphazard and contradictory use of important symbols. If the only choice open to us appears to be this increasing immunization against any appeal, this increasing apathy and callousness, so that photographs of a thousand murdered innocents no longer have any power to move us, the temptation to swing back to authoritarianism may become increasingly great. If, however, we can go on and formulate a system of responsibility appropriate to the age in which we live, a system which takes into account the state of technology [8], the type of mixed economy, the democratic aspirations, and the present dulled sensibilities of the American people, we may prevent such a reaction and, instead, move forward.

Any theory of the way in which responsibility for communications must be developed must deal with the problem of intent, with the beliefs that the communicator has about himself, and about his audience, as well as with the particular constitution and situation of that audience. This facet of the problem is particularly important in America, where the average citizen still identifies his position as a minority one, and so always thinks of power as wielded by THEM, and not by himself or a group to which he belongs. All discussions of the locations of responsibility for the communication stream, in any positive or constructive sense, are likely to stumble over this feeling that responsibility means power, and power is always in the hands of someone else. A set of negative controls, such as the rule that a radio station must discuss both sides of a situation, no matter how imperfectly and destructively each side is presented, is more congenial than any set of positive controls. So also were the teachings of propaganda analysis; the American felt safer in learning how not to respond to a false appeal than in per-

[8] Lyman Bryson, this volume, "Introductory Chapter," p. 7.

mitting any effective development of appeals which would be so good that he would respond to them.

It therefore seems that it is important to arrive at a phrasing of responsibility which will meet this fear of misused power and develop an ethic of communications within a democracy such as ours. Once a climate of opinion expressing such an ethic begins to develop, appropriate institutional forms may be expected to emerge, either slowly or under intensive cultivation.

Such an ethic might take the form of an insistence that the audience be seen as composed of *whole* individuals, not artificial cut outs from crowd scenes, such as are represented on the dust jacket of a recent book [9] on radio. It might take the form of insisting that the audience be seen as composed of individuals who could not be manipulated but could only be appealed to in terms of their systematic cultural strengths. It might include a taboo on seeing any individual as the puppet of the propagandist, and focussing instead on the purposeful cultivation of directions of change. It would then be regarded as ethical to try to persuade the American people to drink orange juice, as a pleasant and nutritional drink, by establishing a style of breakfast, a visual preference for oranges, and a moral investment in good nutrition, but not by frightening individual mothers into serving orange juice for fear that they would lose their children's love, or their standing in the community.

Probably the closest analogue for the development of such sanctions can be found in medical ethics, legal ethics, etc., in which a group of self-respecting practitioners constitute themselves as a final court of appeal upon their own behavior. To the extent that advertising, public relations, market research, and the various communication media experts come to hold themselves and be held by the public in greater respect, such internally self-corrective systems might be developed.

If the contention is justified that democratic institutions represent a more complex integration of society, in which greater or different possibilities are accorded to each individual, we must expect corres-

[9] Paul F. Lazarsfeld and Harry Field, *The People Look at Radio,* University of North Carolina Press, Chapel Hill, 1946.

ponding differences between the communication ethics of societies representative of different degrees of feudalism and capitalism in different political combinations. The wholly feudal state may be said to have localized responsibility for communications within a hierarchical status system, and avoided the problem of power over individuals or trends by regarding that system as fixed and immutable. The totalitarian system which has lost the sanctions of feudalism and cannot depend upon the character structure of its citizens, develops monopolistic communication systems which seek to establish a direction in the society, but which in the interval are seen as operating on identified individuals, playing upon their most vulnerable points to bring them in line with a dictated policy. Whether it is claimed that the availability of concentration camps influence the propagandist or merely makes the audience members vulnerable, the interrelationship is there.

Political democracies have, to date, by insisting on negative sanctions, maintained systems in which the individual was the target of many sorts of propagandic themes but in which he was protected by the existence of contradictions in the appeals made to him. Such negative sanctions are better than none, but the target of American advertising is not a dignified human figure.[10] The target of political campaigns in the United States is not a dignified human figure. The limitation on the sense of power of the advertising agency copy writer or the campaign manager has merely been the knowledge that there were opponents in the field, free to act just as irresponsibly as he and free to present an equally contradictory and destructive set of counter appeals.

This negative approach is challenged whenever the country goes to war and wishes to mobilize its citizens toward common goals. It is doubly challenged when branches of the United States Army or the United States Government are charged with the task of reeducating peoples who have lived under totalitarian regimes. The resistance of the Germans,[11] for example, to the sort of protection of freedom

---

[10] Constantin Fitz Gibbon, "The Man of Fear," *Atlantic Monthly*, January, 1947, pp. 78–81.

[11] Bertram Schaffner, *Father Land, A Study of Authoritarianism in the German Family*. Columbia University Press, New York, 1948.

which is implied in the cultivation of a two party system, challenges American culture to the development of a more positive ethic.

Note: It is the purpose of this paper to raise problems, not to offer ready-made solutions. I shall therefore, in Chapter Thirteen of this book, present a case history of the application of anthropological methods to an even wider problem of communication. M. M.

III

CLASSIC THEORIES OF COMMUNICATION

BY

WHITNEY J. OATES

Classic theories of communication, as they are expressed by Plato and his successors, must be considered in the light of the following proposition: "It is not possible to discuss profitably problems in connection with the communication of ideas merely on the technical level since inevitably the question of the meaning or the significance of that which is communicated arises."

This proposition might be amplified by adding two words as more or less alternatives for "meaning" and "significance," and these are "validity" and "truth." In essence, the proposition, as I have attempted to frame it, constitutes the classic position with respect to communication. Plato first laid down this principle and held to it as he analyzed the problem with its manifold technical complications. He was followed by a long series of rhetoricians, such as Aristotle, the Stoics, Cicero, and Quintilian, who held for the most part to this central position, however much they may have rejected in various respects the metaphysics of the master.

Before we can consider the Platonic position, it is necessary to emphasize three inescapable preconditions to any rigorous speculation on the problem of communication. The first is that the problem of communication as such is extremely difficult, particularly when one undertakes a meticulous philosophical investigation of the question. Plato was completely aware of this fact, and indeed the story is told about his friend, Cratylus, after whom he named one of his dialogues, who was so puzzled, so doubtful about adequate communication via words that he finally gave up in despair and decided that in the future he was only going to point. The second precondition is this: All investigators should be continually aware of the problem of the medium. There are many media of communication—speech, poetry, prose, music, gesture, painting, the dance, scientific formulae, and so on. We must remember that there are certain things which can be communicated in certain media and certain things which cannot be communicated in those media. To emphasize the point, we can call to mind the simple thought that one cannot whistle an algebraic formula. Third, even though the whole phenomenon of communication is complex, ultimately its basic constituent elements are simple. They are three: The communicator, the medium, and the recipient of the communication.

The classic theory as it is found in Plato is confined to communication in words and is consistently given the specific name of rhetoric. To put it rather crudely and bluntly, the theory merely points out the fact that it makes a great deal of difference whether what one says is true or not. Is or is not a proposition so? Therefore the classic theory underscores the fact that inescapably the value of truth is raised whenever anybody says anything. This attitude was explicitly recognized by the Stoic rhetoricians who carried the position so far as to maintain that speaking well was the equivalent of speaking the truth.

A clear illustration of the attitude can be found in a recent statement made by Lyman Bryson to the general effect that the *purpose* of communication was all important, and in referring to the particular type of communication with which he is most concerned, the radio, he added, "The essential problem in mass communication is the management for the public good of something which is by nature monopolistic." We do not need to quarrel about what he means by "monopolistic," but the question which he raises amounts to this, that in some sense that which is for the public good must be true.

Another illustration may serve to express the anti-classical attitude. Not long ago a very enthusiastic classicist, a lawyer by profession, was talking about the values and benefits of classical education. He said, "I have found it tremendously valuable; it puts money in my pocket. I want to tell you how it is done. A client of mine, who was arrested for drunken driving and who had pleaded guilty, found himself in a position involving political complications and it became very necessary for him to be let off. Therefore, I was engaged as his attorney. I didn't know how I was going to get a man off when he had already confessed himself as guilty. So I decided that I would cross examine the doctor who had certified that my client was drunk. After the doctor took the stand I put this question to the witness, 'Doctor, what would you say if I told you that the defendant was a psomophagist?' The doctor scratched his head and said he didn't know; it was probably pretty serious. Then I said, 'What if I should tell you, doctor, that my client is a congenital psomophagist?' The doctor shook his head, 'Pretty serious.' In the meantime, many law attendants were scrambling in the dictionary. After the doctor admitted that it was a very serious condition, I successfully moved that the case be dismissed."

The lawyer had played a simple trick. He merely made up a word from Greek roots: "psomophagist" means nothing except a person who bolts his food. It is very difficult to find in the dictionary. In the first place, it isn't there, and in the second place, it begins with "ps" instead of an "s." Clearly this anecdote illustrates a certain type of communication, and I should say that it is against this kind of thing in its ancient form in classical Greece that Plato moved with all the power of his mind and his thought.

Plato's position on our problem is best expressed in the two dialogues, the *Gorgias* and the *Phaedrus*. But before one considers these works it is necessary to refer to Plato's Theory of Ideas, the central metaphysical theory which provides him with his ultimate criterion of truth. The Theory of Ideas is either explicit or implicit in everything which Plato says. It is his ultimate reference point, the ultimate sanction for the validity of any proposition he may utter. Here it is well to bear in mind that each man's ultimate metaphysical or religious position is that which supplies for him his ultimate criterion of truth. In other words, each man's view of Reality and his final criterion of truth are functionally related. Historically the criteria of truth have differed as metaphysical positions have differed. Some men have espoused "Naturalism," some would hold to a humanism, some would hold to a theism, depending upon whether their views concerning the nature of Reality were primarily "zoocentric," anthropocentric or theocentric. No matter what the differences may be with respect to each individual's view of truth, it is important to remember that Plato believed in truth with a capital "T," and believed that it exists quite apart from what each one or other of us may think it to be, and he further believed that no man, *as man,* could know Truth fully and absolutely.

Plato's Theory of Ideas, in brief, postulates two modes or realms of being. One is the world of phenomena, in space and time, the world of "sights and sounds," as he called it, which is characterized by impermanence and change. However, lying behind the world of phenomena is the world of Ideas or Forms, and for Plato this is the true realm of Reality. In contrast to the phenomenal world, the realm of Ideas, which is non-spatial and non-temporal, is characterized by being permanent, unchanging and eternal. In it are Ideas both of things and of qualities, and Plato insists that in some sense all things and qualities in the space-time world are more or less close reflections of the abstract Ideas at the heart of a total Reality which is thus given more than spatial and temporal dimensions.

The theory is remarkable for its philosophical economy, since it presents a metaphysical system which can function simultaneously in various areas of philosophical inquiry. In the first place, the Theory of Ideas has a logical function. In its terms Plato has a theory of logical universals upon the basis of which the phenomena of predication can be explained. That this function is important is obvious, since ultimately the communication of mind with mind depends upon the existence and validity in some sense of logical universals. Secondly, the Theory of Ideas provides Plato with a theory of a Reality which is hierarchically ordered. Thirdly, the theory forms the basis of his epistemology, and finally, Ideas of qualities are the ultimate norms for Plato in his thinking in the field of value. Thus the Theory of Ideas, in its fourfold aspect in logic, ontology, epistemology, and axiology, really determines Plato's judgment with respect to the validity of any proposition.

The famous dialogue, the *Gorgias,* gives a concentrated picture not only of the rhetoric of the famous Sophists of the fifth century B. C., those prototypes of the traveling lecturer, but also of Plato's sharp opposition to the sophistic theory of communication. In the first section of the dialogue Socrates presses Gorgias to explain just exactly what Gorgias believes rhetoric to be. As they spar at the outset Gorgias asserts that rhetoric deals with "discourse," and as Socrates gently but firmly prods, Gorgias amplifies his statement by saying that rhetoric is discourse about "the greatest and best of human things." At this point the dialogue proceeds as follows:

"*Soc.* . . . What is that which, as you say, is the greatest good of man, and of which you are the creator? Answer us.

"*Gor.* That good, Socrates, which is truly the greatest, being that which gives to men freedom in their own persons, and to individuals the power of ruling over others in their several states.

"*Soc.* And what would you consider this to be?

"*Gor.* What is there greater than the word which persuades the judges in the courts, or the senators in the council, or the citizens in the assembly, or at any other political meeting?—if you have the power of uttering this word, you will have the physician your slave, and the trainer your slave, and the money-maker of whom you talk will be found to gather treasures, not for himself, but for you who are able to speak and to persuade the multitude.

"*Soc.* Now I think, Gorgias, that you have very accurately explained what you conceive to be the art of rhetoric; and you mean to say, if I am not mistaken, that rhetoric is the artificer of persuasion, having this and no other business, and that this is her crown and end. Do you know any other effect of rhetoric over and above that of producing persuasion?

"*Gor.* No: the definition seems to be very fair, Socrates; for persuasion is the chief end of rhetoric." [1]

Socrates proceeds to point out that other arts involve persuasion; for example, arithmetic persuades us of the truth with respect to number. Gorgias then limits the persuasion of rhetoric to the subject matter of the just and the unjust. Socrates next is able to make Gorgias admit that rhetoric in courts and assemblies produces be-

---

[1] Benjamin Jowett, *The Dialogues of Plato*, 3rd edition, Oxford University Press, 1892, 452 d2–453 27.

lief and not knowledge, an admission which obviously will permit Socrates to launch a telling attack on the sophistic position.

Another passage, in which Gorgias attempts to defend his own attitude, reflects the latent immoralism in any view of rhetoric which is anchored in probability and not in truth.

"*Gor.* A marvel, indeed, Socrates, if you only knew how rhetoric comprehends and holds under her sway all the inferior arts. Let me offer you a striking example of this. On several occasions I have been with my brother Herodicus or some other physician to see one of his patients, who would not allow the physician to give him medicine, or apply the knife or hot iron to him; and I have persuaded him to do for me what he would not do for the physician just by the use of rhetoric. And I say that if a rhetorician and a physician were to go to any city, and had there to argue in the Ecclesia or any other assembly as to which of them should be elected state-physician, the physician would have no chance; but he who could speak would be chosen if he wished; and in a contest with a man of any other profession the rhetorician more than any one would have the power of getting himself chosen, for he can speak more persuasively to the multitude than any of them, and on any subject." [2]

The *Gorgias,* even in the two passages cited, makes it perfectly plain that Plato will not accept any theory of rhetoric or of communication which stops at "persuasion" without raising the question of the merits or validity or truth of that which is being communicated. In his other important dialogue which deals with rhetoric, the *Phaedrus,* Plato analyzes the problem further and makes clear what he believes rhetoric should be. The dialogue, one of the most fascinating and difficult of Plato's works, opens with Socrates meeting his young friend, Phaedrus. They take a walk along the banks of the river Ilissus near Athens, and recline in the shade of a plane tree while Phaedrus reads a speech of the very famous orator, Lysias. The speech, on an erotic subject, is clearly a rhetorical *tour de force,* since it attempts to defend the claims of the non-lover over against

[2] *Ibid.,* 456 a7–c6.

the lover, more or less by indicating that a non-lover is a much more pleasant and comfortable person to get along with than a lover.

Phaedrus expresses great admiration for the speech, since he is fascinated by its technical virtuosity, whereupon Socrates avers that he can do better and extemporizes a speech of his own. In the midst of his speech which is partly serious and partly playful, Socrates suddenly stops, saying that he can go no further, since he is doing an impiety to Eros, the great god of love. So he begins again, this time speaking in honor of love and here follows the third speech of the dialogue, a great myth which is one of the most majestic flights of Plato's poetic imagination. The three speeches are then made the subject of the subsequent discussion, as Phaedrus and Socrates take up rhetoric, the art of writing and various questions inherent in literary criticism. The subject most specifically considered is rhetoric as the so-called art in which the practiced speaker must be disciplined, that is, the rhetoric as it was then conventionally taught. The dialogue closes with the consideration of non-written, oral discourse.

Such is the brief outline of the *Phaedrus*. In order to understand this curious dialogue and its relevance to Plato's view of rhetoric, one should recall the Theory of Ideas, and the fact that the theory asserts the greater reality and value of "things not seen." A first and most important consequence of this belief in "things not seen," a point particularly emphasized in the second speech of Socrates, is the assertion of the relatively greater reality and greater value of the soul in man as compared with the body. Plato in this myth contends that the soul is immortal, is that which is capable of initiating motion, *i.e.*, it is a "self-moved mover," is really that which is capable of grasping or apprehending the Ideas, in so far as man may. By "soul" Plato means the totality of man's inner being and his characteristic analysis of it into three constituent elements is reflected in the myth when he likens the soul to a charioteer and two horses. In the *Republic* Plato had maintained that there are three parts of the soul; one, the reason; second, the nobler emotions; and third, the appetitive element, the lower emotions. In the image in the *Phaedrus,* the charioteer is the reason, the nobler emotions are represented by a noble white steed, while the lower emotions are represented by an ugly, mean, black beast. In the myth, the life of the soul is described as the struggle of the reason to control and manage this ill matched team, these two elements, man's higher emotions and his lower desires.

As the conversation turns to the subject of rhetoric and literary criticism, it becomes apparent why Plato dwelt so fully on the nature of man's soul. It is the soul which apprehends that which is communicated, and hence rhetoric addresses itself only to the soul. Consequently it is a matter of utmost importance that rhetoric recognize thoroughly the true nature of man's soul, and that the orator, the public speaker trained by rhetoric, be aware that he is addressing the soul, that part of man which can grasp truth. Hence really the discussion between Socrates and Phaedrus attacks vigorously the conventional rhetoric of persuasion, the rhetoric that plays fast and loose with men's souls, that does not recognize the philosophical fact that men's souls can be twisted or turned either to truth or falsity.

On the other hand, Plato is fully aware of the need for technical proficiency in the speaker, his need, as we might say, for a knowledge of human psychology on the technical level. He also knows that the speaker or writer must be a master of the medium of language, but his view of technical skill is consistently one that regards it only as a means to some further end. It must never be considered as an end in itself, as rhetoricians from his day to this have been so prone to do. Indeed, there is a passage in the *Phaedrus* in which Plato makes great sport of all the rhetorical gadgets and tricks of technique which conventional professors of public speaking invariably taught their clients. Socrates is referring to the super-subtle analysis of an oration:

"*Soc.* And, secondly comes the 'Narrative,' and after it the 'Testimony;' and thirdly 'Evidence;' and fourthly 'Probability.' And, if I don't mistake, that best of wordsmiths, from Byzantium, adds 'Confirmation' and 'Sur-confirmation.'

"*Phaedr.* You mean the very eminent Theodorus?

"*Soc.* Who else? And he has 'Refutation' and 'Sur-refutation'—how to do them in accusation as well as in defense. But the illustrious Parian, Evenus, shall we not bring him to the centre? The inventor of 'Insinuation' and 'Praise Indirect'! And 'Censure Indirect,' which some maintain he put into verse to help the memory! What a savant he was." [3]

In the concluding sections of the dialogue Plato begins to develop his own theory of a dialectical rhetoric which he would urge as a substitute for the rhetoric of persuasion. Dialectical rhetoric he calls ψυχαγωγία, psychagogy, which means an enchantment, a winning of men's souls, a turning of men's souls toward the truth. Plato insists that a speaker or a communicator must say what he has to say always with reference, either explicitly or implicitly, to the first principles that lie deep at the heart of Reality. The rhetoric of persuasion often turns men's souls toward opinion, often falsifies, often operates without reference to first principles or truth. Hence dialectical rhetoric, or psychagogy, demands that the communicator have, first, a profound knowledge of men's souls, and second, a deep awareness, in so far as he can, of the truth, or at least that aspect of the truth which may bear upon the subject at hand. To put it very simply, the communicator is under the high obligation never to falsify, never to say "what is not so."

Plato clarifies his position concerning dialectical rhetoric by introducing the analogy of the physician. He insists that it is not enough for a doctor to have mere technical proficiency, to know by rote his drugs and medicines, but rather he must be a "philosophical" doctor, *i.e.,* he must know the first principles of medicine. He must know when to employ a particular drug in order to achieve a valuable result. In other words, he must know his universal principles and his particulars, and he must be able to establish their relations, over and above the preliminary mastery of medical technique which he must have. Similarly the rhetorician, or speaker, or communicator,

[3] Lane Cooper, *The Phaedrus, Ion, Gorgias and Symposium, with Passages from the Republic and the Laws,* 1st edition, Oxford University Press, New York, 1938, 266 e2–267 a5.

must be able to relate soundly his universals and particulars, for after all this is precisely what every proposition does.

What does this classic theory of communication amount to, this theory of dialectical rhetoric, when it is applied to the problem in our world today? The answer to this question is one which can hardly be overemphasized in our situation which has been complicated by the development of mass media of communication, of statistical techniques, of advertising, propaganda, opinion polls, let alone the advance in the science of semantics. In this welter of material, the fact that communication involves philosophy, that it is ultimately a philosophical enterprise, tends to be forgotten. Plato once and for all in his attack upon the ancient sophists demonstrated the complete futility of dealing with rhetoric merely as technique, with rhetoric which had its only sanction in what an audience might be persuaded to accept as probable, with rhetoric which permitted its practitioners to boast that they could take any side of any argument and overcome the opposition. In contrast, Plato insists that the first question is always, "Does the utterance correspond to the facts?" After this question has been answered in the affirmative, then rhetoric can move on to the secondary problem of techniques of effective communication. This is what Plato means when he says that the communicator must be a "lover of wisdom," a philosopher in the broadest sense of the word, one who has some conception of what he believes to be truth. All of us in our time will do well to listen to him, for in the last analysis, on whatever level communication takes place, there is always the question of truth and validity. No concern for techniques will make it possible to avoid this question, while in philosophy lies the way to the answer.

IV

THE STRUCTURE AND FUNCTION OF
COMMUNICATION IN SOCIETY

BY

HAROLD D. LASSWELL

The Act of Communication

A convenient way to describe an act of communication is to answer the following questions:

> Who
> Says What
> In Which Channel
> To Whom
> With What Effect?

The scientific study of the process of communication tends to concentrate upon one or another of these questions. Scholars who study the "who," the communicator, look into the factors that initiate and guide the act of communication. We call this subdivision of the field of research *control analysis*. Specialists who focus upon the "says what" engage in *content analysis*. Those who look primarily at the radio, press, film and other channels of communication are doing *media analysis*. When the principal concern is with the persons reached by the media, we speak of *audience analysis*. If the question is the impact upon audiences, the problem is *effect analysis*. [1]

Whether such distinctions are useful depends entirely upon the

---

[1] For more detail, consult the introductory matter in Bruce L. Smith, Harold D. Lasswell and Ralph D. Casey, *Propaganda, Communication, and Public Opinion: A Comprehensive Reference Guide,* Princeton University Press, Princeton, 1946.

degree of refinement which is regarded as appropriate to a given scientific and managerial objective. Often it is simpler to combine audience and effect analysis, for instance, than to keep them apart. On the other hand, we may want to concentrate on the analysis of content, and for this purpose subdivide the field into the study of purport and style, the first referring to the message, and the second to the arrangement of the elements of which the message is composed.

Structure and Function

Enticing as it is to work out these categories in more detail, the present discussion has a different scope. We are less interested in dividing up the act of communication than in viewing the act as a whole in relation to the entire social process. Any process can be examined in two frames of reference, namely, structure and function; and our analysis of communication will deal with the specializations that carry on certain functions, of which the following may be clearly distinguished: (1) The surveillance of the environment; (2) the correlation of the parts of society in responding to the environment; (3) the transmission of the social heritage from one generation to the next.

Biological Equivalencies

At the risk of calling up false analogies, we can gain perspective on human societies when we note the degree to which communication is a feature of life at every level. A vital entity, whether relatively isolated or in association, has specialized ways of receiving stimuli from the environment. The single-celled organism or the many-membered group tends to maintain an internal equilibrium and to respond to changes in the environment in a way that maintains this equilibrium. The responding process calls for specialized ways of bringing the parts of the whole into harmonious action. Multi-celled animals specialize cells to the function of external contact and internal correlation. Thus, among the primates, specialization is exemplified by organs such as the ear and eye, and the nervous system itself. When the stimuli receiving and disseminating patterns operate smoothly, the several parts of the animal act in concert in reference to the environment ("feeding," "fleeing," "attacking").[2]

In some animal societies certain members perform specialized roles, and survey the environment. Individuals act as "sentinels," standing apart from the herd or flock and creating a disturbance whenever an alarming change occurs in the surroundings. The trumpeting, cackling or shrilling of the sentinel is enough to set the herd in motion. Among the activities engaged in by specialized "leaders" is the internal stimulation of "followers" to adapt in an orderly manner to the circumstances heralded by the sentinels.[3]

Within a single, highly differentiated organism, incoming nervous impulses and outgoing impulses are transmitted along fibers that make synaptic junction with other fibers. The critical points in the process occur at the relay stations, where the arriving impulse may be too weak to reach the threshold which stirs the next link into action. At the higher centers, separate currents modify one another, producing results that differ in many ways from the outcome when each is allowed to continue a separate path. At any relay station there is no conductance, total conductance or intermediate conductance. The same categories apply to what goes on among members of an animal society. The sly fox may approach the barnyard in a way that supplies too meager stimuli for the sentinel to sound the alarm. Or the attacking animal may eliminate the sentinel before he makes more than a feeble outcry. Obviously there is every gradation possible between total conductance and no conductance.

Attention in World Society

When we examine the process of communication of any state in the world community, we note three categories of specialists. One group surveys the political environment of the state as a whole,

[2] To the extent that behavior patterns are transmitted in the structures inherited by the single animal, a function is performed parallel to the transmission of the "social heritage" by means of education.

[3] On animal sociology see: Warder C. Allee, *Animal Aggregations,* University of Chicago Press, Chicago, 1931; *The Social Life of Animals,* Norton, New York, 1935.

another correlates the response of the whole state to the environment, and the third transmits certain patterns of response from the old to the young. Diplomats, attachés, and foreign correspondents are representative of those who specialize on the environment. Editors, journalists, and speakers are correlators of the internal response. Educators in family and school transmit the social inheritance.

Communications which originate abroad pass through sequences in which various senders and receivers are linked with one another. Subject to modification at each relay point in the chain, messages originating with a diplomat or foreign correspondent may pass through editorial desks and eventually reach large audiences.

If we think of the world attention process as a series of *attention frames,* it is possible to describe the rate at which comparable content is brought to the notice of individuals and groups. We can inquire into the point at which "conductance" no longer occurs; and we can look into the range between "total conductance" and "minimum conductance." The metropolitan and political centers of the world have much in common with the interdependence, differentiation, and activity of the cortical or subcortical centers of an individual organism. Hence the attention frames found in these spots are the most variable, refined, and interactive of all frames in the world community.

At the other extreme are the attention frames of primitive inhabitants of isolated areas. Not that folk cultures are wholly untouched by industrial civilization. Whether we parachute into the interior of New Guinea, or land on the slopes of the Himalayas, we find no tribe wholly out of contact with the world. The long threads of trade, of missionary zeal, of adventurous exploration and scientific field study, and of global war, reach the far distant places. No one is entirely out of this world.

Among primitives the final shape taken by communication is the ballad or tale. Remote happenings in the great world of affairs, happenings that come to the notice of metropolitan audiences, are reflected, however dimly, in the thematic material of ballad singers and reciters. In these creations far away political leaders may be shown supplying land to the peasants or restoring an abundance of game to the hills.[4]

When we push upstream of the flow of communication, we note that the immediate relay function for nomadic and remote tribesmen is sometimes performed by the inhabitants of settled villages with whom they come in occasional contact. The relayer can be the school teacher, doctor, judge, tax collector, policeman, soldier, peddler, salesman, missionary, student; in any case he is an assembly point of news and comment.

More Detailed Equivalencies

The communication processes of human society, when examined in detail, reveal many equivalencies to the specializations found in the physical organism, and in the lower animal societies. The diplomats, for instance, of a single state are stationed all over the world and send messages to a few focal points. Obviously, these incoming reports move from the many to the few, where they interact upon one another. Later on, the sequence spreads fanwise according to a few to many pattern, as when a foreign secretary gives a speech in public, an article is put out in the press, or a news film is distributed to the theaters. The lines leading from the outer environment of the state are functionally equivalent to the afferent channels that convey incoming nervous impulses to the central nervous system of a single animal, and to the means by which alarm is spread among a flock. Outgoing, or efferent impulses, display corresponding parallels.

The central nervous system of the body is only partly involved in the entire flow of afferent-efferent impulses. There are automatic systems that can act on one another without involving the "higher" centers at all. The stability of the internal environment is maintained principally through the mediation of the vegetive or autonomic specializations of the nervous system. Similarly, most of the messages within any state do not involve the central channels of communication. They take place within families, neighborhoods, shops, field

---

[4] Excellent examples are given in Robert Redfield's account of *Tepoztlan, A Mexican Village: A Study of Folk Life*, University of Chicago Press, Chicago, 1930.

gangs, and other local contexts. Most of the educational process is carried on the same way.

A further set of significant equivalencies is related to the circuits of communication, which are predominantly one-way or two-way, depending upon the degree of reciprocity between communicators and audience. Or, to express it differently, two-way communication occurs when the sending and receiving functions are performed with equal frequency by two or more persons. A conversation is usually assumed to be a pattern of two-way communication (although monologues are hardly unknown). The modern instruments of mass communication give an enormous advantage to the controllers of printing plants, broadcasting equipment, and other forms of fixed and specialized capital. But it should be noted that audiences do "talk back," after some delay; and many controllers of mass media use scientific methods of sampling in order to expedite this closing of the circuit.

Circuits of two-way contact are particularly in evidence among the great metropolitan, political and cultural centers in the world. New York, Moscow, London and Paris, for example, are in intense two-way contact, even when the flow is severely curtailed in volume (as between Moscow and New York). Even insignificant sites become world centers when they are transformed into capital cities (Canberra in Australia, Ankara in Turkey, the District of Columbia, U.S.A.). A cultural center like Vatican City is in intense two-way relationship with the dominant centers throughout the world. Even specialized production centers like Hollywood, despite their preponderance of outgoing material, receive an enormous volume of messages.

A further distinction can be made between message controlling and message handling centers and social formations. The message center in the vast Pentagon Building of the War Department in Washington, D.C., transmits with no more than accidental change incoming messages to addressees. This is the role of the printers and distributors of books; of dispatchers, linemen, and messengers connected with telegraphic communication; of radio engineers, and other technicians associated with broadcasting. Such message handlers may be contrasted with those who affect the content of what is said, which is the function of editors, censors, and propagandists. Speaking of the symbol specialists as a whole, therefore, we separate them into the manipulators (controllers) and the handlers; the first group typically modifies content, while the second does not.

Needs and Values

Though we have noted a number of functional and structural equivalencies between communication in human societies and other living entities, it is not implied that we can most fruitfully investigate the process of communication in America or the world by the methods most appropriate to research on the lower animals or on single physical organisms. In comparative psychology when we describe some part of the surroundings of a rat, cat, or monkey as a stimulus (that is, as part of the environment reaching the attention of the animal), we cannot ask the rat; we use other means of inferring perception. When human beings are our objects of investigation, we can interview the great "talking animal." (This is not that we take everything at face value. Sometimes we forecast the opposite of what the person says he intends to do. In this case, we depend on other indications, both verbal and non-verbal.)

In the study of living forms, it is rewarding, as we have said, to look at them as modifiers of the environment in the process of gratifying needs, and hence of maintaining a steady state of internal equilibrium. Food, sex, and other activities which involve the environment can be examined on a comparative basis. Since human beings exhibit speech reactions, we can investigate many more relationships than in the non-human species.[5] Allowing for the data furnished by speech (and other communicative acts), we can investigate human society in terms of values; that is, in reference to categories of relationships that are recognized objects of gratification. In America, for example, it requires no elaborate technique of study to discern that power and respect are values. We can demon-

[5] Properly handled, the speech event can be described with as much reliability and validity as many non-speech events which are more conventionally used as data in scientific investigations.

strate this by listening to testimony, and by watching what is done when opportunity is afforded.

It is possible to establish a list of values current in any group chosen for investigation. Further than this, we can discover the rank order in which these values are sought. We can rank the members of the group according to their position in relation to the values. So far as industrial civilization is concerned, we have no hesitation in saying that power, wealth, respect, well being, and enlightenment are among the values. If we stop with this list, which is not exhaustive, we can describe on the basis of available knowledge (fragmentary though it may often be), the social structure of most of the world. Since values are not equally distributed, the social structure reveals more or less concentration of relatively abundant shares of power, wealth and other values in a few hands. In some places this concentration is passed on from generation to generation, forming castes rather than a mobile society.

In every society the values are shaped and distributed according to more or less distinctive patterns (*institutions*). The institutions include communications which are invoked in support of the network as a whole. Such communications are the ideology; and in relation to power we can differentiate the political *doctrine,* the political *formula* and the *miranda.*[6] These are illustrated in the United States by the doctrine of individualism, the paragraphs of the Constitution, which are the formula, and the ceremonies and legends of public life, which comprise the miranda. The ideology is communicated to the rising generation through such specialized agencies as the home and school.

Ideology is only part of the myths of any given society. There may be counter ideologies directed against the dominant doctrine, formula, and miranda. Today the power structure of world politics is deeply affected by ideological conflict, and by the role of two giant powers, the United States and Russia.[7] The ruling elites view one

[6] These distinctions are derived and adapted from the writings of Charles E. Merriam, Gaetano Mosca, Karl Mannheim, and others. For a systematic exposition see the forthcoming volume by Harold D. Lasswell and Abraham Kaplan.

[7] See William T. R. Fox, *The Super-Powers,* Harcourt, Brace, New York, 1944, and Harold D. Lasswell, *World Politics Faces Economics,* McGraw-Hill, New York, 1945.

another as potential enemies, not only in the sense that interstate differences may be settled by war, but in the more urgent sense that the ideology of the other may appeal to disaffected elements at home and weaken the internal power position of each ruling class.

Social Conflict and Communication

Under the circumstances, one ruling element is especially alert to the other, and relies upon communication as a means of preserving power. One function of communication, therefore, is to provide intelligence about what the other elite is doing, and about its strength. Fearful that intelligence channels will be controlled by the other, in order to withhold and distort, there is a tendency to resort to secret surveillance. Hence international espionage is intensified above its usual level in peacetime. Moreover, efforts are made to "black out" the self in order to counteract the scrutiny of the potential enemy. In addition, communication is employed affirmatively for the purpose of establishing contact with audiences within the frontiers of the other power.

These varied activities are manifested in the use of open and secret agents to scrutinize the other, in counter intelligence work, in censorship and travel restriction, in broadcasting and other informational activities across frontiers.

Ruling elites are also sensitized to potential threats in the internal environment. Besides using open sources of information, secret measures are also adopted. Precautions are taken to impose "security" upon as many policy matters as possible. At the same time, the ideology of the elite is reaffirmed, and counter ideologies are suppressed.

The processes here sketched run parallel to phenomena to be observed throughout the animal kingdom. Specialized agencies are used to keep aware of threats and opportunities in the external environment. The parallels include the surveillance exercised over the internal environment, since among the lower animals some herd leaders sometimes give evidence of fearing attack on two fronts, internal and external; they keep an uneasy eye on both environments. As a means of preventing surveillance by an enemy, well known devices are at the disposal of certain species, *e.g.,* the squid's use of a liquid fog screen, the protective coloration of the chameleon. However, there appears to be 'no correlate of the distinction between the "secret" and "open" channels of human society.

Inside a physical organism the closest parallel to social revolution would be the growth of new nervous connections with parts of the body that rival, and can take the place of, the existing structures of central integration. Can this be said to occur as the embryo develops in the mother's body? Or, if we take a destructive, as distinct from a reconstructive, process, can we properly say that internal surveillance occurs in regard to cancer, since cancers compete for the food supplies of the body?

Efficient Communication

The analysis up to the present implies certain criteria of efficiency or inefficiency in communication. In human societies the process is efficient to the degree that rational judgments are facilitated. A rational judgment implements value-goals. In animal societies communication is efficient when it aids survival, or some other specified need of the aggregate. The same criteria can be applied to the single organism.

One task of a rationally organized society is to discover and control any factors that interfere with efficient communication. Some limiting factors are psychotechnical. Destructive radiation, for instance, may be present in the environment, yet remain undetected owing to the limited range of the unaided organism.

But even technical insufficiencies can be overcome by knowledge. In recent years shortwave broadcasting has been interfered with by disturbances which will either be surmounted, or will eventually lead to the abandonment of this mode of broadcasting. During the past few years advances have been made toward providing satisfactory substitutes for defective hearing and seeing. A less dramatic, though no less important, development has been the discovery of how inadequate reading habits can be corrected.

There are, of course, deliberate obstacles put in the way of communication, like censorship and drastic curtailment of travel. To some extent obstacles can be surmounted by skillful evasion, but in the long run it will doubtless be more efficient to get rid of them by consent or coercion.

Sheer ignorance is a pervasive factor whose consequences have never been adequately assessed. Ignorance here means the absence, at a given point in the process of communication, of knowledge which is available elsewhere in society. Lacking proper training, the personnel engaged in gathering and disseminating intelligence is continually misconstruing or overlooking the facts, if we define the facts as what the objective, trained observer could find.

In accounting for inefficiency we must not overlook the low evaluations put upon skill in relevant communication. Too often irrelevant, or positively distorting, performances command prestige. In the interest of a "scoop," the reporter gives a sensational twist to a mild international conference, and contributes to the popular image of international politics as chronic, intense conflict, and little else. Specialists in communication often fail to keep up with the expansion of knowledge about the process; note the reluctance with which many visual devices have been adopted. And despite research on vocabulary, many mass communicators select words that fail. This happens, for instance, when a foreign correspondent allows himself to become absorbed in the foreign scene and forgets that his home audience has no direct equivalents in experience for "left," "center," and other factional terms.

Besides skill factors, the level of efficiency is sometimes adversely influenced by personality structure. An optimistic, outgoing person may hunt "birds of a feather" and gain an uncorrected and hence exaggeratedly optimistic view of events. On the contrary, when pessimistic, brooding personalities mix, they choose quite different birds, who confirm their gloom. There are also important differences among people which spring from contrasts in intelligence and energy.

Some of the most serious threats to efficient communication for the community as a whole relate to the values of power, wealth and respect. Perhaps the most striking examples of power distortion occur when the content of communication is deliberately adjusted to fit an ideology or counter ideology. Distortions related to wealth not only arise from attempts to influence the market, for instance, but from rigid conceptions of economic interest. A typical instance of inefficiencies connected with respect (social class) occurs when an upper class person mixes only with persons of his own stratum and forgets to correct his perspective by being exposed to members of other classes.

Research on Communication

The foregoing reminders of some factors that interfere with efficient communication point to the kinds of research which can usefully be conducted on representative links in the chain of communication. Each agent is a vortex of interacting environmental and predispositional factors. Whoever performs a relay function can be examined in relation to input and output. What statements are brought to the attention of the relay link? What does he pass on verbatim? What does he drop out? What does he rework? What does he add? How do differences in input and output correlate with culture and personality? By answering such questions it is possible to weigh the various factors in conductance, no conductance and modified conductance.

Besides the relay link, we must consider the primary link in a communication sequence. In studying the focus of attention of the primary observer, we emphasize two sets of influences: Statements to which he is exposed; other features of his environment. An attaché or foreign correspondent exposes himself to mass media and private talk; also, he can count soldiers, measure gun emplacements, note hours of work in a factory, see butter and fat on the table.

Actually it is useful to consider the attention frame of the relay as well as the primary link in terms of media and non-media exposures. The role of non-media factors is very slight in the case of many relay operators, while it is certain to be significant in accounting for the primary observer.

Attention Aggregates and Publics

It should be pointed out that everyone is not a member of the world public, even though he belongs to some extent to the world attention aggregate. To belong to an attention aggregate it is only necessary to have common symbols of reference. Everyone who has a symbol of reference for New York, North America, the Western Hemisphere or the globe is a member respectively of the attention aggregate of New York, North America, the Western Hemisphere, the globe. To be a member of the New York public, however, it is essential to make demands for public action in New York, or expressly affecting New York.

The public of the United States, for instance, is not confined to residents or citizens, since non-citizens who live beyond the frontier may try to influence American politics. Conversely, everyone who lives in the United States is not a member of the American public, since something more than passive attention is necessary. An individual passes from an attention aggregate to the public when he begins to expect that what he wants can affect public policy.

Sentiment Groups and Publics

A further limitation must be taken into account before we can correctly classify a specific person or group as part of a public. The demands made regarding public policy must be debatable. The world public is relatively weak and undeveloped, partly because it is typically kept subordinate to sentiment areas in which no debate is permitted on policy matters. During a war or war crisis, for instance, the inhabitants of a region are overwhelmingly committed to impose certain policies on others. Since the outcome of the conflict depends on violence, and not debate, there is no public under such conditions. There is a network of sentiment groups that act as crowds, hence tolerate no dissent.[8]

From the foregoing analysis it is clear that there are attention, public and sentiment areas of many degrees of inclusiveness in world politics. These areas are interrelated with the structural and functional features of world society, and especially of world power. It

[8] The distinction between the "crowd" and the "public" was worked out in the Italian, French and German literature of criticism that grew up around Le Bon's over-generalized use of the crowd concept. For a summary of this literature by a scholar who later became one of the most productive social scientists in this field, see Robert E. Park, *Masse und Publikum; Eine methodologische und soziologische Untersuchung,* Lack and Grunau, Bern, 1904. (Heidelberg dissertation.)

is evident, for instance, that *the strongest powers tend to be included in the same attention area,* since their ruling elites focus on one another as the source of great potential threat. The strongest powers usually pay proportionately less attention to the weaker powers than the weaker powers pay to them, since stronger powers are typically more important sources of threat, or of protection, for weaker powers than the weaker powers are for the stronger.[9]

The attention structure within a state is a valuable index of the degree of state integration. When the ruling classes fear the masses, the rulers do not share their picture of reality with the rank and file. When the reality picture of kings, presidents and cabinets is not permitted to circulate through the state as a whole, the degree of discrepancy shows the extent to which the ruling groups assume that their power depends on distortion.

Or, to express the matter another way: If the "truth" is not shared, the ruling elements expect internal conflict, rather than harmonious adjustment to the external environment of the state. Hence the channels of communication are controlled in the hope of organizing the attention of the community at large in such a way that only responses will be forthcoming which are deemed favorable to the power position of the ruling classes.

The Principle of Equivalent Enlightenment

It is often said in democratic theory that rational public opinion depends upon enlightenment. There is, however, much ambiguity about the nature of enlightenment, and the term is often made equivalent to perfect knowledge. A more modest and immediate conception is not perfect but equivalent enlightenment. The attention structure of the full time specialist on a given policy will be more elaborate and refined than that of the layman. That this difference will always exist, we must take for granted. Nevertheless, it is quite possible for the specialist and the layman to agree on the

---

[9] The propositions in this paragraph are hypotheses capable of being subsumed under the general theory of power, referred to in footnote 6. See also Harold D. Lasswell and Joseph M. Goldsen, "Public Attention, Opinion and Action," *The International Journal of Opinion and Attitude Research,* Mexico City, I, 1947, pp. 3–11.

broad outlines of reality. A workable goal of democratic society is equivalent enlightenment as between expert, leader and layman.

Expert, leader and layman can have the same gross estimate of major population trends of the world. They can share the same general view of the likelihood of war. It is by no means fantastic to imagine that the controllers of mass media of communication will take the lead in bringing about a high degree of equivalence throughout society between the layman's picture of significant relationships, and the picture of the expert and the leader.

Summary

The communication process in society performs three functions: (a) *surveillance* of the environment, disclosing threats and opportunities affecting the value position of the community and of the component parts within it; (b) *correlation* of the components of society in making a response to the environment; (c) *transmission* of the social inheritance. In general, biological equivalents can be found in human and animal associations, and within the economy of a single organism.

In society, the communication process reveals special characteristics when the ruling element is afraid of the internal as well as the external environment. In gauging the efficiency of communication in any given context, it is necessary to take into account the values at stake, and the identity of the group whose position is being examined. In democratic societies, rational choices depend on enlightenment, which in turn depends upon communication; and especially upon the equivalence of attention among leaders, experts and rank and file.

V

SPEECH AND PERSONALITY

WENDELL JOHNSON

Communication reduces to the event, both commonplace and awesome, of Mr. A. talking to Mr. B. And most commonplace and strange of all—possibly the most distinctively *human* occurrence to be found or imagined—is the case in which Mr. A. and Mr. B. are one and the same person: a man talking to himself.

Every speaker is, of course, his own listener, even when (if not *especially* when) he is speaking in public. In fact, even when he is alone, a man speaking to himself is by no means removed psychologically from his social context. What he talks about, to whom (in imagination) and for what purpose, are matters which are never independent of his concerns, associations and motivations as a social being. Mr. A. talking to Mr. B. is, therefore, a social phenomenon, whether or not Mr. A. and Mr. B. are one or two persons. And it is communication, viewed as Mr. A. talking to Mr. B., with respect to both its individual and social implications, that is here to be examined, with particular attention to the relationship between speech and personality. The essential point to be made in this discussion is that when speech is frustrated, personality is frustrated, too, whether personality be viewed as a process of self-realization or with respect to the role it plays in effective social interaction.

Speech is, of course, a form of language behavior and reflects the characteristics of language regarded in its broader aspects. It reflects, in fact, the basic features of symbolic systems generally, so that whatever we may say in the present discussion concerning speech and personality will have implications with respect to the relationships between personality and the uses of other symbolic forms and media as well. The consequences and causes of speech frustration are in some ways and in some measure the consequences and the causes of frustration .of the processes involved in graphic artistic expression, in mathematizing, in the dramatic interpretation of experience, in music, architecture, law, or any of the other facets of symbolic functioning. The science which treats of symbolisms and symbolizations, in themselves and in their interrelationships with one another and with individual and social phenomena, is known as general semantics, and to the extent that it encompasses the scope of consideration here indicated, this discussion presents a general semantic approach to problems of communication.

The present discussion is focused upon speech frustration and its significance so far as personality is concerned, not from any desire on the part of the writer to play up the more negative aspects of the situation, but rather in order to facilitate the organization of an obviously comprehensive problem and to point up the problem in a manner that may be expected to engage the serious attention of a relatively large proportion of all those who are in various ways concerned with the communication of ideas. The frustration of speech, and the consequences of such frustration, are of peculiarly vital concern to everyone who is sensitive to the role that effective speech plays in the democratic process, in scientific, educational and political affairs, and in the growth and ripening of individual personalities.

Restricted Verbal Output

Speech frustration may be observed and considered in various ways. Clearly, of course, it is to be observed in the restriction of verbal output. What the speech pathologists call delayed or retarded speech development is an obvious case in point. Verbal output may be restricted in any degree, with respect to differing aspects of speech behavior, under different sorts of circumstances, and with varying effects. The causative factors may range from the predominately organic, as in cases of aphasia due to brain damage, through the ordinary semantic blockages affecting all of us in varying degrees, to the predominately psychogenic, as in the relative mutism of gravely depressed psychiatric patients.

Restricted verbal output may be accompanied by various personal characteristics and behavior tendencies, in relation to which its significance, from different points of view, is to be appraised. Quiet contentment is not at all like sullen reticence; a bashful child is quite different from a patient psychologist who listens sympathetically to the agitated outpourings of a clinical case. Silence can be, indeed, to one who has learned to judge it well, as richly expressive as any spoken words could ever be. Restricted verbal output is not to be evaluated without regard to its motivations, its setting, and its effects. In the form of effective listening it can be strongly conducive to personal development, cooperation, and group morale. We are at present concerned with it in those instances in which its motivations are individually disorienting and socially disruptive, and in which it is inappropriate to the circumstances under which it occurs.

Stages of the Process of Communication

In addition to generally restricted verbal output, various distortions of verbal expression may constitute the manifestations of speech frustration. The communicative potentialities of speech may be thwarted by forms of expression that are vague or factually meaningless, that involve over or understatement, or that are lacking in reliability and validity. And it is to be considered, of course, that these distortions of communication may be a function of the listener as well as the speaker. Indeed, statements that are by reasonable standards clear, valid and sufficiently comprehensive may be interpreted—even grossly translated—by the listener in ways which are decidedly eccentric and disruptive of the communicative process. Many speakers allow themselves the luxury of an utterly unwarranted sense of security because of a naïve faith in the communicative effects of "defining their terms"—for definitions, too, are subject to the evaluative idiosyncracies of listeners. What Professor Quine of Harvard has called "the uncritical assumption of mutual understanding," which is undoubtedly reinforced by the common practice of "defining our terms," would appear to be one of the most formidable obstacles to effective communication.

FIGURE 1. Schematic stage by stage representation of what goes on when Mr. A. talks to Mr. B.—the process of communication.

KEY:

1. An event occurs (any first order fact serving as a source of sensory stimulation)
2. which stimulates Mr. A. through eyes, ears, or other sensory organs, and the resulting
3. nervous impulses travel to Mr. A.'s brain, and from there to his muscles and glands, producing tensions, preverbal "feelings," etc.,
4. which Mr. A. then begins to translate into words, according to his accustomed verbal patterns, and out of all the words he "thinks of"
5. he "selects," or abstracts, certain ones which he arranges in some fashion, and then
6. by means of sound waves and light waves, Mr. A. speaks to Mr. B.,
7. whose ears and eyes are stimulated by the sound waves and light waves, respectively, and the resulting
8. nervous impulses travel to Mr. B.'s brain, and from there to his muscles and glands, producing tensions, preverbal "feelings," etc.,
9. which Mr. B. then begins to translate into words, according to *his* accustomed verbal patterns, and out of all the words *he* "thinks of"
10. he "selects," or abstracts, certain ones, which he arranges in some fashion and then Mr. B. speaks, or acts, accordingly, thereby stimulating Mr. A.—or somebody else—and so the process of communication goes on, and on—with complications, as indicated in the accompanying text.

(Adapted from Wendell Johnson, *People in Quandaries: The Semantics of Personal Adjustment,* Harper and Brothers, New York, 1946, p. 472. For elaboration see accompanying outline of the process of communication, with discussion, *Ibid.,* pp. 469–481.)

The restrictions and distortions of speech with which we are concerned can be particularly well appreciated in terms of the diagram of the process of communication shown in Figure 1. The diagram provides a convenient organizing scheme for dealing in an orderly manner with an exceedingly complex pattern of events. By breaking the pattern down into a series of stages it becomes possible to examine the functions and the possible disorders at each stage, as well as the conditions importantly related to these functions and disorders.

If we begin by having a look at stage 6, as represented in the diagram, and then work back toward stage 1, perhaps we shall gain most quickly the clearest possible view of the communicative process as it is here presented. So far as spoken language is concerned, what passes in any physical sense between the speaker and the listener are sound waves and, in cases where the speaker is visible to the listener, light waves. These waves may be sufficiently mysterious, but at least they set definite limits to such mystery as there may be in the transmission of whatever the speaker has to communicate to the listener. Anything in the way of "spiritual influence," value," or "the intangibilities of personality" that Mr. A. may succeed in conveying to Mr. B. is to be described ultimately by the physicist conversant with optics and acoustics.

Undeniable as this may be, however, our understanding of communication is to be considerably abetted if we move back a step and examine the events of stage 6 in relation to the functions and the possible disorders involved in stage 5. Limiting our considerations to speech—rather than writing, musical performance, painting, etc. —we see that the functions at this stage are those involved in the use of appropriate symbol systems, such as the English language, for example, including words and the forms according to which they are arranged. The chief functions involved in speech at this stage are those of phonation and articulation of sounds. Auxiliary functions include gesture, posture, facial expression, and general bodily action. It is also to be considered that the manipulation of the situation is involved—the arrangement of background or setting for the spoken words. This may include the use of music, banners, sound effects, color, lighting, clothes, etc. Finally, the means of transmission are to be taken into account—the use of radio, television, motion pictures with sound, telephone, speech recordings, or face to face communication.

The possible disorders affecting these functions fall generally into the following categories: speech and voice defects; anxiety tension reactions, such as are involved in stage fright or feelings of inferiority, which noticeably affect speech; paralyses, diseases, or characteristics of physical appearance which interfere with expressive bodily action, or which tend to call forth unfavorable reactions on the part of listeners; lack of skill in the use of background or staging techniques, together with defects, such as radio static, in the means and conditions of transmission.

Common Speech and Voice Defects

Speech and voice defects may be classified as (a) defective articulation, (b) fluency anxiety (stuttering), (c) general non-fluency, (d) disorders of voice, and (e) ineffective word usage and arrangement.

Defects of articulation take the forms of sound omission (*pay* for *play*), sound substitutions (*wun* for *run*), and sound distortions ("whistling" *s,* or slighted, indistinct sounds). These defects may be due chiefly to faulty training, or lack of sufficient and proper stimulation. They may, in certain of their forms, constitute foreign or regional dialects. They may also be expressive of mental deficiency, or of such common maladjustments as infantilism, shyness and the like, or they may be accompaniments of psychoneurotic or psychotic states. In other cases, they are demonstrably due, in some degree at least, to such organic conditions as cleft palate, dental irregularities, muscular spasticity, or paralysis, or to deficiencies of hearing.

Fluency anxieties, or stuttering, constitute a particularly interesting form of speech frustration. Stuttering, viewed as overt behavior, involves excessive tension, centering in the speech musculatures but spreading with varying degrees of intensity and in varying patterns throughout the organism. No two stutterers are exactly alike with regard to these tensions and, in fact, no two stutterings may be reasonably assumed to be identical in all respects. The practical effect of the hypertension is that of a stoppage, or at least a constriction, of speech. Overtly, this effect is to be observed mainly as prolongation of sounds and as full pauses; other phenomena are repetition of sounds or words and interjection of extraneous sounds or words. The stoppage tensions are to be observed as excessive contraction of the lips, holding of the tongue against the teeth or palate, and holding of the breath and interference with phonation by means of contraction of the pharyngeal and laryngeal musculatures and of the muscles subserving breathing. The excessive tensions are not to be well understood, however, aside from a consideration of the motivations underlying them. These motivations may be meaningfully summarized by the term *anxiety*. The anxiety appears to be primarily a concern on the part of the stutterer as to his ability to speak without stuttering. In this sense, it may be said that stuttering constitutes an attempt on the part of the stutterer to keep from stuttering.

This is no more paradoxical than the statement, which will doubtless seem quite reasonable to practically everyone, that what the tight rope walker does in falling off the rope constitutes in the main his attempts to avoid falling off the rope. Good tight rope walkers are probably not particularly conscious of devoting any significant share of their attention or activity to the negative purpose of not falling. Just so, normal speakers seem not to give any systematic thought to considering how they might keep their speech from becoming blocked. Stutterers, however, as stutterers, testify to a preoccupation with the problem of avoiding non-fluency. To wrap up the problem in a particularly flamboyant verbal package, a stutterer is someone who tries to stop speaking every so often because he is afraid to go ahead, on the chance that if he does he will stutter, an understandable reaction for one who has developed an inclination to try too hard to talk too well in order to please too many people too much.

Stuttering Not a Physical Defect

Scientific investigations, of which there have been a relatively large number and variety, have not served to demonstrate any organic or physical cause for stuttering. The most defensible statement to be made on the basis of all the data so far assembled would appear to be that stuttering is a form of learned behavior. It is unusually illuminating to the present discussion in that it constitutes a rather obvious form of speech frustration occasioned primarily by relatively high and overly uniform social standards with respect to speech fluency. Studies done in the University of Iowa Speech Clinic and Preschools indicate that the average child between the ages of two and five years repeats (a syllable, word, or phrase) about forty-five times per thousand words in free-play speech. So-called beginning "stutterers" do not appear to be excessively repetitious or otherwise non-fluent on the basis of this norm. What seems quite definitely to be the case is that some parents—especially those who stutter themselves, or who have stuttered, or who have known stuttering in their own families—become concerned about the *normal* non-fluency of their children. Through their anxious efforts to "help" the child to speak better they succeed only in making him disturbingly self-conscious about his speech. Adopting the anxieties of his parents, he comes to exert effort to avoid the *normal* non-fluencies that have been disapproved, and goes on to develop the hypertonic avoidance reactions which constitute stuttering in the significant clinical sense of the term. Here we see a clean cut effect, in the form of speech frustration, of an unrealistic social standard.

General non-fluency, not complicated by anxiety tensions as in stuttering, are to be observed as repetitive, jerky, irregular, or labored speech. Such speech patterns may be due to faulty training, lack of certain kinds of speaking experience, lack of preparation and other common, non-pathological factors. In some cases, however, their significance is colored by their association with psychoneurosis, psychosis, or mental deficiency—or, in other cases, with organic pathology, such as cerebral palsy, aphasia, paralyses, etc.

Non-fluencies, whether represented by anxiety-tensions as in stuttering, or as "mental blocking," simple hesitancy, or predominately motor disturbance, constitute a particularly obvious form of speech frustration with causes and consequences having an important bearing on personality development and on the interactions of speaker and listener.

Related particularly to the fluency problems involving anxiety-tensions, there are the anxiety-tension manifestations which are customarily termed stagefright. As overt behavior, stagefright—

which is, of course, not confined to the stage—involves a more or less serious disturbance of speech. It is appallingly common. In an investigation which one of the writer's research students, Mr. Floyd Greenleaf, conducted at the University of Iowa during 1946, a majority of first year students have reported mild to severe degrees of stagefright. The effects on speech are both disintegrative and restrictive.

Communication may be distractingly affected by disorders of voice, also. Characteristics of the pitch, loudness, and quality of a speaker's voice are, of course, influential in determining the degree of effectiveness of his communicative efforts. The more important disorders in this connection are pitch and loudness that are excessively high, low, monotonous, or inflexibly patterned, and quality defects such as nasality, hoarseness and harshness, extending to the severe extreme of aphonia. These conditions of voice may be associated with organic pathology, hearing deficiencies, and personality maladjustments involving infantilism and hypertension particularly, or they may be due to training and vocal abuse, as occasioned by prolonged and strained speaking or shouting.

Word usage may also be faulty, as observed in inappropriate or ineffective word choice, grammatical ineptitudes, or mispronunciations. Such imperfections are most extreme in severe cases of aphasia, are sometimes quite marked in the retarded speech of children and in certain cases of foreign or regional dialects, and are to be observed in ordinary varieties and degrees in the speech of normal but relatively untutored persons. Generally speaking, a distinction is to be made between misarticulation in the production of speech sounds and mispronunciation of whole words.

In some instances communication is adversely affected by certain characteristics of the speaker. Sheer physical size may even be a factor: It has been reported that the average Senator wears a hat a bit larger than the average Representative in Congress! More obvious in their effects, however, are such physical characteristics as paralyses and other crippling conditions, apparent diseases or deformities, and other conditions interfering with expressive gesture, posture and other bodily action. The list is to be extended to include physical unattractiveness, characteristics of shape and size and skin color, which tend to call forth unfavorable reactions on the part of listeners. In this latter connection it is the evaluative reaction of the listener, of course, rather than the characteristics of the speaker, that is responsible in large part, if not entirely, for any failure of communication. As a matter of fact, listeners in our culture are often markedly impressed even by the clothes worn by speakers. A uniform, or the lack of a uniform, can play a crucial role in many a communicative situation.

No sharp line can be drawn between such considerations and those having to do with the effects on communication of lack of skill in staging. Banners, music, sound effects, advance publicity, introductions, sponsoring authorities, platform and auditorium arrangements, dress, the timing of entrances and exits and all the other aspects of showmanship play a clearly important role in determining the reactions of Mr. B. to Mr. A. This is obvious under conditions of public address, but it is no less true in many instances of professional counseling, bargaining, or even private conversation.

The effect on communication which factors of staging or setting appear to have is due fundamentally, of course, to the evaluative tendencies of the listener, but this does not relieve the speaker who wishes to be effective from the obligation of manipulating the communicative situation as adroitly as possible. Lack of skill in the handling of situational factors is one of the notable sources of communicative ineffectiveness. In some cases, of course, certain aspects of the situation may be beyond the speaker's control. Radio static, for example, may scuttle the best laid plans of the most competent speaker, and even poor lighting or acoustic properties in an auditorium—or distracting heat and humidity—may not be entirely subject to correction in particular situations.

These disorders have been discussed in relation to stages 5 and 6 of the process of communication, as diagrammed (Figure 1), not because they are exclusively limited to these stages, but because they are more readily observed at these points in the process. In representing the communicative process as a series of stages, there is no intention of implying that the stages are discrete or independent of each other. Stuttering, for example, is most apparent as a disturbance of overt verbal expression, but as a manifestation of anxiety tension it is to be traced back through at least stages 4 and 3 and may even affect the basic sensory functions represented as stage 2 in the diagram.

The disorders which have been mentioned are perhaps the ones which are most commonly recognized. Their effects on communication are no doubt generally acknowledged, and although in our schools and colleges little enough is done about them their importance seems to be appreciated by most people at least in a naïve sort of way. In fact, their *communicative* significance would appear to be out of all proportion to their actual effects on the intelligibility of speech. And the reason for this is probably to be found in the relatively high and uniform social standards that we tend to maintain with respect to the superficial aspects of speech. That is, we seem inclined to pay more attention to how a speaker says what he says than to what he says. We pay more attention to the package than to the contents.

General Semantic Principles and Disturbances

Certain other disorders of speech, which are more significant from a communicative standpoint than the ones we have discussed, are far less commonly known. In fact, until the recent development of semantics and general semantics many of these disorders were for practical purposes unrecognized; some had not even been named. The more important ones are to be most meaningfully discussed in relation to stage 4 of our diagram. This is the stage of preliminary verbal formulation, the stage at which the preverbal tensions resulting from a sensory stimulation are transformed into words. How vacuously we take speech for granted is to be sensed from a moment of intensive contemplation of this amazing transformation of nonverbal goings on within the nervous system, and throughout the organism, into the curiously codified motor responses that we so glibly refer to as "spoken words"!

One can at least be appropriately humble in recognizing the fact that no one understands very well just how this fateful transformation is brought about. But humility need not be carried to the point of swooning. The fact that does appear to be clear enough, although it is widely disregarded, is that what we verbalize is not—as the "practical minded" seem chronically to take for granted—anything that can be called "external reality." To say, for example, "The room is hot," is not, by any stretch of imagination, to make a statement about the room, as such, "in and of itself." As our diagram indicates, at least four discernible stages are passed through before we utter a statement at all. To stick with our homely example, there is first of all some source of sensory stimulation in what we call "the room"—some sort of "energy radiations" (stage 1) which play upon the sensory end organs in our skin. The effect of these "energy radiations" is that activity is aroused in the nerve endings, with consequent nervous currents which travel into the spinal cord and brain. This we represent in our diagram as stage 2. The resulting "disturbance" (stage 3), which we call "preverbal tensions," is determined in part by the character of the sensory nerve impulses coming into the nervous system and in part by the condition existing in the nervous system at the moment of their arrival. Moreover, the incoming impulses are relayed out to muscles and glands where the resulting activities give rise to proprioceptive stimulation, with subsequent incoming nerve impulses which complicate and intensify the effects of the original sensory stimulation. It is this whole complex process which we represent in our diagram as the preverbal tensions at stage 3. *And it is these preverbal tensions that we verbalize.*

The crucial significance of this fact is that basically we always talk about ourselves. Our statements are the verbalizations of our preverbal tensions. It is these organismic tensions—not the external reality of rooms, chairs, people, sound waves, light waves and pressures—that we transform into words. What we talk about, then, is a joint product of reality (regarded as a source of sensory stimulation) and of the conditions existing within our nervous systems at the time of stimulation. This joint product is represented as stage 3 in our diagram. The preliminary verbalizations of it are represented as stage 4.

The basic function occurring in stage 4 is that of symbolic formulation. This function is affected in a determinative way by the structure of the speaker's available symbolic systems. In the case of speech, the symbolic system is the speaker's acquired language, or languages—his vocabulary and the rules according to which he uses it, the information it represents, the flexibility or rigidity with which he operates with it, and the insight and ingenuity with which he abstracts, from all the verbal formulations possible to him, those few statements which he actually utters.

The disorders to be considered in relation to stage 4 are to be identified accordingly. They fall roughly into three main categories. There are, first, deficiencies in vocabulary and grammatical form. While a quite limited store of words, arranged in relatively simple sentences, might well serve for most purposes of common conversation and small talk, nevertheless present day communal living and technological specialization require very considerable language skills of any citizen who presumes to maintain an intelligent grasp of the wide range of affairs by which his life is affected. Much can be done, of course, to simplify the discussion of even relatively complex social and scientific matters, as has been demonstrated by Rudolf Flesch in his provocative book, *The Art of Plain Talk,* and by I. A. Richards and C. K. Ogden in their publications concerning Basic English (for an unusually practical presentation see I. A. Richards' twenty-five cent *Pocket Book of Basic English*). What these inventive students of language recommend as techniques of simplification, however, demand, for their adroit application, a degree of linguistic skill that is not to be come by without effort. The language skill of a school child who describes a movie, using short simple sentences and a limited vocabulary, is definitely to be contrasted with that of a university professor who manages to discuss psychoanalysis or atomic fission in equally short and simple sentences and with an equally limited vocabulary. In the case of the school child there is to be observed a deficiency, perhaps even a very grave deficiency, of language development, while in the simplified speech of the professor there is to be noted a linguistic subtlety and sophistication rarely achieved. It is probably as difficult for a highly trained scientific specialist to explain his work to a second grader as it is for the second grader to explain the scientist's work to the kid in the next seat.

Vocabulary deficiency, that is to say, works both ways; a vocabulary may be too limited or too elaborate for specific purposes of communication. One's vocabulary can be lacking in complexity—or in simplicity. The language used in the present discussion, for example, is probably lacking more in simplicity than in complexity, generally speaking.

The basic point to be emphasized in this connection is that the language, or languages, available to us are such that they tend to make for oversimplification and overgeneralization. Reality—that is, the sources of sensory stimulation—is, so far as we know, decidedly process-like, highly dynamic, ever changing. Our language, on the other hand, is by comparison quite static and relatively inflexible. The six hundred thousand or so words in the English language must serve to symbolize millions—indeed, billions—of individual facts, experiences and relationships. Moreover, the average individual does not use or readily understand as many as ten per cent of the six hundred thousand words making up the English language. In a recent study by one of the writer's students (Helen Fairbanks, *The Quantitative Differentiation of Samples of Spoken Language,* Psychological Monographs, 56, 1944, pp. 19–28), a total of thirty thousand words was obtained from a group of superior university freshmen, and the same size of speech sample was obtained from a group of mental hospital patients diagnosed as schizophrenic. Each individual talked, interpreting fables, until he had produced a sample of three thousand words. For the freshmen just forty-six different words made up half of the thirty thousand words in the total sample. For the schizophrenic patients the comparable figure was thirty-three words. (In fact, *one* word, the one most frequently used by the schizophrenic patients, which was the word *I,* made up over eight percent of their entire thirty thousand words.)

Thus the magnitude of the discrepancy between reality and language, with respect to variability, is by no means adequately indicated by reference to the six hundred thousand words which make up the approximate total for the English language. The discrepancy is more meaningfully indicated by reference to the few hundred—at best, the few thousand—words which make up the practical daily use vocabulary of an ordinary person. In this general sense, we all suffer from vocabulary deficiency. The basic fact is that, at best, there are far more things to speak about than there are words with which to speak about them.

We have already noted that what a speaker has to verbalize is an organismic condition (stage 3) which is a joint product of the sensory stimulation arising from reality and the state of his organism at the moment of stimulation. We have now to add that what a speaker has to communicate (stage 5) is a joint product of this organismic condition (stage 3) and the language structure of the speaker, together with his habits of employing it (stage 4). What a speaker eventually says can hardly be anything but a far cry from the supposedly relevant first order facts (stage 1). And what the listener makes of what the speaker says is something else again! Anyone able to read a headline or twist a radio knob knows that there is no dearth of misunderstanding in the world—and anyone with even an elementary knowledge of the process of communication can only wonder that there is not more misunderstanding and confusion than there seem to be.

Disturbances Due to Ignorance

We have so far considered only a part of the difficulty, however. A second considerable source of communicative inefficiency is sheer ignorance. The number of factual subjects which the average person is able to discuss in detail and with a thorough grasp of important relationships and implications has never been determined with statistical refinement, but it is doubtless lower than any college president would find to be gratifying. The "Quiz Kids" provide a thin ray of hope, but even that is dustied up a bit by the fact that we are seldom given an opportunity to find out whether they are thinkers or mere collectors of odds and ends of information. At best, of course, only a small portion of the little information most of us have is first hand; most by far of what we know we have gained verbally, and most of this has come to us in the form of relatively high order generalization rather than detailed descriptive report. Thus, we are not only drastically limited by our common verbal means of symbolizing fact and experience, but we are also appallingly limited in our reliable knowledge of fact and experience. There is almost always a significant degree of probability that discourse involving two or more individuals will result in misunderstanding, confusion and the intensification of conflict. There is considerable hope of decreasing this probability, however, so long as the obstacles to communication are clearly recognized so that allowance can be made for them in a forthright, impersonal and even good humored manner. On the other hand, a naïve confidence in the constructive possibilities of discussion, an uncritical faith in the power of words, can be disastrously misleading and socially as well as individually disruptive. It obscures both the sources of misunderstanding and the possibilities of agreement and cooperative action.

Disturbances Due to Pre-scientific Orientation

A third large category of disorders affecting communication adversely are those due mainly to the generally pre-scientific orientation so common in our culture. It is this particular class of disorders that general semantics serves to highlight effectively. The disorders constitute violations of fundamental semantic principles. One is handicapped in discussing them briefly, however, because the principles themselves can hardly be presented in a few pages, and the particular frame of reference which they represent, so far from being generally familiar, constitutes in certain respects a major break from our traditional orientation. While a general suggestion of the relevant disorders can be given in the present discussion, any serious reader will insist upon a fuller knowledge of them and of general semantics itself than can possibly be provided in this chapter.[1]

---

[1] The principles and procedures which provide the basic framework of general semantics, and a relatively detailed discussion of the disorders in question, are presented in Wendell Johnson, *People in Quandaries: The Semantics of Personal Adjustment,* Harper and Brothers, New York, 1946. See also the following: Alfred Korzybski, *Science and Sanity: An Introduction to Non-Aristotelian Systems and General Semantics,* Science Press, Lancaster, 2nd ed., 1941; S. I. Hayakawa, *Language in Action,* Harcourt, Brace, New York, 1941; Irving J. Lee, *Language Habits in Human*

Identification

The most pervasive of these disorders is that which Korzybski first described systematically as undue identification.[2] He gave this term a special meaning, which can best be approximated, perhaps, for our present purposes, by saying that undue identification involves a factually unwarranted degree of categorical thinking. Differences among individuals, and differences within given individuals from time to time, are relatively disregarded, because broad group trends and characteristics, and the general tendencies of individuals, are overemphasized. For example, no particular attention is paid to an individual Charles Brown, because he is evaluated by a process of identifying him with—of regarding him as identical with—all other "Negroes." The supposed attributes of the category "Negro" are taken as the basis of evaluation of each and every individual Negro. One who is grossly addicted to identification, therefore, thinks in terms of verbal fictions, or high order abstractions, rather than the extensional, or factual, sources of data and experience. Statements involving undue identifications constitute, therefore, overgeneralizations. It is to be emphasized, however, that generalization, as such, is not being indicted; it is unwarranted generalization, untested and uncorrected, to which reference is being made.

Class names—categorical nouns, verbs, adjectives and adverbs—play a crucial role in the process of identification. The unreflective use of such class words makes automatically for identification, for overgeneralization and the relative disregard of individual differences and specific data. Discussions carried on in terms of such words as "Democrats" and "Republicans," "Communists" and "capitalists," "the Russian," "the Englishman," "the underprivileged," "the consumer," etc., tend, unless conducted with extraordinary semantic consciousness and care in qualification, to degenerate into almost meaningless manipulation of vacuous verbal forms.

Affairs, Harper and Brothers, New York, 1941; *ETC.: A Review of General Semantics,* published quarterly by the Society for General Semantics, Chicago, Illinois.

[2] Korzybski, *op. cit.*

Class names serve to lump together as identical indefinite numbers of different individuals. What this amounts to is the identification of—the failure to differentiate—high order abstractions and lower order abstractions. The principles of general semantics are principles of abstracting. In terms of our diagram (Figure 1), we abstract from the sources of sensory stimulation (stage 1) only so much as our sensory end organs and their functional connections within the nervous system are able to abstract. What we call an object, therefore, an orange, for example, as perceived by us, is a joint product of whatever the orange may be, independently of our perceptions of it, and whatever perceptions of it we are able to make. What appears to be the most reasonable assumption is that we leave out an indefinite number of details which we might be able to abstract if only we possessed different sensory and perceptive apparatus.

Going another step, any description we might make of this orange "manufactured by our nervous system" can be no more than an abstract of somewhat higher order. No matter how thorough we make it, our description can never be complete. Some details will be disregarded or left out of account. We seldom deal, however, with thorough descriptions. The statements we make about even first order experiences are usually partial to an extreme degree, mere summaries, often nothing but a word or two, or just names. A child experiences a complex experience of observation, for example, and we help him to verbalize it by saying, "That? Oh, that's a steamshovel." There should be no difficulty in noting in such an instance the process of abstracting. It is a process of leaving out details—of ignoring the unique in favor of the general, of putting the individual fact under the blurring dim light of the undifferentiating category, of identification.

One may speak of levels of abstraction: the levels, for example, of first order fact or direct experience (the non-verbal orange as seen, felt, or tasted), of naming or description, of inference from description, and of inference of higher order from inference of lower order practically without end. And the level of first order is made up of events which we cannot completely observe or experience, but about which we can imagine or infer as elaborately as we are able in such terms as electrons, protons, hereditary predispositions, immunities and other hypothetical constructs.

Now, identification, as general semanticists use the term, refers most fundamentally to a failure to differentiate the levels of abstraction. Thus, one may exhibit identification by reacting to a name as though it were an object—as in the word magic of certain primitive peoples, or in the reactions made by some persons in our own culture to such words as *syphilis, labor union,* or *expert.* Or, one may exhibit identification by reacting to the object, to what one sees or smells, for example, as though it were the event—as in the behavior of persons with food dislikes, many of whom have never eaten the foods in question, having always responded to the food, as seen, as though it were the food, as digested. Again, one may show identification by reacting to a high order verbal abstract, such as the present discussion, as though it were a highly detailed descriptive report. Having read the present chapter, for example, some readers might announce to their friends that they "know all about" general semantics, and even proceed to pass quite conclusive judgments one way or another concerning it.

The more highly conscious one is of the identifying tendencies of our language processes, the more effectively one may take them into account and even counteract them. Language necessarily involves varying degrees of identification, and for purposes of essential and fruitful generalization identification is indispensable. Precisely because it is both unavoidable and necessary, there is constant need for awareness of it. That is to say, since abstracting is a process of leaving out details, adequate abstracting, and so effective communication, necessitate an awareness of the details left out—and of those left in—in any act of observation or of verbal statement. This awareness is for practical purposes our only effective safeguard against undue and maladjustive identifications.

Projection

Another basic aspect of the abstracting process, which can be misused with unfortunate effects, is that of projection. Since all we have to verbalize (stages 4 and 5) is an internal condition (stage 3), we are able to have any knowledge of, or to communicate anything about, reality (stage 1) only by projecting our internal condition "into" the external events. That is, if Mr. A. is to speak about an orange as a public event, so that Mr. B. might share his experience of it, or check his statements about it, he must project the orange as he experiences it, as "manufactured by his nervous system," into the orange as an object independent of himself. He must, in other words, speak about the orange (stage 3) "as if" it were outside himself (stage 1). If Mr. A. says, "There is an orange on the. table," he is projecting, since all he has to verbalize is a condition inside his own nervous system. But if Mr. B. replies, "Yes, I see the orange," Mr. A.'s projection is thereby, to that extent, justified. If, however, Mr. A. says, "There is a green lizard on the wall," and Mr. B. replies, "I don't see a green lizard," we might, with sufficient evidence, conclude that Mr. A. is exhibiting the sort of illegitimate projection that we call hallucination.

There is nothing abnormal about projection, as such. In fact, it is, like identification, unavoidable and necessary. It is an integral aspect of the process of abstracting. What is essential, for purposes of effective abstracting and communication, is that there be adequate consciousness of projection. We may, for practical emphasis, speak of consciousness of projection as "to-me-ness." That is to say, Mr. A. exhibits consciousness of his own projecting when he says, "It seems to me that there is a green lizard on the wall," or, "This orange tastes sour to me. How does it taste to you?" In this way he indicates an awareness that what he reports is a personal experience, not a universal truth—a personal experience, or evaluation, which depends for its reliability as a social fact on the degree to which others concur in it. Lack of "to-me-ness" is to be observed particularly ·in language that is highly "is-y"—in such statements as "This orange is sour," as though the sourness were in the orange rather than a quality of the experience of tasting the orange. To someone else the orange might taste sweet. Statements like "John is stupid," "Mary is beautiful," "Taxes are high," suggest, at least, a lack of consciousness of projection on the part of the speaker.

So long as the listener is aware of the speaker's projection, the listener, at least, can allow for it and respond accordingly. This is exemplified by a competent psychiatrist's manner of responding to the deluded statements of a patient who is indulging to an extreme degree in unconscious projection. The psychiatrist at least does not argue with the patient, and thereby sets us all an object lesson of great promise. He may go further, of course, and does whenever possible, to help the patient become sufficiently aware of his projecting to recapture a useful degree of self-critical ability. Participants in discussion groups and forums might well study closely the psychiatrist's techniques in bringing about such a beneficent transformation. If, in our schools, we ever get around to doing something systematically about teaching pupils how to listen, it would appear that one of the things most worth doing would be that of giving them a psychiatric attitude toward speakers who are relatively lacking in "to-me-ness."

Just so, in the teaching of speech, from the preschool ages on through graduate school and beyond, doubtless much can be done to improve communication by training speakers in consciousness of projection. This would amount to training speakers to listen effectively to themselves, out of due deference to the fact that every speaker is, as a rule, his own most affected listener. Such training would also involve attention to developing the speaker's skill in allowing for the lack, in those listeners in whom there is a notable lack, of awareness of the role of projection in verbal expression.

Unconscious projection would appear to be a mechanism fundamental in the development of delusional states, hysterical paralysis, fatigue and other symptoms, as well as prejudices of various kinds. It goes without saying that such reaction tendencies militate pervasively against effective communication. They limit the possibilities of adequate abstracting, and they make for systematic distortion of the verbal formulation of experience.

Two Valued Evaluation

Undue identification and unconscious projection give rise to a considerable variety of disorders of abstracting and symbolic expression. One of the more common of these is to be seen as an excessive tendency to formulate issues and situations in a two valued, either-orish manner; people are evaluated as good or bad, policies as right or wrong, organizations as American or un-American, etc. With such an orientation, there are only two sides to any question, and one of them is to be rejected. This is the formula of conflict: The number of choices is reduced to two, and a choice is insisted upon. A two valued scheme of classification automatically enforces a vicious sorting of people into Jews and non-Jews, Americans and aliens, acceptable and non-acceptable. Identification without due regard to individual differences, together with unconscious projection of the resulting categorical evaluations, more or less inevitably results in an unrelenting either-orishness, conducive to conflict, prejudice, confusion and injustice. It appears to be essentially futile to attempt to counteract specific prejudices, delusions, or fixed attitudes of any sort, so long as the underlying two valued orientation, arising out of relatively unconscious identification and projection, is left unexamined and undisturbed.

Related Disturbing Factors

Further analysis of the semantic disorders operating particularly, though not exclusively, at stage 4 of the communicative process, as diagrammed, would extend this discussion unduly. The more fundamental mechanisms of misevaluation have been indicated, unconscious identification and projection, and excessive either-orishness. The specific effects of these mechanisms are too numerous and varied to be catalogued readily and briefly.[3] The effects are to be observed in an impressive variety of distortions and frustrations of the symbolic functions involved in speech and in interpretations of the spoken word. The consequences for personality development and for interpersonal relationships are disintegrative in varying forms and degrees.

At stage 3 of the process of communication the basic functions are those of the transmission of nerve currents from the sensory end organs (eye, ear, etc.) to the spinal, thalamic and cortical levels

[3] See Johnson, *op. cit.*, chapters 5 through 12, and pp. 469–481.

of the central nervous system, and the relaying of these nerve currents out to muscles and glands, with consequent bodily changes from which further afferent nerve impulses arise to travel back to the central nervous system, elaborating and complicating the bodily condition later to be verbalized in stages 4 and 5.

Impaired transmission of nerve currents, the main disorder involved in stage 3, may manifest itself as failure of response, or as incoordination of response, to stimuli. The impaired transmission may be due to physical or semantic factors. That is, it may be due to damage to nerve tracts resulting from infections, tumors, inherited defects, etc. Or, it may be due to acquired or learned semantic blockages, as seen in inattentiveness, disinterest, aversion to colors, etc.; undelayed preverbal reactions of rejection, or overreactions of uncritical acceptance; fear responses, reactions of self-defensiveness, "bristling," etc.; fainting in response to certain odors, or in response to certain situations such as large crowds or small enclosures. Such reactions would appear to be dependent upon the characteristic identifications and projections discussed in relation to stage 4, but they are here identified with stage 3 because they are to be observed chiefly as highly conditioned organismic, preverbal responses to sensory stimulation. Perhaps they can best be characterized in a general sense as undelayed overreactions.

With respect to stage 2, the main function is sensory stimulation, and the chief disorder is that of sensory deficiency or defect, such as impaired vision, or blindness, and impaired hearing acuity, or deafness. Aside from the commonly recognized physical causes of such sensory defects, there are to be duly considered also the semantogenic (roughly psychological) factors responsible for hysterical or psychoneurotic blindness or deafness, for example. The mechanisms described in connection with stage 4 appear to have pervasive effects throughout the abstracting and communicative process.

It remains to be said of stage 1, the sources of sensory stimulation, that these sources play a less determinative role in most communication than might be commonly assumed. As we have noted, we do not verbalize in any direct or complete sense the "facts" of so-called reality. A relatively elaborate series of evaluative and transformative processes intervene between the sources of sensory stimulation (stage 1) and overt expression (stage 5). Nevertheless, it is the responsibility of the speaker to see to it that his statements mirror, as reliably as these intervening processes will allow, the facts to which his statements presumably refer. And reliability, in this case, is to be gauged in terms of the agreement among speakers and their listeners as to the factual dependability of given statements. Our common world of agreed upon facts is a kind of average of the abstracting, evaluating and reporting in which we all share. Public opinion, that fateful product of general communication, can be no more reliable than the common consciousness of abstracting, of identification and projection, will permit it to be. A population ignorant of the abstracting processes involved in communication can, with little difficulty, be led off in the fruitless or disastrous pursuit of red herrings and verbal mirages. Delusion can be made epidemic, as has been often and unfortunately demonstrated. Fifty million Frenchmen can be wrong—and never suspect it.

Concluding Considerations

When the processes of abstracting, evaluating and reporting essential to speech are distorted and frustrated by the mechanisms which have been indicated, personality, however defined, is correspondingly affected. Viewed as self-realization, personality is affected by the disorders described in ways that are reflected in self-defensive anxiety tensions, in aggressiveness, withdrawing tendencies, feelings of inferiority and guilt, schizoid rigidities and resistances to growth, provincial or local loyalties, fears and discouragements, personalized resentments, etc. Personalities so affected, viewed with respect to their effects on social interaction, tend to be disintegrative, conducive to conflict, and preventive of constructive cooperation. The possibilities of change, in terms of personal development, are obscured by overgeneralizations, rigidly held and untested. Similarly, "other persons" are grossly identified and evaluated in terms of categories which tend to obliterate the promising variations in the individuals involved. Language, under the spell of unconscious identification and projection, not only renders our capacities for communication untrustworthy, but at the same time it impairs our very powers of observation. The effects on personality need hardly be labored.

There is scant mystery in the more obvious effects on personality of the disorders discussed in relation to stage 5. To the extent that stuttering, lisping, or disorders of voice, for example, render communication difficult or unsatisfying, they tend to occasion a reduction in verbal output and some degree of seclusiveness on the part of the speaker. The psychology of the speech defective is largely the psychology of frustration and withdrawal. And these effects on personality are by no means without subsequent effect on the speech behavior of the person concerned. It is a vicious circle, or spiral, phenomenon: nothing fails like failure.

These remarks owe their significance in our culture, however, at least to considerable degree, to our prevailing social standards. The importance we attach to fluency and to the conventionalities of diction and grammar is hardly warranted by considerations of intelligibility alone. We are slaves of fashion, and of tradition, in speech as in so many other things. A great deal of the speech correction we do in our schools and clinics is apparently motivated on purely esthetic grounds. To this extent it is on a par with beauty culture. This is to say that it reflects a need for training in listening. Ineffectiveness of communication appears to lie, very often, in the evaluative habits of listeners who allow a lisp, or a stutter, or the color of a speaker's skin, to distract them from giving due attention to what the speaker says. Many a speaker who would function adequately, so far as the communication of ideas is concerned, in a culture dedicated to essentials, is in our culture rated as "defective." The relatively high and uniform social standards which we insist upon with respect to the superficialities of speech create problems that would not otherwise exist either for speakers or for listeners. The personality maladjustments of many of the individuals whom we call speech defectives are due as much, or more, to the reactions of their listeners as to the characteristics of their own speech.

Generally speaking, the relationship between speech and personality is so close that the two terms may hardly be disentangled.

Whatever we might care to mean by personality is judged largely by whatever occurs at stage 5 in our diagram—and it is "understood" largely on the basis of whatever occurs in stages 2 to 4. Speech is not only the evidence of personality, but it is also probably the chief means by which it is molded. It seems hardly possible that either term could have any significant meaning in isolation from the other. Communication may be viewed as the interaction of personalities through the medium of speech, and it is when the speaker is his own listener that the closeness of the relationship between speech and personality becomes strikingly apparent.

It has been the burden of this discussion to formulate this relationship with reference to the process of communication, and to point up some of the basic problems of communication by reducing the process to a series of stages, defined in terms of the functions and possible disorders occurring at each stage. If the commonplace event of Mr. A. speaking to Mr. B. has been made thereby to appear somewhat elaborate, or even nearly impossible, it is to be hoped that at the same time a case has been made out for taking it less for granted than both Mr. A. and Mr. B. appear customarily to do.

VI

THE PSYCHOLOGIST'S CONTRIBUTION
TO
THE COMMUNICATION OF IDEAS

BY

IRVING LORGE

When the professor says to his class, "Please take out your note-books," he expects that some students will do as directed. He even expects that some will make preparations to record his remarks. The simple order, given in a classroom, brings out a variety of reactions: a few students will be startled into attention, others will take out their notebooks and get ready to write, and a few will be elated with the notion that the professor has something important to say. There may be another few who will interpret the remark as an indication that the lecture was prepared. The effects of the simple assertion involve acts of attending to the speaker, comprehending the order, acting in certain ways because of the order, evaluating and interpreting the comment, and other behavior like thinking, dreaming, and anticipating. Usually, the full range of behavior does not take place in the same individual, but it can, even though infrequently.

When the professor gets to the content of his lecture, the variety of effects may be extended considerably. Usually, the college professor is concerned with the level of concept or the number of ideas. He usually makes the assumption that since he is speaking English, he will be understood; or he makes the assumption that since he (or some student) understands the material, his auditors will. The large collection of "boners" selected from examination papers demonstrates the error of his ways. In formal lectures, in text presentation, in music, and in the arts, the error is in the assumption that if

79

an individual understands, the audience, the mass of readers and listeners, will behave like an aggregate of such comprehending individuals. A corrective for such a prejudice is in discussion or in conversation with the students. In rapid exchange of roles between speaker and hearer, the lack of communication and the misunderstandings, may become apparent. The speaker may clarify or enrich the message by specific instances, by analogy, by illustration, or by other devices in his repertoire. By questions and responses, the genuine communication process achieves an increase in the probability of the transmission of the message.

In the more formal communications, the adequacy of the transaction must be checked by more formal means. By adequacy is meant some evaluation of the hearer's understanding or comprehension of the speech or the text. It is true that communication implies a relationship between an expresser and an understander. Yet, regardless of whether the expresser's intent is to communicate a fact, an act, a feeling or an idea, it is the actual response by the understander that is crucial. Basically, what the adequacy of the communication is, depends upon what the hearer or the writer does as a consequence of the communication transaction. The mass communication of ideas is an abstraction. At best, mass communication is an account of what happens in individuals. Mass communication usually is a description of the responses of many individuals when they hear presumably identical speeches or when they read presumably identical texts.

Psychologists, for the past fifty years, have recognized that from the hearer's or the reader's side communications have varied in their effects upon different individuals. For instance, they have been concerned with amount of comprehension of the spoken or the written word. The understanding of sentences, paragraphs, passages, and books is an elaborate but individual process. The testing of the amount of comprehension usually may proceed by asking the reader, let us say, to tell what the passage means, or what the author intended; or it may start by asking questions purporting to reveal what the reader grasped. An illustration of the latter form of measuring comprehension is given in the little exercise below. The reader is ordinarily allowed about eight minutes to read and answer the questions on it.

Read this paragraph and then write answers to the six questions. Read it again if you need to.

There are two principal characteristics which, taken in conjunction, may serve to distinguish what is properly called slang from certain other varieties of diction that in some respects resemble it. The first of these is that slang is a conscious offence against some conventional standard of propriety. A mere vulgarism is not slang, except when it is purposely adopted, and acquires an artificial currency, among some class of persons to whom it is not native. The other distinctive feature of slang is that it is neither a part of the ordinary language, nor an attempt to supply its deficiencies. The slang word is a deliberate substitute for word of the vernacular, just as the characters of a cipher are substitutes for the letters of the alphabet or as a nickname is a substitute for a personal name. The latter comparison is the more exact of the two; indeed nick-names, as a general rule, may be accurately described as a kind of slang. A slang expression, like nicknames, may be used for the purpose of con-cealing the meaning from uninitiated hearers, or it may be employed sportively or out of aversion to dignity or formality of speech. The essential point is that it does not, like the words of ordinary language, originate in the desire to be understood. The slang word is not invented or used because it is in any respect better than the accepted term but because it is different. No doubt it may accidentally happen that a word which origi-nates as slang is superior in expressiveness to its regular synonym (much as a nickname may identify a person better than his name does), or that in time it develops a shade of meaning which the ordinary language cannot convey. But when such a word comes to be used mainly on ac-count of its intrinsic merit, and not because it is a wrong word, it is already ceasing to be slang. So long as the usage of good society continues to proscribe it, it may be called a vulgarism, but unless the need which it serves is supplied in some other way, it is likely to find its way into the standard speech.

1. What does *in conjunction* mean?

2. What other variety of diction which resembles slang in some ways is carefully distinguished from it in the paragraph?

3. If you found that there was no English word in regular use to describe persons born of the same parents and invented a word *sibs* to mean such, would *sibs* be slang?

4. Which is the more inclusive term, slang or vulgarism?

5. According to the paragraph, what happens to a slang word or phrase when it proves more expressive of some important meaning than any ordinary word is?

The little test has been given to thousands of high school graduates seeking admission to college. The variety of responses to each question are extraordinary. For question 1, for instance, the sense of *in conjunction* was given adequately as "together" or "at the same time and connected with one another" or "together, in connection with each other." Less adequate but not erroneous senses were "together to form a whole," "joined in connection with," and "together in order of importance." Vague, inadequate responses include "taking the two and comparing them," and "compared together." The responses, thus illustrated, range from completely adequate to vague. There are other responses, however, that are less than vague, they are incorrect, *e.g.,* "in addition," "acting in the same direction," "into thought," and "apart from each other."

Obviously, missing the sense of words or collocations, such as *in conjunction,* distorts the meaning of the passage for the reader. For the second question, the resemblance to slang was given correctly by "vulgarism," and "Mere vulgarism," less adequately by "vulgarism, substituted part of language, ciphers for letters, nicknames," and incorrectly by "nicknames," "a slang word is not a form of diction," "special words used in various occupations," and "a word which is originated and is superior in expressiveness."

To the third question almost as many answered, "Yes," (which is incorrect) as answered "No." And, for the fourth question, many believed "slang" more inclusive than "vulgarism." For the fifth question, the majority obtained the correct answer "it ceases to be slang," or its equivalent, but there a few answered with "a vulgarism." If credit were given for each response to each question with credit like +3 for a completely adequate answer, 0 for a vague one, and —2 for an incorrect one, high school graduates would make scores ranging from +15 to —7. The range of points would indicate a comprehension score from adequacy of communication to confusion, misunderstanding, and contradictions.

Recently, this same exercise was given to a class in the psychology of communication. All the students were college graduates. The range of scores was from +3 to a perfect score of +15. Of the group, 21 per cent made a score of +8 or less, 42 per cent made a score of +9 or +10, and only 14 per cent made a perfect score of +15. In this class of college graduates, wrong answers to the questions were as vague and incorrect as they were for high school graduates, although not nearly as frequent.

The psychologist, by his observations, recognizes that comprehension of a spoken or a written passage will range from satisfactory communication to misconception and error. It is important, however, to emphasize that the kind of questions asked in the passage about slang deals with the manifest aspects of the communication, *i.e.,* the specific information given in the passage. The subtler nuances regarding the attitudes, orientations, and intentions of the writer were not appraised by the reader. The variation of understanding, undoubtedly, would be greater for such subtler communications than for the manifest aspects.

The act of interrogating each individual definitely affects the comprehension of the passage. The questions, as a matter of fact, may have the force of directing the reader's attention and of aiding his understanding of the material. Without the questions, the material might have been skimmed and glossed over. Even though the process of questioning may augment the amount of comprehension, the important fact of individual differences among readers is clearly demonstrated. Not only have psychologists demonstrated the wide range in understandings of printed texts, but also they have shown similar variations in the comprehension of speeches. The poorer the average score on a test on written or spoken materials, the greater will be its apparent difficulty. Such difficulty is undoubtedly attributable to a lack of community between the expresser and *each* understander. Every communication involves an interaction between the knowledges, attitudes, and skills of the writer (or speaker) and those of the reader (or hearer). Yet, as must be evident from the range of scores in college graduates, the reader has no way of evaluating his own understanding of the message. Too frequently, the reader's error is that he is certain that he has comprehended the passage. He is utterly dismayed by the objective demonstration of the error of his reading ways.

The differences in the degrees of understanding from person to person, then, are in part attributable to the unwillingness of individuals to admit that they do not, or cannot, comprehend the text read or heard. For those who feel that they missed something, moreover, the tendency is to avoid the situation completely. Individuals avoid the reading of, or the listening to, material that gives them a sense of frustration or a feeling of being stupid. In general, in communication, the individual tends to use the least effort to get the message. He will not look up the meanings of words, or consider the analogy or the metaphors used or take time to *reason* out the implications of the passage.

Of course, part of the differences in communicability are attributable to the writer or the speaker. He, too, goes by the law of least effort. In general, his error is the greater for he fails to consider the audience—their knowledge of the subject matter, their skill in getting the material through the medium, their knowledge of the vocabulary of the field, their attitudes and prejudices about the material and so on. Since understanding both spoken and written texts is a matter of experience, of habits, of purposes of the understander, the expresser must, for maximum interaction, plan his text in those terms.

The improvement of communication, therefore, may be achieved in two ways. Firstly, educators may try to give children and adults greater skill in understanding the spoken or the printed word. Such communication skills involve not only the understanding of words but the equally important interpretations of graphs and pictures, of gestures and bodily movement, and of rhythms and music. Education can improve the understanding of people by increasing the range of experiences, direct and vicarious, and has done so. The greater the commonality of background, the greater will be the basis for communication.

Communication, however, can also be augmented by the expresser.

Not only must he have reasonable command of the skills of speaking and of writing, but he must acquire a sense of audience. Each expresser, for effectiveness, must think of the individual he is trying to reach. The expresser should think of the interests of his audience, of their sense of reality, of their knowledge of vocabulary, of the number of ideas that they can grasp in a short span of text (or time). From the text on the *slang* passage, it is apparent that part of the difficulty is due to the failure to understand fully the meaning of *in conjunction* or of *inclusive,* or of *intrinsic,* etc. Difficulty, also, may be partially accounted for by the complexity of the sentence structure with its variety of restrictive clauses and phrases like *except when, just as,* and *so long as.* Moreover, the difficulty may also be related to the large number of different ideas expressed in the passage.

Educators have been particularly concerned with estimates of the relative difficulty of printed texts. Their objective was to select those textbooks most appropriate to the grade level of the pupils. Many researches have been attempted trying to relate some aspects of internal structure of the passage (vocabulary, sentence structure and the like) to the general difficulty of the passage. Difficulty of the passage, usually, was estimated on the basis of the average score of a sample of the population. For instance, the average on the *slang* passage could be used as an index of its difficulty. To gain comparability between passages, however, the passage difficulty is related to an outside criterion like a reading test. Different passages would have different scores; thus the higher the average, the easier the text. Of course, such an average obscures the variations that may be an outcome from the differences among individuals in their reading interests and purposes.

After each passage had been assigned some number indicative of its relative ease, the researcher tried to determine if some measure of internal structure or some combination of such measures would predict difficulty. In general, four categories of internal structure have been found to be indicative of difficulty. The four classifications deal with vocabulary difficulty, complexity of sentence structure, the density of ideas, and some measure of the *personalness* of the approach. Vocabulary difficulty usually deals with some estimate of the rarity of lexical units, or the number of different words, or the number of abstract words, or the unusualness of the meanings of the words. Basically, all studies seem to agree that passages using a large proportion of words which are infrequent in occurrence, or that are abstract, or that are used in unusual senses, make for greater difficulty of the passage or for less complete communication. The most important variable in passage difficulty is *vocabulary load*.

Contributing to difficulty, however, is sentence structure. Again, the studies seem to concur in the generalization that difficulty is increased by a relatively greater frequency of compound or complex sentences, or in restrictive phrases. Related to sentence complexity, but yet adding to the difficulty of texts is the number of different ideas per hundred words. When the expresser has to say everything he knows in a few words, he condenses the exposition by liberal use of prepositional phrases or parenthetical expressions.

So far, the only empirically discovered factor that tends to show reduction in the difficulty of passages is some measure of the amount of human interest in the passage. The human interest factor has been appraised by words related to fundamental life experiences, *e.g., home, mother, baby.* Other methods for measuring this factor are the number of personal pronouns, and words learned early in life.

Formulae for predicting the relative ease or difficulty of passages have been developed by several research workers. Primarily, by weighting measures of the vocabulary, sentence structure, idea density, and human interest within a passage, an estimate of the difficulty of the passage is obtained. These estimates, however, do not measure the *readability* with great precision. To the professional writer or speaker, it is fairly obvious that communication is not only easy words, simple sentences, and many personal references. He would recognize the requirement of interesting the reader and of presenting the ideas in coherent form.

The search for panaceas in communication, however, has blinded many people as to the limitations of readability formulae. At best, formulae give only an estimate of difficulty; they do not provide a rule for writing. Donald R. Murphy, editor of *Wallace's Farmer and Iowa Homestead,* has provided an excellent illustration of the fact that readability is more than meeting the requirements of a formula. Mr. Murphy, as a forward looking editor, is searching for ways to increase the *readership* of the articles he publishes. He goes at his job scientifically. He has two versions of an article published in his journals so that a representative sample of the farmers read each version. Then, later, field workers go from farm family to farm family checking on the readership of the articles.

Below are two articles: version A and version B.

A

WHAT WILL YOU DO
WITH YOUR CORN?

The method of handling the present corn crop may affect farm profits this year and have some influence on farm profits for a year or two ahead.

There are several different ways in which farmers might market their 1946 corn. The first way is to turn every possible bushel on the market this fall, keeping only enough corn to feed until new oats come along next summer.

Another method is to feed hogs to heavy weights, raise more early spring pigs, and feed your own cattle or buy cattle to feed.

Still another method is to put corn in storage on the farm selling just enough to pay farm expenses, or sell the corn and take a government loan.

B

WHAT WILL YOU DO
WITH YOUR CORN?

What will you do with the big corn crop? The answer may tell you how much money you will make this year and even next year. Here are suggestions:

1. Turn every possible bushel on the market this fall. Keep only enough corn to feed until new oats arrive next summer.

2. Feed as much as possible of the corn to hogs. Raise early spring pigs to eat more of this corn crop. Buy and feed cattle.

3. Store all the corn on the farm that the cribs will hold. Sell just enough corn to pay expenses. Or, sell corn for ready cash.

Version A, it is true, has relatively longer sentences, more difficult words and fewer personal references than version B. The difference, however, is greater that that. B starts with a quiz, and structures the answer in 1–2–3 order. Version A, on the contrary, is rambling and unclear. The superiority of the B version is attested by field appraisal. On checking readership, B was read by 66 per cent more people than was version A. Studies such as Murphy's have confirmed the generalization that communication is more than simple words, sentences and few thoughts. The most significant feature of readable understandable communication is appeal to the reader's motives and an organization of content so that it can be apprehended.

Thus, the psychologist and educator have produced two important devices for appraising communication, first, the comprehension test, and second, the readability index. These two methods are, of course, related. Generally, the various aspects of research in the communication of ideas are interwoven. For instance, just as there are tests for measuring the understanding of passages, there are tests for the appraisal of word knowledge. Since vocabulary is so dominant a determiner of vocabulary difficulty, the assessment of word knowledge of individuals is also important. What does understanding a word mean? Understanding represents the synthesis of many experiences (or their lack) that the individual has had with the senses of the word. The psychologist tries to get at the meaning of words in a variety of ways. He may ask "What does —— mean?" or he may say "Give me a synonym for ——." Some of the test forms for appraising vocabulary knowledge are given below:

Type   I **Action**—What does action mean?

Type   II Look at the first word. Find the other word in the line which means the same or nearly the same.

>   **action**   1 play — 2 deed — 3 mention — 4 opinion — 5 crime

Type III Look at the first word. Find the other words in the line which mean the same or nearly the same.

>   **action**   1 battle — 2 scene— 3 deed — 4 activity — 5 lawsuit

Type IV Look at the first word. It means several different things. Read the sentences *a, b, c, d* and *e*. Put a check before each sentence in which it is used correctly. Put a cross before each sentence in which it is used incorrectly.

average a. The average of 2 and 4 is 3.
        b. The average temperature this summer was **very** high.
        c. Irving is only an average student.
        d. Ginger ale is a cooling average for summer days.
        e. Alice's marks are about like the average.

Type V Look at the three words a) alternate, b) cardinal, c) assimilate. Then look at the column of twelve definitions. Put the letter **a** before those definitions that belong to alternate, the letter **b** for those definitions that belong to cardinal, the letter **c** for those definitions that belong to assimilate, put an x before those definitions that do not belong to alternate or cardinal or assimilate.

a. **alternate**   ——Roman Catholic official
b. **cardinal**   ——digest
c. **assimilate**   ——take turns
                ——a bird
                ——make like
                ——close-fitting jacket
                ——principal
                ——arrange one after the other
                ——to be absorbed
                ——substitute
                ——became like
                ——figure of speech

In the first example, the respondent may say, "It's when you do something," or "being busy," or "an act," or "a deed," or "part of a play," and so on. Since any idea or sense of the meaning of "action" commonly accepted is adequate, each of the answers is considered correct. The many different ways of responding to the question, "What does action mean?" suggest, firstly, that individuals may respond to the query with a response in terms of use, of description, of example, of synonym, or of genus species; and suggests, secondly, that any of a wide variety of different senses may be used. In the Oxford English Dictionary, for instance, more than three hundred different definitions are recorded for the word "run."

Partially to restrict the number of different responses, type II is used. In this form, the student is asked to choose the one correct meaning from the five options. This item type indicates a kind of passive knowledge of a sense of the word. The difference between type II and the following type III is that the latter tries to get at the number of different senses of the word an individual knows.

Types IV and V attempt to get at nuances of meaning and usage. From all these types, and particularly from the last three, the psychologist gets an indication of the variety of the meanings, usages, and discriminations in meaning a person has and understands. The results, however, from the different methods of appraising vocabulary knowledge indicate that the five forms are measuring the same kind of knowledge or ability. While each form gives a different estimate of the number of words or senses of a word a person knows, the five methods indicate that in any age group, or in any educational group, the knowledge of the lowest scorers is about one third that of the highest scorers, or even worse.

The wide range in vocabulary knowledge reemphasizes the wide range in comprehension. If, in addition to measuring the knowledge of meanings of words, the variety of notions about names like Lincoln, Roosevelt, Republican, and Democrat had also been appraised, the material would again have indicated a variety of different responses varying from adequate to completely wrong. When names of people, places or things are used metaphorically, the sense may be confused. Suppose somebody described Gandhi as the *Lincoln of India,* would there be a unanimity of comprehension and understanding? Undoubtedly, no. Recently, bankers were asked to define "financial independence," "communism," and "collective bargaining." In a select group of bankers, the most impressive fact was the lack of agreement in the interpretation of the words or collocations. Part of the variability in meaning was due to the fact that some bankers interpreted these words with a confounded mixture of their knowledge *and* their prejudices.

Thus, the psychologist has shown that the comprehension of sentences and paragraphs will be quite variable, that part of this variation may be due to the wide range of understandings of specific words and part is attributable to the fact that people read, listen, and misunderstand with their prejudices and their ignorances. If readers and listeners were autocritical about their comprehension, the problem of communication would be somewhat easier.

In addition to appraising individuals' comprehension of passages, or of the meaning of words out of context or in it, or of estimating the difficulty of passages, psychologists and educators have produced lists of words occurring with the greatest frequency, and also lists of the grammatical constructions used most often. The vocabulary of English or American English is tremendous, both written and spoken. In the repository of a standard abridged dictionary there are upwards of one hundred and thirty-five thousand entries; in an unabridged dictionary, there are about four hundred and fifty thousand entries. If to these, were added the words in slang, jargon, technical terminology, and the names of places and people used figuratively or metaphorically, there would be upwards of a million different lexical units. Obviously not each of these words is equally likely to occur. The relative frequency of occurrence has been obtained by counting the number of times each word appeared in print.

Usually a sample of material representative of printed English would be assembled. Then, workers would tabulate how many times each word would occur. For printed English about forty million running words have been counted. In Thorndike and Lorge's "The Teachers Word Book of 30,000 Words," published in 1944, are listed the thirty thousand most frequent words based on a count of twenty-five million words. In this count is given not only a general appraisal of the frequency of occurrence for all kinds of literature, but also separate counts for books for children, and also for popular magazines.

The five hundred most frequently occurring words accounted for almost sixty-seven per cent of the five million words counted in the high circulation magazines, *Saturday Evening Post, Woman's Home Companion, Ladies Home Journal, True Story* and *Reader's Digest*. These five hundred words include *a, about, above, became, because, become, case, cause, chance, dollar, done, don't, every, everything, eye* and *from, front, full*.

Special word counts have also been made by the telephone engineers of the words used in five hundred telephone conversations. As might be expected, the commonest words were "I" and "you." The total number of different words used in the equivalence of eight hours of telephoning was two thousand two hundred and forty. Of these, there were about a thousand different nouns and four hundred and fifty different verbs. *Things* are more frequent than *actions,* or the same actions can be accomplished by, or on, a variety of things.

In addition, counts have been made in French, German, and Spanish. Helen Eaton collected the word frequency for each language, controlling on concept, to develop her "Semantic Frequency List for English, French, German, and Spanish." This was published in 1940. In this book, the six or seven thousand most frequent concepts were collected. The Eaton count was begun while the semantic count for English was in progress.

The *semantic* count was made to correct for the apparent error in *word* counts. Even though the facts about the frequency of words be known, more information is needed about the meanings words may have. Even common words may cause confusion. Take the word *game*. It has been used by various writers in at least fifteen senses: (1) amusement; (2) diversion; (3) diversion in the nature of a contest; (4) such games played in ancient Greece and Rome, *e.g.,* Olympic Games, and by extension, the Modern Olympic Games; (5) the proper method of play; (6) a proceeding, intrigue followed up like a game; (7) a person's policy; (8) a definite portion of play; (9) position or advantage in play; (10) the quarry; (11) the flesh of wild animals used as food; (12) spirited or plucky; (13) lame; (14) to play, sport, jest, or make sport of; (15) to gamble for a prize or wager. Each of these meanings actually occurred in the reading of some five million words.

In general, teachers, psychologists, philologists, linguists, editors, script writers, and lexicographers cannot estimate the relative frequency of the occurrence of each of the different senses of a word. Despite the interpretation via context, many readers will lack the knowledge of some of the senses of the word. Some linguistic scientists believed that since the most frequent words are known, a fundamental vocabulary of seven hundred, eight hundred, or a thousand words would be ample for communication. Unfortunately, the facts are not so simple. For example, *Basic English's* eight hundred and fifty words have not less than twelve thousand five hundred different senses and upwards of eighteen thousand different meanings. About half the words in *Basic English* have from three to thirteen different senses; certain verbs (operators) like *come* have sixty-nine, *go* has ninety-four, and *will* has fifty-eight meanings to add confusion to context.

The Semantic Count of Lorge and Thorndike was based on five million words from a wide variety of sources. The frequency of the occurrence of each meaning was classified by the senses defined in the *Oxford English Dictionary*. The facts for the frequency with which each meaning of each word is used are recorded. Hence, in addition to vocabulary control, the writer and speaker can check the relative unusualness of the sense of the word. Even though primers could certainly be clarified by careful attention to the facts of word and sense frequency, radio speeches and magazine articles would benefit more from such a check.

The words that are used in speech or in writing, or are heard or read, are usually multi-sensed. While it is true that the expresser may have had only one meaning in mind, not every individual will get that meaning by context and by whatever connections he has formed with the word. Thus, the reader (or hearer) will range in his grasp of the sense of the word from practical correspondence with that of the speaker (or writer) to complete independence of it. The kind of meaning or the quality of the idea that the understander gets will only occasionally coincide with that of the expresser; the different individuals in the group will not get the same sense since their backgrounds will differ.

The psychologist, therefore, suggests that it is possible to control vocabulary and meaning to a degree, within materials. He recognizes, fully, that though care in the use of words may minimize communication difficulties, understanding and interpretation are essentially an individual reaction. The mass effort is not the sum of the individual understandings, it is generally less. Misunderstanding of communication in even a few individuals may penalize the communion of communication for all.

VII

MASS COMMUNICATION, POPULAR TASTE AND
ORGANIZED SOCIAL ACTION

BY

PAUL F. LAZARSFELD AND ROBERT K. MERTON

Problems engaging the attention of men change, and they change not at random but largely in accord with the altering demands of society and economy. If a group such as those who have written the chapters of this book had been brought together a generation or so ago, the subject for discussion would in all probability have been altogether different. Child labor, woman suffrage or old age pensions might have occupied the attention of a group such as this, but certainly not problems of the media of mass communication. As a host of recent conferences, books and articles indicate, the role of radio, print and film in society has become a problem of interest to many and a source of concern to some. This shift in public interest appears to be the product of several social trends.

Social Concern with the Mass Media

Many are alarmed by the ubiquity and potential power of the mass media. A participant in this symposium has written, for example, that "the power of radio can be compared only with the power of the atomic bomb." It is widely felt that the mass media comprise a powerful instrument which may be used for good or for ill and that, in the absence of adequate controls, the latter possibility is on the whole more likely. For these are the media of propaganda and Americans stand in peculiar dread of the power of propaganda. As the British observer, William Empson, recently remarked of us: "They believe in machinery more passionately than we do; and modern propaganda is a scientific machine; so it seems to them obvious that a mere reasoning man can't stand up against it. All this produces a curiously girlish attitude toward anyone who might be doing propaganda. 'Don't let that man come near. Don't let him tempt me, because if he does I'm sure to fall.' "

The ubiquity of the mass media promptly leads many to an almost magical belief in their enormous power. But there is another and, probably, a more realistic basis for widespread concern with the social role of the mass media; a basis which has to do with the changing types of social control exercised by powerful interest groups in society. Increasingly, the chief power groups, among which organized business occupies the most spectacular place, have come to adopt techniques for manipulating mass publics through propaganda in place of more direct means of control. Industrial organizations no longer compel eight year old children to attend the machine for fourteen hours a day; they engage in elaborate programs of "public relations." They place large and impressive advertisements in the newspapers of the nation; they sponsor numerous radio programs; on the advice of public relations counsellors they organize prize contests, establish welfare foundations, and support worthy causes. Economic power seems to have reduced direct exploitation and turned to a subtler type of psychological exploitation, achieved largely by disseminating propaganda through the mass media of communication.

This change in the structure of social control merits thorough examination. Complex societies are subject to many different forms of organized control. Hitler, for example, seized upon the most visible and direct of these: organized violence and mass coercion. In this country, direct coercion has become minimized. If people do not adopt the beliefs and attitudes advocated by some power group —say, the National Association of Manufacturers—they can neither be liquidated nor placed in concentration camps. Those who would control the opinions and beliefs of our society resort less to physical force and more to mass persuasion. The radio program and the institutional advertisement serve in place of intimidation and coercion. The manifest concern over the functions of the mass media is in part based upon the valid observation that these media have taken on the job of rendering mass publics conformative to the social and economic *status quo*.

A third source of widespread concern with the social role of mass media is found in their assumed effects upon popular culture and the esthetic tastes of their audiences. In the measure that the size of these audiences has increased, it is argued, the level of esthetic taste has deteriorated. And it is feared that the mass media deliberately cater to these vulgarized tastes, thus contributing to further deterioration.

It seems probable that these constitute the three organically related elements of our great concern with the mass media of communication. Many are, first of all, fearful of the ubiquity and potential power of these media. We have suggested that this is something of an indiscriminate fear of an abstract bogey stemming from insecurity of social position and tenuously held values. Propaganda seems threatening.

There is, secondly, concern with the present effects of the mass media upon their enormous audiences, particularly the possibility that the continuing assault of these media may lead to the unconditional surrender of critical faculties and an unthinking conformism.

Finally, there is the danger that these technically advanced instruments of mass communication constitute a major avenue for the deterioration of esthetic tastes and popular cultural standards. And we have suggested that there is substantial ground for concern over these immediate social effects of the mass media of communication.

A review of the current state of actual knowledge concerning the social role of the mass media of communication and their effects upon the contemporary American community is an ungrateful task, for certified knowledge of this kind is impressively slight. Little more can be done than to explore the nature of the problems by methods which, in the course of many decades, will ultimately provide the knowledge we seek. Although this is anything but an encouraging preamble, it provides a necessary context for assessing the research and tentative conclusions of those of us professionally concerned with the study of mass media. A reconnaissance will suggest what we know, what we need to know, and will locate the strategic points requiring further inquiry.

To search out "the effects" of mass media upon society is to set upon an ill defined problem. It is helpful to distinguish three facets of the problem and to consider each in turn. Let us, then, first inquire into what we know about the effects of the existence of these media in our society. Secondly, we must look into the effects of the particular structure of ownership and operation of the mass media in this country, a structure which differs appreciably from that found elsewhere. And, finally, we must consider that aspect of the problem which bears most directly upon policies and tactics governing the use of these media for definite social ends: our knowledge concerning the effects of the particular contents disseminated through the mass media.

The Social Role of the Machinery of Mass Media

What role can be assigned to the mass media by virtue of the fact that they exist? What are the implications of a Hollywood, a Radio City, and a Time-Life-Fortune enterprise for our society? These questions can of course be discussed only in grossly speculative terms, since no experimentation or rigorous comparative study is possible. Comparisons with other societies lacking these mass media would be too crude to yield decisive results and comparisons with an earlier day in American society would still involve gross assertions rather than precise demonstrations. In such an instance, brevity is clearly indicated. And opinions should be leavened with caution. It is our tentative judgment that the social role played by the very existence of the mass media has been commonly overestimated. What are the grounds for this judgment?

It is clear that the mass media reach enormous audiences. Approximately seventy million Americans attend the movies every week; our daily newspaper circulation is about forty-six million, and some thirty-four million American homes are equipped with radio, and in these homes the average American listens to the radio for about three hours a day. These are formidable figures. But they are merely supply and consumption figures, not figures registering the effect of mass media. They bear only upon what people do, not upon the social and psychological impact of the media. To know the number of hours people keep the radio turned on gives no indication of the effect upon them of what they hear. Knowledge of consumption data in the field of mass media remains far from a demonstration of their net effect upon behavior and attitude and outlook.

As was indicated a moment ago, we cannot resort to experiment by comparing contemporary American society with and without mass media. But, however tentatively, we can compare their social effect with, say, that of the automobile. It is not unlikely that the invention of the automobile and its development into a mass owned commodity has had a significantly greater effect upon society than the invention of the radio and its development into a medium of mass communication. Consider the social complexes into which the automobile has entered. Its sheer existence has exerted pressure for vastly improved roads and with these, mobility has increased enormously. The shape of metropolitan agglomerations has been significantly affected by the automobile. And, it may be submitted, the inventions which enlarge the radius of movement and action exert a greater influence upon social outlook and daily routines than inventions which provide avenues for ideas—ideas which can be avoided by withdrawal, deflected by resistance and transformed by assimilation.

Granted, for a moment, that the mass media play a comparatively minor role in shaping our society, why are they the object of so much popular concern and criticism? Why do so many become exercised by the "problems" of the radio and film and press and so few by the problems of, say, the automobile and the airplane? In addition to the sources of this concern which we have noted previously, there is an unwitting psychological basis for concern which derives from a socio-historical context.

Many make the mass media targets for hostile criticism because they feel themselves duped by the turn of events.

The social changes ascribable to "reform movements" may be slow and slight, but they do cumulate. The surface facts are familiar enough. The sixty hour week has given way to the forty hour week. Child labor has been progressively curtailed. With all its deficiencies, free universal education has become progressively institutionalized. These and other gains register a series of reform victories. And now, people have more leisure time. They have, ostensibly, greater access to the cultural heritage. And what use do they make of this unmortgaged time so painfully acquired for them? They listen to the radio and go to the movies. These mass media seem somehow to have cheated reformers of the fruits of their victories. The struggle for freedom for leisure and popular education and social security was carried on in the hope that, once freed of cramping shackles, people would avail themselves of major cultural products of our society, Shakespeare or Beethoven or perhaps Kant. Instead, they turn to Faith Baldwin or Johnny Mercer or Edgar Guest.

Many feel cheated of their prize. It is not unlike a young man's first experience in the difficult realm of puppy love. Deeply smitten with the charms of his lady love, he saves his allowance for weeks on end and finally manages to give her a beautiful bracelet. She finds it "simply divine." So much so, that then and there she makes a date with another boy in order to display her new trinket. Our social struggles have met with a similar denouement. For generations, men fought to give people more leisure time and now they spend it with the Columbia Broadcasting System rather than with Columbia University.

However little this sense of betrayal may account for prevailing attitudes toward the mass media, it may again be noted that the sheer presence of these media may not affect our society so profoundly as is widely supposed.

Some Social Functions of the Mass Media

In continuing our examination of the social role which can be ascribed to the mass media by virtue of their "sheer existence," we temporarily abstract from the social structure in which the media find their place. We do not, for example, consider the diverse effects of the mass media under varying systems of ownership and control, an important structural factor which will be discussed subsequently.

The mass media undoubtedly serve many social functions which might well become the object of sustained research. Of these functions, we have occasion to notice only three.

THE STATUS CONFERRAL FUNCTION. The mass media *confer* status on public issues, persons, organizations and social movements.

Common experience as well as research testifies that the social standing of persons or social policies is raised when these command favorable attention in the mass media. In many quarters, for example, the support of a political candidate or a public policy by *The Times* is taken as significant, and this support is regarded as a distinct asset for the candidate or the policy. Why?

For some, the editorial views of *The Times* represent the considered judgment of a group of experts, thus calling for the respect of laymen. But this is only one element in the status conferral function of the mass media, for enhanced status accrues to those who merely receive attention in the media, quite apart from any editorial support.

The mass media bestow prestige and enhance the authority of individuals and groups by *legitimizing their status*. Recognition by the press or radio or magazines or newsreels testifies that one has arrived, that one is important enough to have been singled out from the large anonymous masses, that one's behavior and opinions are significant enough to require public notice. The operation of this status conferral function may be witnessed most vividly in the advertising pattern of testimonials to a product by "prominent people." Within wide circles of the population (though not within certain selected social strata), such testimonials not only enhance the prestige of the product but also reflect prestige on the person who provides the testimonials. They give public notice that the large and powerful world of commerce regards him as possessing sufficiently high status for his opinion to count with many people. In a word, his testimonial is a testimonial to his own status.

The ideal, if homely, embodiment of this circular prestige-pattern is to be found in the Lord Calvert series of advertisements centered on "Men of Distinction." The commercial firm and the commercialized witness to the merit of the product engage in an unending series of reciprocal pats on the back. In effect, a distinguished man congratulates a distinguished whisky which, through the manufacturer, congratulates the man of distinction on his being so distinguished as to be sought out for a testimonial to the distinction of the product. The workings of this mutual admiration society may be as non-logical as they are effective. The audiences of mass media apparently subscribe to the circular belief: "If you really matter, you will be at the focus of mass attention and, if you *are* at the focus of mass attention, then surely you must really matter."

This status conferral function thus enters into organized social action by legitimizing selected policies, persons and groups which receive the support of mass media. We shall have occasion to note the detailed operation of this function in connection with the conditions making for the maximal utilization of mass media for designated social ends. At the moment, having considered the "status conferral" function, we shall consider a second: the enforced application of social norms through the mass media.

THE ENFORCEMENT OF SOCIAL NORMS. Such catch phrases as "the power of the press" (and other mass media) or "the bright glare of publicity" presumably refer to this function. The mass media may initiate organized social action by "exposing" conditions which are at variance with public moralities. But it need not be prematurely assumed that this pattern consists *simply* in making these deviations widely known. We have something to learn in this connection from Malinowski's observations among his beloved Trobriand Islanders. There, he reports, no organized social action is taken with respect to behavior deviant from a social norm unless there is *public* announcement of the deviation. This is not merely a matter of acquainting the individuals in the group with the facts of the case. Many may have known privately of these deviations—*e.g.,* incest among the Trobrianders, as with political or business corruption, prostitution, gambling among ourselves—but they will not have pressed for public action. But once the behavioral deviations are made simultaneously public for all, this sets in train tensions between the "privately tolerable" and the "publicly acknowledgeable."

The mechanism of public exposure would seem to operate somewhat as follows. Many social norms prove inconvenient for individuals in the society. They militate against the gratification of wants and impulses. Since many find the norms burdensome, there is some measure of leniency in applying them, both to oneself and to others. Hence, the emergence of deviant behavior and private toleration of these deviations. But this can continue only so long as one is not in a situation where one must take a public stand for or against the norms. Publicity, the enforced acknowledgment by members of the group that these deviations have occurred, requires each individual to take such a stand. He must either range himself with the non-conformists, thus proclaiming his repudiation of the group norms, and thus asserting that he, too, is outside the moral framework or, regardless of his private predilections, he must fall into line by supporting the norm. *Publicity closes the gap between "private attitudes" and "public morality."* Publicity exerts pressure for a single rather than a dual morality by preventing continued evasion of the issue. It calls forth public reaffirmation and (however sporadic) application of the social norm.

In a mass society, this function of public exposure is institutionalized in the mass media of communication. Press, radio and journals expose fairly well known deviations to public view, and as a rule, this exposure forces some degree of public action against what has been privately tolerated. The mass media may, for example, introduce severe strains upon "polite ethnic discrimination" by calling public attention to these practices which are at odds with the norms of non-discrimination. At times, the media may organize exposure activities into a "crusade."

The study of crusades by mass media would go far toward answering basic questions about the relation of mass media to organized social action. It is essential to know, for example, the extent to which the crusade provides an organizational center for otherwise unorganized individuals. The crusade may operate diversely among the several sectors of the population. In some instances, its major effect may not be so much to arouse an indifferent citizenry as to alarm the culprits, leading them to extreme measures which in turn alienate the electorate. Publicity may so embarrass the malefactor as to send him into flight as was the case, for example, with some of the chief henchmen of the Tweed Ring following exposure by *The New York Times*. Or the directors of corruption may fear the crusade only because of the effect they anticipate it will have upon the electorate. Thus, with a startlingly realistic appraisal of the communications behavior of his constituency, Boss Tweed peevishly remarked of the biting cartoons of Thomas Nast in *Harper's Weekly:* "I don't care a straw for your newspaper articles: my constituents don't know how to read, but they can't help seeing them damned pictures." [1]

The crusade may affect the public directly. It may focus the attention of a hitherto lethargic citizenry, grown indifferent through familiarity to prevailing corruption, upon a few, dramatically simplified, issues. As Lawrence Lowell once observed in this general connection, complexities generally inhibit mass action. Public issues must be defined in simple alternatives, in terms of black and white, to permit of organized public action. And the presentation of simple alternatives is one of the chief functions of the crusade. The crusade may involve still other mechanisms. If a municipal government is not altogether pure of heart, it is seldom wholly corrupt. Some scrupulous members of the administration and judiciary are generally intermingled with their unprincipled colleagues. The crusade may strengthen the hand of the upright elements in the government, force the hand of the indifferent and weaken the hand of the corrupt. Finally, it may well be that a successful crusade exemplifies a circular, self-sustaining process, in which the concern of the mass medium with the public interest coincides with its self-interest. The triumphant crusade may enhance the power and prestige of the mass medium, thus making it, in turn, more formidable in later

---

[1] James Bryce, *The American Commonwealth,* Volume 2. Copyright 1898 by Macmillan and Company; 1910, 1914 by The Macmillan Company; 1920 by The Right Honorable Viscount Bryce.

crusades, which, if successful, may further advance its power and prestige.

Whatever the answer to these questions, mass media clearly serve to reaffirm social norms by exposing deviations from these norms to public view. Study of the particular range of norms thus reaffirmed would provide a clear index of the extent to which these media deal with peripheral or central problems of the structure of our society.

THE NARCOTIZING DYSFUNCTION. The functions of status conferral and of reaffirmation of social norms are evidently well recognized by the operators of mass media. Like other social and psychological mechanisms, these functions lend themselves to diverse forms of application. Knowledge of these functions is power, and power may be used for special interests or for the general interest.

A third social consequence of the mass media has gone largely unnoticed. At least, it has received little explicit comment and, apparently, has not been systematically put to use for furthering planned objectives. This may be called the narcotizing dysfunction of the mass media. It is termed *dys*functional rather than functional on the assumption that it is not in the interest of modern complex society to have large masses of the population politically apathetic and inert. How does this unplanned mechanism operate?

Scattered studies have shown that an increasing proportion of the time of Americans is devoted to the products of the mass media. With distinct variations in different regions and among different social strata, the outpourings of the media presumably enable the twentieth century American to "keep abreast of the world." Yet, it is suggested, this vast supply of communications may elicit only a superficial concern with the problems of society, and this superficiality often cloaks mass apathy.

Exposure to this flood of information may serve to narcotize rather than to energize the average reader or listener. As an increasing meed of time is devoted to reading and listening, a decreasing share is available for organized action. The individual reads accounts of issues and problems and may even discuss alternative lines of action. But this rather intellectualized, rather remote connection with organized social action is not activated. The interested and informed citizen can congratulate himself on his lofty state of interest and information and neglect to see that he has abstained from decision and action. In short, he takes his secondary contact with the world of political reality, his reading and listening and thinking, as a vicarious performance. He comes to mistake *knowing* about problems of the day for *doing* something about them. His social conscience remains spotlessly clean. He *is* concerned. He *is* informed. And he has all sorts of ideas as to what should be done. But, after he has gotten through his dinner and after he has listened to his favored radio programs and after he has read his second newspaper of the day, it is really time for bed.

In this peculiar respect, mass communications may be included among the most respectable and efficient of social narcotics. They may be so fully effective as to keep the addict from recognizing his own malady.

That the mass media have lifted the level of information of large populations is evident. Yet, quite apart from intent, increasing dosages of mass communications may be inadvertently transforming the energies of men from active participation into passive knowledge.

The occurrence of this narcotizing dysfunction can scarcely be doubted, but the extent to which it operates has yet to be determined. Research on this problem remains one of the many tasks still confronting the student of mass communications.

The Structure of Ownership and Operation

To this point we have considered the mass media quite apart from their incorporation within a particular social and economic structure. But clearly, the social effects of the media will vary as the system of ownership and control varies. Thus to consider the social effects of American mass media is to deal only with the effects of these media as privately owned enterprises under profit oriented management. It is general knowledge that this circumstance is not inherent in the technological nature of the mass media. In England, for example, to say nothing of Russia, the radio is to all intents and purposes owned, controlled and operated by government.

The structure of control is altogether different in this country. Its salient characteristic stems from the fact that except for movies and books, it is not the magazine reader nor the radio listener nor, in large part, the reader of newspapers who supports the enterprise, but the advertiser. Big business finances the production and distribution of mass media. And, all intent aside, he who pays the piper generally calls the tune.

Social Conformism

Since the mass media are supported by great business concerns geared into the current social and economic system, the media contribute to the maintenance of that system. This contribution is not found merely in the effective advertisement of the sponsor's product. It arises, rather, from the typical presence in magazine stories, radio programs and newspaper columns of some element of confirmation, some element of approval of the present structure of society. And this continuing reaffirmation underscores the duty to accept.

To the extent that the media of mass communication have had an influence upon their audiences, it has stemmed not only from what is said, but more significantly from what is not said. For these media not only continue to affirm the *status quo* but, in the same measure, they fail to raise essential questions about the structure of society. Hence by leading toward conformism and by providing little basis for a critical appraisal of society, the commercially sponsored mass media indirectly but effectively restrain the cogent development of a genuinely critical outlook.

This is not to ignore the occasionally critical journal article or radio program. But these exceptions are so few that they are lost in the overwhelming flood of conformist materials. The editor of this volume, for example, has been broadcasting a weekly program in which he critically and rationally appraises social problems in general and the institution of radio in particular. But these fifteen minutes in which Mr. Bryson addresses himself to such questions over one network constitute an infinitesimally small drop in the weekly flood of materials from four major networks, from five hundred and seventy or so unaffiliated stations, from hundreds of magazines and from Hollywood.

Since our commercially sponsored mass media promote a largely unthinking allegiance to our social structure, they cannot be relied upon to work for changes, even minor changes, in that structure. It is possible to list some developments to the contrary, but upon close inspection they prove illusory. A community group, such as the PTA, may request the producer of a radio serial to inject the theme of tolerant race attitudes into the program. Should the producer feel that this theme is safe, that it will not antagonize any substantial part of his audience, he may agree, but at the first indication that it is a dangerous theme which may alienate potential consumers, he will refuse, or will soon abandon the experiment. Social objectives are consistently surrendered by commercialized media when they clash with economic gains. Minor tokens of "progressive" views are of slight importance since they are included only by grace of the sponsors and only on the condition that they be sufficiently acceptable as not to alienate any appreciable part of the audience. Economic pressure makes for conformism by omission of sensitive issues.

Impact Upon Popular Taste

Since the largest part of our radio, movies, magazines and a considerable part of our books and newspapers are devoted to "entertainment," this clearly requires us to consider the impact of the mass media upon popular taste.

Were we to ask the average American with some pretension to literary or esthetic cultivation if mass communications have had any effect upon popular taste, he would doubtlessly answer with a resounding affirmative. And more, citing abundant instances, he would insist that esthetic and intellectual tastes have been depraved by the flow of trivial formula products from printing presses, radio stations and movie studios. The columns of criticism abound with these complaints.

In one sense, this requires no further discussion. There can be no doubt that the women who are daily entranced for three or four hours by some twelve consecutive "soap operas," all cut to the same dismal pattern, exhibit an appalling lack of esthetic judgment. Nor is this impression altered by the contents of pulp and slick magazines, or by the depressing abundance of formula motion pictures replete with hero, heroine and villain moving through a contrived atmosphere of sex, sin and success.

Yet unless we locate these patterns in historical and sociological terms, we may find ourselves confusedly engaged in condemning without understanding, in criticism which is sound but largely irrelevant. What is the historical status of this notoriously low level of popular taste? Is it the poor remains of standards which were once significantly higher, a relatively new birth in the world of values, largely unrelated to the higher standards from which it has allegedly fallen, or a poor substitute blocking the way to the development of superior standards and the expression of high esthetic purpose?

If esthetic tastes are to be considered in their social setting, we must recognize that the effective audience for the arts has become historically transformed. Some centuries back, this audience was largely confined to a selected aristocratic elite. Relatively few were literate. And very few possessed the means to buy books, attend theaters and travel to the urban centers of the arts. Not more than a slight fraction, possibly not more than one or two per cent, of the population composed the effective audience for the arts. These happy few cultivated their esthetic tastes, and their selective demand left its mark in the form of relatively high artistic standards.

With the widesweeping spread of popular education and with the emergence of the new technologies of mass communication, there developed an enormously enlarged market for the arts. Some forms of music, drama and literature now reach virtually everyone in our society. This is why, of course, we speak of *mass* media and of *mass* art. And the great audiences for the mass media, though in the main literate, are not highly cultivated. About half the population, in fact, have halted their formal education upon leaving grammar school.

With the rise of popular education, there has occurred a seeming decline of popular taste. Large numbers of people have acquired what might be termed "formal literacy," that is to say, a capacity to read, to grasp crude and superficial meanings, and a correlative incapacity for full understanding of what they read.[2] There has developed, in short, a marked gap between literacy and comprehension. People read more but understand less. More people read but proportionately fewer critically assimilate what they read.

Our formulation of the problem should now be plain. It is misleading to speak simply of the decline of esthetic tastes. Mass audiences probably include a larger number of persons with cultivated esthetic standards, but these are swallowed up by the large masses who constitute the new and untutored audience for the arts. Whereas yesterday the elite constituted virtually the whole of the audience, they are today a minute fraction of the whole. In consequence, the average level of esthetic standards and tastes of audiences has been depressed, although the tastes of some sectors of the population have undoubtedly been raised and the total number of people exposed to communication contents has been vastly increased.

But this analysis does not directly answer the question of the effects of the mass media upon public taste, a question which is as complex as it is unexplored. The answer can come only from disciplined research. One would want to know, for example, whether mass media have robbed the intellectual and artistic elite of the art forms which might otherwise have been accessible to them. And this involves inquiry into the pressure exerted by the mass audience upon creative individuals to cater to mass tastes. Literary hacks have ex-

---

[2] *Ibid.,* Part IV, Chapter LXXX, James Bryce perceived this with characteristic clarity: "That the education of the masses is nevertheless a superficial education goes without saying. It is sufficient to enable them to think they know something about the great problems of politics: insufficient to show them how little they know. The public elementary school gives everybody the key to knowledge in making reading and writing familiar, but it has not time to teach him how to use the key, whose use is in fact, by the pressure of daily work, almost confined to the newspaper and the magazine. So we may say that if the political education of the average American voter be compared with that of the average voter in Europe, it stands high; but if it be compared with the functions which the theory of the American government lays on him, which its spirit implies, which the methods of its party organization assume, its inadequacy is manifest." *Mutatis mutandis,* the same may be said of the gap between the theory of "superior" cultural content in the mass media and the current levels of popular education.

isted in every age. But it would be important to learn if the elec-
trification of the arts supplies power for a significantly greater proportion of dim literary lights. And, above all, it would be essential to
determine if mass media and mass tastes are necessarily linked in
a vicious circle of deteriorating standards or if appropriate action on
the part of the directors of mass media could initiate a virtuous circle of cumulatively improving tastes among their audiences. More
concretely, are the operators of commercialized mass media caught
up in a situation in which they cannot, whatever their private preferences, radically raise the esthetic standards of their products?

In passing, it should be noted that much remains to be learned
concerning standards appropriate for mass art. It is possible that
standards for art forms produced by a small band of creative talents
for a small and selective audience are not applicable to art forms
produced by a gigantic industry for the population at large. The
beginnings of investigation on this problem are sufficiently suggestive
to warrant further study.[3]

Sporadic and consequently inconclusive experiments in the raising
of standards have met with profound resistance from mass audiences.
On occasion, radio stations and networks have attempted to supplant
a soap opera with a program of classical music, or formula comedy
skits with discussions of public issues. In general, the people supposed
to benefit by this reformation of program have simply refused to be
benefited. They cease listening. The audience dwindles. Researches
have shown, for example, that radio programs of classical music tend
to preserve rather than to create interest in classical music and that
newly emerging interests are typically superficial. Most listeners to
these programs have previously acquired an interest in classical
music; the few whose interest is initiated by the programs are caught
up by melodic compositions and come to think of classical music
exclusively in terms of Tschaikowsky or Rimsky-Korsakow or
Dvorak.

Proposed solutions to these problems are more likely to be born
of faith than knowledge. The improvement of mass tastes through
the improvement of mass art products is not as simple a matter as

[3] *Cf.* Chapter XVI.

we should like to believe. It is possible, of course, that a conclusive effort has not been made. By a triumph of imagination over the current organization of mass media, one can conceive a rigorous censorship over all media, such that nothing was allowed in print or on the air or in the films save "the best that has been thought and said in the world." Whether a radical change in the supply of mass art would in due course reshape the tastes of mass audiences must remain a matter of speculation. Decades of experimentation and research are needed. At present, we know conspicuously little about the methods of improving esthetic tastes and we know that some of the suggested methods are ineffectual. We have a rich knowledge of failures. Should this discussion be reopened in 1976, we may, perhaps, report with equal confidence our knowledge of positive achievements.

At this point, we may pause to glance at the road we have traveled. By way of introduction, we considered the seeming sources of widespread concern with the place of mass media in our society. Thereafter, we first examined the social role ascribable to the sheer existence of the mass media and concluded that this may have been exaggerated. In this connection, however, we noted several consequences of the existence of mass media: their status conferral function, their function in inducing the application of social norms and their narcotizing dysfunction. Secondly, we indicated the constraints placed by a structure of commercialized ownership and control upon the mass media as agencies of social criticism and as carriers of high esthetic standards.

We turn now to the third and last aspect of the social role of the mass media: the possibilities of utilizing them for moving toward designated types of social objectives.

Propaganda for Social Objectives

This final question is perhaps of more direct interest to you than the other questions we have discussed. It represents something of a challenge to us since it provides the means of resolving the apparent paradox to which we referred previously: the seeming paradox arising from the assertion that the significance of the sheer existence of the mass media has been exaggerated and the multiple indications that the media do exert influences upon their audiences.

What are the conditions for the effective use of mass media for what might be called "propaganda for social objectives"—the promotion, let us say, of non-discriminatory race relations, or of educational reforms, or of positive attitudes toward organized labor? Research indicates that, at least, one or more of three conditions must be satisfied if this propaganda is to prove effective. These conditions may be briefly designated as (1) monopolization (2) canalization rather than change of basic values and (3) supplementary face to face contact. Each of these conditions merits some discussion.

Monopolization

This situation obtains when there is little or no opposition in the mass media to the diffusion of values, policies or public images. That is to say, monopolization of the mass media occurs in the absence of counter propaganda.

In this restricted sense, monopolization of the mass media is found in diverse circumstances. It is, of course, indigenous to the political structure of authoritarian society, where access to the media of communication is wholly closed to those who oppose the official ideology. The evidence suggests that this monopoly played some part in enabling the Nazis to maintain their control of the German people.

But this same situation is approximated in other social systems. During the war, for example, our government utilized the radio, with some success, to promote and to maintain identification with the war effort. The effectiveness of these morale building efforts was in large measure due to the virtually complete absence of counter propaganda.

Similar situations arise in the world of commercialized propaganda. The mass media create popular idols. The public images of the radio performer, Kate Smith, for example, picture her as a woman with unparalleled understanding of other American women, deeply sympathetic with ordinary men and women, a spiritual guide and mentor, a patriot whose views on public affairs should be taken seriously. Linked with the cardinal American virtues, the public images of Kate Smith are at no point subject to a counter propaganda. Not that she has no competitors in the market of radio advertising. But there are none who set themselves systematically to question what she has said. In consequence, an unmarried radio entertainer with an annual income in six figures may be visualized by millions of American women as a hard working mother who knows the recipe for managing life on fifteen hundred a year.

This image of a popular idol would have far less currency were it subjected to counter propaganda. Such neutralization occurs, for example, as a result of preelection campaigns by Republicans and Democrats. By and large, as a recent study has shown, the propaganda issued by each of these parties neutralizes the effect of the other's propaganda. Were both parties to forego their campaigning through the mass media entirely, it is altogether likely that the net effect would be to reproduce the present distribution of votes.

This general pattern has been described by Kenneth Burke in his *Attitudes Toward History* ". . . businessmen compete with one another by trying to *praise their own commodity* more persuasively than their rivals, whereas politicians compete by slandering the *opposition*. When you add it all up, you get a grand total of absolute praise for business and grand total of absolute slander for politics."

To the extent that opposing political propaganda in the mass media are balanced, the net effect is negligible. The virtual monopolization of the media for given social objectives, however, will produce discernible effects upon audiences.

Canalization

Prevailing beliefs in the enormous power of mass communications appear to stem from successful cases of monopolistic propaganda or from advertising. But the leap from the efficacy of advertising to the assumed efficacy of propaganda aimed at deeprooted attitudes and ego involved behavior is as unwarranted as it is dangerous. Advertising is typically directed toward the canalizing of preexisting behavior patterns or attitudes. It seldom seeks to instil new attitudes or to create significantly new behavior patterns. "Advertising pays" because it generally deals with a simple psychological situation. For Americans who have been socialized in the use of a toothbrush, it makes relatively little difference which brand of toothbrush they use. Once the gross pattern of behavior or the generic attitude has been established, it can be canalized in one direction or another. Resistance is slight. But mass propaganda typically meets a more complex situation. It may seek objectives which are at odds with deeplying attitudes. It may seek to reshape rather than to canalize current systems of values. And the successes of advertising may only highlight the failures of propaganda. Much of the current propaganda which is aimed at abolishing deep-seated ethnic and racial prejudices, for example, seems to have had little effectiveness.

Media of mass communication, then, have been effectively used to canalize basic attitudes but there is little evidence of their having served to change these attitudes.

Supplementation

Mass propaganda which is neither monopolistic nor canalizing in character may, nonetheless, prove effective if it meets a third condition: supplementation through face to face contacts.

A case in point will illustrate the interplay between mass media and face to face influences. The seeming propagandistic success achieved some years ago by Father Coughlin does not appear, upon inspection, to have resulted primarily from the propaganda content of his radio talks. It was, rather, the product of these centralized propaganda talks *and* widespread local organizations which arranged for their members to listen to him, followed by discussions among themselves concerning the social views he had expressed. This combination of a central supply of propaganda (Coughlin's addresses on a nationwide network), the coordinated distribution of newspapers and pamphlets and locally organized face to face discussions among relatively small groups—this complex of reciprocal reinforcement by mass media and personal relations proved spectacularly successful.

Students of mass movements have come to repudiate the view that mass propaganda in and of itself creates or maintains the movement. Nazism did not attain its brief moment of hegemony by capturing the mass media of communication. The media played an ancillary role, supplementing the use of organized violence, organized distribution of rewards for conformity and organized centers of local indoctrination. The Soviet Union has also made large and impressive use of mass media for indoctrinating enormous populations with appropriate ideologies. But the organizers of indoctrination saw to it that the mass media did not operate alone. "Red corners," "reading huts" and "listening stations" comprised meeting places in which groups of citizens were exposed to the mass media in common. The fifty-five thousand reading rooms and clubs which had come into being by 1933 enabled the local ideological elite to talk over with rank and file readers the content of what they read. The relative scarcity of radios in private homes again made for group listening and group discussions of what had been heard.

In these instances, the machinery of mass persuasion included face to face contact in local organizations as an adjunct to the mass media. The privatized individual response to the materials presented through the channels of mass communication was considered inadequate for transforming exposure to propaganda into effectiveness of propaganda. In a society such as our own, where the pattern of bureaucratization has not yet become so pervasive or, at least, not so clearly crystallized, it has likewise been found that mass media prove most effective in conjunction with local centers of organized face to face contact.

Several factors contribute to the enhanced effectiveness of this joining of mass media and direct personal contact. Most clearly, the local discussions serve to reinforce the content of mass propaganda. Such mutual confirmation produces a "clinching effect." Secondly, the central media lessen the task of the local organizer, and the personnel requirements for such subalterns need not be as rigorous in a popular movement. The subalterns need not set forth the propaganda content for themselves, but need only pilot potential converts to the radio where the doctrine is being expounded. Thirdly, the appearance of a representative of the movement on a nationwide network, or his mention in the national press, serves to symbolize the legitimacy and significance of the movement. It is no powerless, inconsequential enterprise. The mass media, as we have seen, confer status. And the status of the national movement reflects back on the status of the local cells, thus consolidating the tentative decisions of its members. In this interlocking arrangement, the local organizer ensures an audience for the national speaker and the national speaker validates the status of the local organizer.

This brief summary of the situations in which the mass media achieve their maximum propaganda effect may resolve the seeming contradiction which arose at the outset of our discussion. The mass media prove most effective when they operate in a situation of virtual "psychological monopoly," or when the objective is one of canalizing rather than modifying basic attitudes or when they operate in conjunction with face to face contacts.

But these three conditions are rarely satisfied conjointly in propaganda for social objectives. To the degree that monopolization of attention is rare, opposing propagandas have free play in a democracy. And, by and large, basic social issues involve more than a mere canalizing of preexistent basic attitudes; they call, rather, for substantial changes in attitude and behavior. Finally, for the most obvious of reasons, the close collaboration of mass media and locally organized centers for face to face contact has seldom been achieved by groups striving for planned social change. Such programs are expensive. And it is precisely these groups which seldom have the large resources needed for these expensive programs. The forward looking groups at the edges of the power structure do not ordinarily have the large financial means of the contented groups at the center.

As a result of this threefold situation, the present role of mass media is largely confined to peripheral social concerns and the media do not exhibit the degree of social power commonly attributed to them.

By the same token, and in view of the present organization of business ownership and control of the mass media, they have served to cement the structure of our society. Organized business does approach a virtual "psychological monopoly" of the mass media. Radio commercials and newspaper advertisements are, of course, premised on a system which has been termed free enterprise. Moreover, the world of commerce is primarily concerned with canalizing rather than radically changing basic attitudes; it seeks only to create preferences for one rather than another brand of product. Face to face contacts with those who have been socialized in our culture serve primarily to reinforce the prevailing culture patterns.

Thus, the very conditions which make for the maximum effectiveness of the mass media of communication operate toward the maintenance of the going social and cultural structure rather than toward its change.

VIII

COMMUNICATION AND THE ARTS

BY

LENNOX GREY

Art and the Ordinary Man

In a day when names like Picasso, Chagall, Bartok, Stein, Joyce and T. S. Eliot are hailed as master keys in various arts, the ordinary man is likely to feel that Art with a capital "A" leads more often to deliberate mystification than to communication, and that it is no important business of his. Since an almost equally common intuition of our time holds that the ordinary man is likely to be right more often than not, his feeling seems worth looking into at the start of this inquiry into the role of the arts as communication.

Granting that it is good for an artist to be self-expressive—is it also good for an art to be broadly communicative?

Let us look at the ordinary American's taste in art—at the feeling of broad rather than inclusive community he seeks—noting a number of angles from which the subject may be approached and finally focusing on one.

While a good deal must be said here about popular arts and particularly about motion pictures, no effort will be made to gain the coverage of Gilbert Seldes' still lively treatment of *The Seven Lively Arts* (1924), or his and others' more recent studies of motion pictures. While also a fair amount must be said about "exclusiveness" in various arts, no attempt will be made to cover that question with the admirable historical perspectives of the chapter on "The Arts, the Snobs, and the Democrat" in Jacques Barzun's *Of Human Freedom* (1939). Both are recommended for their larger dimensions. Here, instead, emphasis falls on a limited number of ideas, vibrantly communicated by the arts in our time, particularly ideas about man's relation to what Mumford has called man's second greatest work of art, the modern city,[1] which has established conditions of mass audiences and mass media affecting all other arts.

The phenomenon of urbanized writers like Stein, Joyce and Eliot, at least, might have been in the mind of the anthropological linguist, Edward Sapir, when he wrote about certain deliberate barriers to communication in his article on "Communication" in the *Encyclopaedia of the Social Sciences:*

It is a question whether the obvious increase of overt communication is not constantly being corrected, as it were, by the creation of new obstacles to communication. The fear of being too easily understood may, in many cases, be more aptly defined as the fear of being understood by too many—so many indeed, as to endanger the psychological reality of the image of the enlarged self confronting the not-self.[2]

If this is a reasonable psychological explanation of the expatriate American behavior of Stein and Eliot, and the superpatriot Irish behavior of Joyce—*i.e.,* that they were afraid or otherwise unwilling to meet the gross mass audience in its largest dimensions—then the ordinary man is intuitively right in feeling that they are no important business of his. He would be intruding on deliberate privacy. To be sure, popular journalists establish Stein, Joyce and Eliot as symbols of unintelligibility and to that extent violate their privacy, perhaps, and make them symbols in mass communication; yet the ordinary man accepts these symbols as *curious* without compelling *much curiosity.* The less ordinary man, eager perhaps to belong to a somewhat exclusive group and so sustain his image of a special kind of self, may become one of a circle of initiates.

This is an extreme interpretation of limited communication of the fine arts, of course, which will offend many a resolute lover of literature and art who has gone to considerable pains to become an initiate

---

[1] "The city is both a physical utility for collective living and a symbol of those collective purposes and unanimities that arise under such favoring circumstances. With language itself, it remains man's greatest work of art." Lewis Mumford, *The Culture of Cities,* Harcourt, Brace and Company, New York, 1938, p. 5.

[2] *Encyclopaedia of the Social Sciences,* copyright 1930 by The Macmillan Company, New York, IV, p. 80.

in one art or another. It will bring forth familiar protests of "anti-intellectual" and "a typical literary (or scientific, or bourgeois) attitude." Yet it is hard not to see, with Barzun, a considerable amount of truth in it, verified by one's own recognizable impulses to be exclusive, and the similar behavior of many of one's fellows. The connection of art with magic, "mysteries," and prestige and power practices of various aristocracies, rather than with lucid communication, is an old story to all students of culture.

To hold that popular art is *ipso facto* worthier would be an equally extreme interpretation. We know too much about low common denominators and promotion rackets in a field which includes comic strips, magazine covers and advertising, the shapes and colors of ten cent store articles, the staples of radio and juke box music, movie stereotypes and the prevailing automobile design and architectural stereotypes. By the devotee of exclusive art, all these are likely to be condemned as esthetically bad. Yet they probably have about the same proportion of esthetically good and bad as the sum total of all that is produced in the name of fine art. All is not bad, surely, in the Disneys and Currys and Grant Woods and Winslow Homers and Norman Rockwells, the Currier and Ives prints, the Stephen Fosters and the Gershwins, the Kitty Foyles and Mr. Deeds, the Chaplins and Ingrid Bergmans, the Radio Cities and neo-Gothic cathedrals and neo-New England churches, the transplanted Cape Cod and neo-Spanish and geometrical-functional houses, the intaglio soap and the playful "container," the streamlined cars and trains and fountain pens. They convey emotions. They have design. They show considerable dexterity.

"But are they Art?"

If Art is symbolic expression of feeling and idea in significant design—whether in language, colors, tones, wood, stone, steel, or other materials, singly or in combination, then they are art even though they may be qualitatively less "significant" in certain respects than a Picasso or a Stein. But who dares then to argue that the evoking of response of large audiences to certain common symbols and the values they stand for is a less significant function of art than the capturing of new visions, aspects, and values of human experience?

At any rate, George H. Mead, pioneer philosopher of communication, offers in *Mind, Self & Society* what seems to be an important corrollary to Sapir's observation on exclusive art:

> The organization . . . of social responses makes it possible for the individual to call out in himself not simply a single response of the other but the response, so to speak, of the community as a whole . . . As a scientist, we will say, one's community consists of all his colleagues, but this community includes anyone who can understand what is said. The same is true of literature. The size of its audience is a functional one; if the achievement of organization is obtained, it may be of any size. Bigness may in this sense be an indication of qualitative achievement.[3]

Many an art critic will protest that the very mention of science and literature in one breath lets art out, that emotional art is the very opposite of non-emotional science, that literature with its devotion to story is too often the betrayer of art, that art has its own pure essence of form according to the special genius of the material used.

All this needs looking into, even if with only brief associational glances, as a way of taking bearings.

Pure and Mixed Arts

According to current truisms the fine arts tend to be pure, while the popular arts are almost always mixed. Obviously purity is better than its opposite. Therefore . . .

But is the supposed purity of our finer arts, *i.e.,* the refinement of forms in a single medium, really anything more admirable than making the most of *limited* resources? Naturally, the artist who for reasons of economy or temperament chooses or is compelled to work only with canvas, or clay, or ink and paper, lovingly rationalizes his medium and his control of it—and even his garret—into the most admirable of things. Very good. But may not a mastery of several media at once be more admirable, especially if it can enlist responses from persons of differing kinds of responsiveness—auditory, visual, kinesthetic? A Shakespeare play, popular alike with galleries and groundlings in Elizabethan London, shows artful mastery of words

[3] George H. Mead, *Mind, Self & Society,* University of Chicago Press, Chicago, 1934, pp. 267–268.

and action and music hardly inferior to the pure lines and colors of a
Mondrian, or the precision of a Paul Klee, or the shapely protoplasms
of a Miro.

For that matter, some of the modern giants in the fine arts seem to
be abandoning the purity; whether because they find interesting
varieties of materials at hand, or because they feel the need of more
varied materials to capture the complex feelings of modern life, or
both. What of Picasso's fusions of the effects of sculpture and stained
glass in his paintings, or his actual mixing of various kinds of
materials in three dimensional montages?[4] Or Van Gogh's heavy
paint suggesting a kind of *bas relief* of feeling? Or the new hanging
"mobiles" of string, wire and painted cardboard or sheet metal cut
outs, not only mixing materials but adding motion to printed and
sculptural dimensions?

All this may simply be momentary aberration within the fine arts.
Yet it throws the theory of pure art as finer art into considerable
doubt. It may remind us that our preference for Greek statues without
their original paint is probably due as much to the fact that we are
comfortably used to the paintless forms as that those forms are purer.
The early painted forms of gods and heroes were designed to bring
them close to the ancient Greek as painted madonnas and Christuses
were meant to come close to folk in a later day. Today for various
reasons which may have little to do with art, sophisticated people prefer, as some of the later Greeks doubtless preferred, to keep at the
greater psychological distance which pure stone or plain wood com-
pels.

Technically, of course, the chance of fumbling and failure to work
out a harmony increases with the number of factors involved in a
work of art. So critics are doubtless wise to advise young artists to
master one medium. But paradoxically they still give highest praise to
works of greatest dimension and even of mixed appeal—a Ninth
Symphony, an epic poem, a Last Supper, a Sistine Chapel, a Chartres
Cathedral. Aristotle's "magnitude and order" still hold good, apparently. As for magnitude, is the magnitude of the audience of no

[4] See Helen F. Mackenzie, *Understanding Picasso*, University of Chicago Press,
Chicago, 1940, Plates VI, VIII, XI, XII, XIX.

account? Or may the art of moving a very large audience through a carefully harmonized combination of appeals be a significant factor in measuring the magnitude of a creative act? Again, if artists and critics deny such possibility of *any* mixture of media, or *any* relation between artist and instrument and audience, are they not making the arts much less free than artists usually profess them to be?

There may be dangers in "slavery" to an audience, but there are perhaps greater dangers in "slavery" to a medium. When the artist becomes enamored of the materials with which he works, his experience in working with that material may become his most exciting experience, and he may become chiefly concerned with showing his power over that material. In that case he is hardly different from the scientist intent on showing his power over the materials in a laboratory. Both can be valuable to mankind in exploring new possibilities in "pure art" or "pure science," but both are in danger of selfish and irresponsible self-indulgence.

The Literary Taint

The literary taint is, of course, the chief current offender against purity in music or pictorial art. It calls for extra inquiry, since language symbols are obviously factors in social communication before they become factors of self-expression, while the substances of other arts seem to have another kind of existence. The sounds of rushing wind or footfalls, or the shape and texture of a stick of wood or a lump of clay or a stone, or the stain of berries on fibers, or the modern counterparts of these primitive materials for art, are not born of any demonstrable communicative impulse, and so may be considered essentially different. Yet a Plato has conceived the sculptor's task to be simply the finding of the speaking image already in the stone and men "pathetically" persist in thinking of nature as speaking to them in many signs and voices.

The peculiar genius of paint is presumably color and light and shadow and perspective in contracted space. The genius of stone is its three dimensionality whether for intimacy or monumentality—not to forget its durability. The genius of music is its tonal flow in time. The genius of words is their multi-symbolic combination of explicitness and suggestiveness. Certainly these distinctive powers should be

developed to their fullest possibilities. In this respect the artist is hardly
different from the artisan or machinist proud of his mastery of a
material. But to the rejection of other powers, so that they exert less
than their full power?

Specifically, just how bad is it for a painting or a piece of music to
tell a story, to be "literary"? If a painter chooses to tell in paint a story
that he might better tell in words, he may be misguided. Yet his paint
may tell certain parts of the story with an immediacy and simultaneity
of effects that would be impossible in words. Some human stories *are*
wordless; but not toneless or shapeless. His own genius may be for
such wordless stories. And are we sure, after all, that any human experience can be freed from the chronological, cause and effect, story
dimension? Or that it is the better for being freed, or for having this
dimension concealed? Probably not, in spite of the modern quest for
the *essence* of the material. What would the "Nude Descending a
Staircase" be without its playful title? The life of word-using man is
a narrative undergoing constant revision. To remove anything wholly
from this narrative context is to dehumanize it, the very thing which
the artist resents in the scientist, the so-called "dehumanization" of
surrealism notwithstanding.

This leads to another set of questions, about humanization and the
Humanities generally.

If one may not reason from literature to the other arts, or from the
other arts to literature, then American college education in the past
fifteen years has been moving headlong in the wrong direction. For
the most conspicuous recent development in college education has
been the development of comprehensive Humanities programs in
which pictorial and plastic art, music and literature are studied together for their common symbolic expression of human values. In
1931 there were four such college programs. Now there must be a
hundred of them in our leading colleges and universities. These
colleges may be wrong. But it seems more likely that our highly
specialized artists and critics who insist that each art is unique in
essence are wrong, and are indulging in medicine man mysteries to
enhance their own "magic." For the ultimate essence of art is in man,
his impulse to express and communicate symbolically.

Similar testimony comes from even more inclusive studies in communication, both in our colleges and in non-academic enterprises. In our developing philosophies of communication, primary emphasis is on symbols of communication rather than the "human values" of the humanities, although symbols obviously imply values. A book like Smith, Lasswell and Casey's *Propaganda, Communication and Public Opinion,* published in 1946 by the Princeton University Press, reports hundreds of studies in communication. Practically every one focuses on man's symbolic behavior. Many of the findings are still hypothetical, among them those on the intricacies of the symbolic process. Yet the grosser stages in man's symbolic behavior seem clear, the process of selecting from a flood of impressions one or more that seem most significant, the establishing of abbreviated images or other signs to stand for them in the mind, and the expression of them in words, pictures, music, gestures.

Sapir, from the essentially unbiased position of the anthropologist, does not conceive of language as essentially different at root from non-verbal symbolization.

It is best to admit that language is primarily a vocal actualization of the tendency to see reality symbolically.[5]

Mead's observation on the symbolic nature of language in *Mind, Self and Society* may also be extended to all the arts:

The significant symbol is nothing but that part of the act which serves as a gesture to call out the other part of the process, the response of the other . . .[6]

Susanne K. Langer, after warning us not to generalize too freely from one art to another, and particularly not to press the phrase "a language of music" in a literal sense, has this to say of the symbolic nature of music:

The belief that music is essentially a form of self-expression meets with a paradox in very short order; philosophically it comes to a stop almost at its beginning. For the history of music has been a history of more and more integrated, disciplined, and articulated *forms,* much like the history of

[5] *Encyclopaedia of the Social Sciences,* copyright 1933 by The Macmillan Company, IX, p. 159.
[6] Mead, *op. cit.,* p. 268.

language, which waxes important only as it is weaned from its ancient source in expressive cries . . . *Sheer self-expression requires no artistic form.*

. . . Let us now explicitly abandon the problems of music as stimulus and music as emotive symptom, since neither of these functions (though both undoubtedly exist) would suffice to account for the importance we attach to it; and let us assume that its "significance" is in some sense that of a symbol.

. . . *Music articulates forms which language cannot set forth.*

Because the forms of human feeling are much more congruent with musical forms than with forms in language, music can *reveal* the nature of feelings with a detail and truth that language cannot approach.

I strongly suspect, though I am not ready to assert it dogmatically, that the import of artistic expression is broadly the same in all arts as it is in music—the verbally ineffable, yet not unexpressible law of vital experience, the patterns of affective and sentient being. This is the "content" of what we perceive as "beautiful form," and this formal element is the artist's "idea" which is conveyed by every great work. . . . That is presumably what Walter Pater meant by his much-debated doctrine, "All art aspires to the condition of music." [7]

In *Signs, Symbols and Behavior,* Charles Morris goes farther than Susanne Langer in calling all arts *languages:*

I see no compelling reason for not regarding the arts as languages . . . less adequate than spoken language for some purposes of communication but more adequate for others.

Such arts as music and painting may . . . signify in any of the modes of signifying . . . designatively informative, appraisively valuative, and so on.

The separation of the fine arts within the arts—however made in detail —is less important than the recognition that non-vocal signs occur in all modes of signifying and are used for all purposes. [8]

In the last analysis the very *commonness* of the literary is probably the chief cause of condescension or condemnation, bringing us back

---

[7] Susanne K. Langer, *Philosophy in a New Key,* Harvard University Press, Cambridge, 1942, pp. 216–235.

[8] Charles Morris, *Signs, Language, and Behavior,* Prentice-Hall, New York, 1946, pp. 193–195.

inescapably to the exclusiveness analyzed by Sapir. Familiarity can breed either admiration or contempt. Note the change of attitude of those folk who loved Tschaikowsky's "Waltz of the Flowers" or Schubert's "Unfinished Symphony" so long as familiarity with them was a mark of status in the exclusive company of symphony lovers, but who condescend to them now that Tschaikowsky and Schubert have become familiar favorites of even a modestly large number of radio listeners. George Inness's paintings similarly were touchstones of the cognoscenti until prints of the "Home of the Heron" began to grace every picture framer's window. Obviously there has been no change in the art quality or design of these works. The change has come in the audience or audiences. Art then seems to be not a pure or absolute quality, but a condition of the time, place, and circumstance of communication also, whether narrow communication or wide. Some people want to possess it only if it is rare, possessed by few others or no others. So with the works of art in the Duke of Ferrara's "Last Duchess." So even with the ladies of the vanished Browning Clubs. This question of familiarity deserves more inquiry, with particular reference to some of the American popular arts cited earlier.

Familiarity and Popularity, Love and Contempt

Can art be good and be popular? Can the "best" art become popular and remain best? Is fine art the finer art? Does art fulfill its prime social function until it is widely known and understood, *i.e.,* communicated or commonly shared? And particularly, how are we to think of these things in America?

The prestige arts have not always been so far removed from the common or so sharply separated from one another as they are in America today. The medieval cathedral remains a symbol of a highly communicative and also self-expressive union of the arts. It moves people of all levels and faiths. It could move a highly sophisticated and doubting American like Henry Adams to a book like *Mont St. Michel and Chartres,* and lift Longfellow's nineteenth century language to rare heights in his sonnets on the *Divina Commedia*—as in the one beginning:

How strange the sculptures that adorn these towers
This crowd of statues in whose folded sleeves
Birds build their nests; while canopied with leaves,
Parvis and portal bloom like trellised bowers,
And the vast minster seems a cross of flowers!
But fiends and dragons on the gargoyled eves
Watch the dead Christ between the living thieves!

and ending

Uprose this poem of the earth and air,
This medieval miracle of song.

Both the cathedral and Longfellow's sonnet are presumably to be classed as "literary" arts. For the cathedral also tells a story. Partly it is the "literary" story of Christ, partly the architectural story of the dark and secret vaults of the early worshippers pushed above ground and pointed until they dominated all the land around, yet still kept dark and vaultlike. In turn, Longfellow's sonnet—one of the few works of Longfellow still regarded by connoisseurs as high art—takes unto itself the virtues of architecture. Would either be better for being purer? Or for being less literary? Or less familiar?

Architecture constantly remembers the story of its own growth—fluted columns remembering early buildings of reeds and wattles, stone corbels the early wood supports. Similarly literature grows on literature—Longfellow on Dante, and both on the Bible. So with music and painting. Here is communication through *time* as well as over *space*. A considerable measure of familiarity is evidently essential.

In America our widespread adoption of ecclesiastical Gothic and its first cousin, collegiate Gothic, has come, of course, in the face of a strong counter impulse symbolized in the white New England church. Born of Protestant and pioneer plainness, the New England church provides the text for a deeprooted, widespreading American attitude toward several arts which must not be ignored. Functionalism in architecture and furniture in the New England church became beauty. And although music and painting never advanced beyond simple symbols of unity in the tune of an old hymn and the whiteness of preserving paint, familiarity has given them a kind of fitness or beauty. While thus functionalism has become one of our chief values —and a very admirable one—the lack of status given to art, particularly music and painting, resulted in limitations of popular experience with these arts and a contempt of unfamiliarity only now being widely overcome (sometimes with a vengeance!) through the inventions of movies, radio, recordings and color printing.

This is not simply an American matter, of course. Our British preceptors have been similar victims of Protestantism, Pragmatism, and —yes, here even the defender of literature must complain against one aspect of literature—Printing. The matter is important enough to call for several paragraphs.

It was no accident that Printing and Puritanism sprang up together in Britain in the fifteenth and sixteenth centuries. Printing made possible the widespread reading of the Bible, and reading of the Bible by common folk provided the basis for Puritanism, with its suspicion of graven images and the other arts of Babylon. Yet it is conceivably historical accident that printing came before other kinds of art reproduction, and that literature became a matter of letters instead of pictures, as indeed it has become a matter of pictures for many "readers" of comic books today.

What if, by some accident plus man's inventiveness, medieval man had discovered some cheap form of color lithography before he had developed letter press, and had been able to give wide circulation to picture stories before he developed inexpensive books? Would he have come to depend on letter press for communication as he did increasingly between the fifteenth and twentieth centuries? Would he have come to be so color blind as he came to be when he got his color more and more (as color in dress and furnishings declined) through descriptions of color in black and white letter press? Or would writers have gone to the pains to describe landscape or costume if they could have had true colored illustrations at hand?

Or consider another possibility. What if Leonardo only a few years after Gutenberg had discovered that a stylus on a wax disc could reproduce the human voice, and had developed cheap sound reproduction? Would people have been put to the same pains to learn how to read? Would we have become so print minded and tone deaf as many of us are?

We may argue, of course, that print could provide the impression of color, picture or music, sometimes remarkably well, as well as be very explicit about ideas, and provide it in a durable form that man could come back to readily. But granting the probability that letter press books would have become important even if color reproduction and sound reproduction had come earlier, those books would not have carried so much burden or been so set apart that literature, music and pictorial art now seem to many people, common and expert alike, to have quite separate functions, instead of complementary communicative appeals to several senses.

Print seemed pragmatically sufficient for communication for many people in Britain and America. Why go to the pains of cultivating other arts? It did not pay; it was a mark of upper classes who could afford luxuries and non-essentials. Just so, the Bible seemed sufficient as a guide to life, including all one needed to know of communication. In seventeenth century Puritan America children learned to read so that they could read the Book. They saw few pictures. Their music established communication in one important sense: It gave them a feeling of community, of being together. But these Puritans were a wordminded and houseminded people, and their descendants have remained largely so today, whether they are in New England or in those large sections of the Middle West to which many of them migrated. Since they came to be the symbols of the oldest and best in American culture, their example was widely followed. Art loving Southerners might have changed the story if they had not come into conflict with these literal minded Yankees, but they did come into conflict and their love of art became a picturesque and alien legend, along with the society which had cultivated it. Some of these questions of Puritan influence were hotly debated some twenty-five years ago, you may recall, by an anti-Puritan critic from Baltimore and a liberal Yankee professor from Illinois. Mencken thought we must fight for release from our Puritanism if our arts were ever to come of age. Stuart Sherman thought we must make the best of our Puritanism and develop our arts on the basis of it. Their quarrel seems quaint to many readers today, but the issue was real and is with us still. A familiar "literary" approach to art is inevitable for most Americans.

American or European

To most Americans the fine arts have been synonymous with Europe. This has been so for the pragmatic native Americans. It has been so, in another sense, for the immigrants from Europe. To American artists or patrons of art, it meant looking to Europe, or, better, going to Europe. It meant European standards. And European standards meant something alien to most Americans. In Europe the artist has been interested in variations from a well defined epic. In America the artist still has to define the epic. Hence our quest for the great American novel, the great American symphony. The very critics who most vigorously applauded European art found the transplanting of European techniques inept.

Yet in spite of these frustrations, Americans have developed sub-arts that have come to status—not as folk expression exactly (for they were not produced by the folk) but as folk communication in keeping with American mechanical prowess (for they were produced for the folk by machine and received by them). The most influential is the motion picture.

Even the few questions raised so far seem to point the need for a new social esthetic closely allied to studies in communication. Any lover of the arts wishes it were possible to use as text certain arresting lines of John Dewey:

> In the end, works of art are the only media of complete and unhindered communication between man and man that can occur in a world full of gulfs and walls that limit community of experience.[9]

But it needs so much qualification that it embarrasses more than it helps.

This new esthetic must go into four questions, particularly:

(1) How far is familiarity a condition of esthetic creation and re-

[9] John Dewey, *Art as Experience,* p. 105, copyright 1934 by John Dewey, courtesy of G. P. Putnam's Sons.

sponse—loving what one knows, confirming what one believes?

(2) At what point does familiarity become a drag on response—breeding contempt and a spirit of rebellion?

(3) Under what conditions is directly functional usefulness likely to be a prime condition for pleasurable response?

(4) Under what conditions is a "plus element"—functional for the observer but not necessarily "functional" in the material object —a necessary condition for continued esthetic satisfaction?

The remaining two sections apply these questions to other popular items named earlier.

Mass Production and Mass Communication

Disney, Chaplin, Norman Rockwell, Currier and Ives, Stephen Foster, Gershwin, Kitty Foyle, Mr. Deeds, Ingrid Bergman, streamlined trains and automobiles and fountain pens—all are the results of American mass communication in tune with American mass production.

Bigness has been a prime condition of American life, bigness in natural resources, bigness in distances, bigness in population, bigness of industry, bigness of cities. It may be, as Mead intimates, a prime mover in distinctly American art.

It is no accidental result that Americans have invented telegraphs, telephones, high speed presses, motion pictures, phonographs, airplanes, skyscrapers, assembly lines, to cope with bigness. They were necessary for the American community. Mass art is necessary also for community—common perceptions, common values—in terms other than those of localized folk art. They tend to come together in works like Benton's or in Federal Art Project murals, which invite participant response for people of rural memories.

Disney's mechanized folk fable, like much comic strip and animated cartoon work, serves various purposes, but particularly to reduce complexities of urban behavior to natural simplicities—in the ingenuities of Mickey Mouse (*cf.* Herriman's Krazy Kat and Ignatz Mouse for an earlier more sophisticated version), the comic frustrations of Donald Duck, the psychologically based fantasies of *Snow White* and *Fantasia*.

Chaplin's pre-Disney service in reducing bewildering complexity to satirically esthetic simplicity has drawn this comment from J. B. Priestley in *Bright Day:*

. . . Given a night off by Aunt Hilda, I would go to the second "house" of the Imperial Music-Hall . . . Looking back soberly at those music-hall shows, and making every allowance for my youth and for the infectious enjoyment of Uncle Miles, I see now that in those noisy smoky halls, with their brassy orchestras, their plush and tarnished gilt, their crudely coloured spotlights raying down from the gallery, we were basking in the brilliant Indian Summer of a popular art, a unique folk art that sprang out of the gusto and irony, the sense of pathos and the illimitable humour of the English industrial people, braving it out in their mills and foundries and dingy crowded towns; an art that flourished, withered and decayed well within a man's lifetime, but that, before it lost all vitality, scattered its seeds, its precious seeds of rich warm humanity, all over the darkening world, and sent an obscure droll called Chaplin as far as California so that his flickering image could go out to conquer the earth.[10]

Familiarity is plainly a key element in these, familiarity of folk figures and stories, as Disney dolls and Chaplin "nights" have testified. Yet they have lasted, too, because there was depth to the familiarity, not simply surface likeness. Depth is essential to hold off boredom and contempt, the boredom that comes soon with the trick tune or trick gesture or trick design. It is essential for lasting popular art as well as lasting fine art.

Functional usefulness also is essential in anything that is often repeated. Disney and Chaplin qualify here again because they give certain needed communication gestures toward life's common incongruities not provided by loftier art and literature. Pantomimic exaggeration can be admirably played up by the motion picture medium. Yet it can be played up well also with paint or clay. Action adds something more. It gives heightened significance, for instance, to the varied types of suspenders and buttons with which clothing stays more or less in place on hoboes and on animal figures. If one

[10] J. B. Priestley, *Bright Day,* Harper and Brothers, New York, 1946, pp. 32–33.

lets his fancy play on these saucer like buttons and safety pinned suspenders, and their relation to child life and adult life generally, he has a fairly good illustration of the "depth below depth" in all lasting art. These satirical "plus elements" are made integral with the rest. Decoration can add to depth even when it is no more essential than the cameo figures on a Wedgwood plate.

Norman Rockwell? Currier and Ives? They may be shrugged off as Americana, *genre* art, the art of our cultural adolescence. But they, too, have depths that invite reexamination. In the Currier and Ives prints, there are appreciative depths of space relations, other than perspective, and time relations other than narratives of Thanksgiving Days or Steamboat Races or Transcontinental Trains, space relations of a day when people had elbow room and time relations of a day when people had time, and when they apparently sensed a danger of losing both. That is more than nostalgia, though nostalgia is a legitimate part of it. Matters of space and time are profoundly important in the designs of lives, and they are important in art for the same reasons.

Norman Rockwell has some of these same rural and village qualities as Currier and Ives, saying with gentler humor than Aristophanes that urban man had better hold on to some of the old values; but his plus element, like Winslow Homer's, is his visual sense of texture of homely realities. Texture happens to be one of Picasso's concerns also. Rockwell's sense of texture is less dramatic than Winslow Homer's feeling for the fisherman's oilskins, or a bronze bell, or the tarry planks of a Nassau schooner; nevertheless Rockwell is very revealing. Manhattan born, Vermont adopted, Rockwell has said some important things about the relative textures of urban and rural things and people—as to what textures we had better hold onto in this day of stone and steel. This is far more than "mere representation." In a day when Hollywood, too, is concerned with textures, mostly slick, it may be quite as important to express texture in this American manner as to express the quality of light in the bridges and ponds and railway stations of French impressionists. If one can express two things together, story and texture, integrally, each may gain from the other.

Currier and Ives, Winslow Homer, Rockwell, all are "mass reproduction" art, and have done well with the limitations of mass reproduction processes—which have their "disciplines" also.

Gershwin . . . Stephen Foster . . . "Rhapsody in Blue" . . . "Swannee River." Here is the "story" of the homeless the world over. The Jew, the Negro, the urban people of all colors. These mixed elements must be harmonized and unified. They are America's greatest challenge. Here the artist has gone farther to meet it than the statesman. "Swannee River" sought its harmony in the rural love song pattern of its day, with still poignant depths of meaning for white and black, North and South, child and parent, lover and loved. A "Rhapsody in Blue" with longer perspective and tougher-mindedness, reaches back from its initial fire siren wail to the work songs and spirituals of the plantation Negro (*cf.* Gershwin's "Porgy and Bess"). We feel them become hectic and more homeless as they take on the ragtime rhythms of New Orleans life; then, moving up river, yield to the Memphis and St. Louis blues; then turning east, catch the crash and jangle of Chicago and the "Chicago School"; and finally become merged in New York with an ancient melody of the Jewish people whose whole history has been a quest for home. With its companion piece, "An American in Paris," it says things that cannot be adequately caught in words, and that seem to be more profound than thematic variations on a Negro Spiritual in Dvorak's "New World" Symphony. Hearing "A Rhapsody in Blue" on a summer night in Lewisohn Stadium in New York leaves little doubt that the breathless audience is there for something deeper than trick tunes, something which brings chaotic life and people into significant form, as Whitman sought to do for an untuned audience in the preceding century.

Kitty Foyle and Mr. Deeds . . . or Ginger Rogers and Gary Cooper, if you prefer? Are they epic symbols or Hollywood stereotypes? It is hard to tell where one leaves off and the other begins, as the poet of "Lonesome Train" observed of Lincoln and the people. Gary Cooper, not unlike Lincoln in face and frame, is perennially the frontiersman or countryman facing the city. Ginger Rogers, versatile, not too pretty for belief, is the white collar girl also facing the city. To be sure, Christopher Morley had to write his novel of Kitty Foyle backward to get her taken seriously (rather than sensationally in the manner of the drugstore bachelor girl romance), but that device was within the range of the popular audience.

One more minor query before turning to the question of the ultimate symbols for which American popular artists are questing. At first glance this last one may appear trivial: What of *streamlining?* It is something more than an application of faddish, intrinsically non-functional racy lines to kitchen mixers or baby carriages. It says something, even in those objects, about a need to integrate science and art in our hurried lives. In the streamlined train and plane and automobile, laggard as the latter is in reaching true artistic functionalism (in part because the customer is said to prefer only modest departures from the familiar), the adaptation of form to economical movement through space has gone far. In the building of homes, "streamlining" took an unhappy start, suggesting that objects were about to take off into space. Then came a happy deflection into the idea of economical space enclosure rather than swift movement through space, but with some suitable hint of moveableness still. Streamline pens? The advertisements of the most shapely of the pens play up their well balanced shapeliness in the hands of artists, by a well known semi-popular, semi-prestige artist. Doubtless there is something of talisman appeal here, and also some illusion that the streamlines will spell swiftness in writing. Yet when the novelty of the present suggestion is gone, the artist can show where the streamlined function is equally valuable, slipping easily into a vest pocket and leaving no square edges to block or catch pocket notebooks or glasses cases. The pen may serve here as a symbol of a great range of industrial art on which Read and others have written seriously as well as "popularly."

The Ultimate Symbol?

The ultimate question of popular communicative art in America turns of course on the *movies—cinema* to the exclusive. The present faint lines of demarcation between radio and movies, growing fainter every day as Hollywood takes over the personnel or supplies it, will be obliterated in another generation if television takes over radio.

The movies are America's chief contribution in the arts, for good or bad. They have made certain other contributions in the arts an almost inseparable if not integral part of themselves—Afro-American jazz, streamlining of various sorts, montage effects, skyscraper perspectives, sloganeering. Can these ever be brought into a satisfying integral composite symbol—*ultimate,* of course, only in the sense that it captures the pattern of what is most significant in the current phase of our complicated, technical, urbanized life?

In an earlier day we used to hear a good deal of serious talk about a mythical "great American novel." (It was matched, of course, by similar dreams of the great American symphony, opera, and architecture, if not painting.) Today we hear of the "great American novel" only in a playful sense. It was to capture the shape and to symbolize all that was most significant in a *balanced* rural and industrial society, to serve as the modern epic, not in verse but in an idiom that Whitman was trying to anticipate in his compromise between verse and prose. The impressionistic critic Huneker said probably the wisest words about that old literary dream: "The great American novel will be in the plural; thousands, perhaps . . ."

The novel did very well, in an inclusive way, for frontier and rural America, and for the first stage of growth of our cities: *Uncle Tom's Cabin, The Hoosier Schoolmaster, Zury, The Rise of Silas Lapham, The Cliff Dwellers, My Antonia, Ethan Frome*—although for popularity, novels still could not compete with the Bible, into whose symbols of migratory, rural life Americans had learned to read their own epic.

But the novel, despite notable achievements, has failed to capture in any truly satisfying comprehensive way a modern urban pattern into which everyone can fit himself—fully granting the grasp of Norris, Dreiser, Herrick, Edith Wharton, Poole, Dos Passos, Farrell, and the magnitudinous Wolfe. After twenty years of searching study of the American urban novel, I am convinced that there is nothing the novel can do that the movies cannot do more artfully, more effectively, more economically—in short, that this is the movie's great job. The great advantage of the movie turns on its superior portrayal of the hard-to-grasp, often fantastic simultaneities of city life. (Parenthetically, here, I suspect that the popularity of the mystery novel is due in no small part to the fact that here, for highbrow and lowbrow alike, the incongruous simultaneities of urban violence and orderliness are most satisfyingly combined, and always with the reassuring knowledge that there is a precise solution to the riddle for the ingenious man to find. Is it possible that in this unpretentious guise our most promising approach to "the great American urban novel," in the plural, has stolen on us unawares?) On this crucial point of incongruous simultaneity plus design, music, painting, dance, architecture are all superior to print, which must present its observations one at a time. The movie can combine them all. It is still inferior to the stage in actual three-dimensionality, in the sense of people around one instead of simply in front of one, but is not inferior to the novel in that respect. When a novelist does not seek this effect of urban simultaneity—Dos Passos has probably been the most successful—he forthwith uses devices of movies (the Camera Eye, Newsreel, montage), music, architectural perspectives, and modern paintings of masses and thrusts.

In the opening paragraphs from the chapter "Skyscraper" in *Manhattan Transfer,* Dos Passos plays on such fantastic simultaneities to good effect, here chiefly in architectural perspectives and a montage of street signs.

Jobless, Jimmy Herf came out of the Pulitzer Building. He stood beside a pile of pink newspapers on the curb, taking deep breaths, looking up the glistening shaft of the Woolworth. It was a sunny day, the sky was a robin's egg blue. He turned north and began to walk uptown. As he got away from it the Woolworth pulled out like a telescope. He walked north through the city of shiny windows, through the city of scrambled alphabets, through the city of gilt letter signs.

Spring rich in gluten . . . Chockful of golden richness, delight in every bite, THE DADDY OF THEM ALL, spring rich in gluten. Nobody can buy better bread than PRINCE ALBERT. Wrought steel, monel, copper, nickel, wrought iron. *All the world loves natural beauty.* LOVE'S BARGAIN at Gumpel's best value in town. Keep that schoolgirl complexion . . . Joe Kiss, starting, lighting, ignition and generators.

Everything made him bubble with repressed giggles. It was eleven o'clock. He hadn't been to bed. Life was upside down, he was a fly walking on the ceiling of a topsyturvy city.[11]

But Dos Passos could do a more powerful piece in shorter time than it takes to read these paragraphs, if he could work with Frank Capra—and better still if he had the further collaboration of a John Marin and a Gershwin. One could do worse than combine Marin's painting of "Downtown New York" (with a hint of the Singer building thrusting up from a street sign and a chaotic groundwork to a pale patterned sky), Gershwin's thrusting, jumbled opening of "A Rhapsody in Blue," and Dos Passos' skyscraper paragraphs—for all are saying the same things. And they might have been fitted into the Capra continuity of "Mr. Deeds Goes To Town" with excellent effect. In an army film, Capra did, in fact, introduce parts of "A Rhapsody in Blue" into selected sequences from the Steiner-Lorenz-Mumford-Copeland documentary "The City."

Better still, however, would be a new film, or many films, reaching beyond "The City" and "Mr. Deeds," Grade AA. Here such artists could catch the magnitude and underlying order (techniques) of the city, the incredible simultaneities of apartment life ten stories deep and business life eighty stories deep, the elbowing communities which give people some feeling of identity in these "cities of villages" (Greenwich Village is the symbol, after its fashion), the street vignettes which lie around every corner (as they pop up where least expected in *The New Yorker* magazine), and not simply Times Square, Fifth Avenue, and the Empire State Building or Radio City. We need the homely textures as well as the slick.

Only a motion picture could do all this. Anyone who has seen the early documentary films on Paris and Berlin, or "The City," can hardly doubt that potentiality.[12] Would it be worth doing? In my opinion, no emotional or intellectual need is so great today as the need for our artists to make clear the form and meaning of life of cities so that people may become masters of cities rather than be mastered by them. This is the idea taking shape in much modern art, fine and popular. For ours is increasingly an urban America, groping

---

[11] John Dos Passos, *Manhattan Transfer*, Penguin Books, New York, 1946, p. 322.
[12] Even though the latest, *The Naked City*, hardly proves it.

for the meaning of a way of life that has replaced the rural way of life. So long as our life was essentially a rural way of life, the Bible of the rural Jews could provide readily applicable symbols of values. As Whitman sensed nearly a century ago, we have need for an enlarged Bible, a new epic of our own, both urban and rural, communicated not in one art but in all available arts.

Would this supplant the need for works of personal expression, or of communication that might be highly limited at first? Not at all. We shall never cease to need works of bold pioneer expression which can be produced as inexpensively as a poem, or a painting, or a song. Out of them come new symbols for new experience, sometimes adopted with surprising speed by our modern movie trained, symbol conscious populace. Consider the speed with which the surrealist perspectives of Salvador Dali have become known. Dali is gradually coming to signify the middle position between pioneer unintelligibility and fairly widespread communication, thanks to the advertisers' recognition of Dali's show window power to focus attention on a perfume bottle set out on a bare "perspective" plain with long shadows, or on grotesquely monumental cantilever rocks, or limp watches fantastically playing upon our concepts of time, or human chests of drawers which play upon our fantastic urban feelings of not being sure where ourselves leave off and our furniture begins, or Dali's fantasies in Hitchcock's "Spellbound." Here is the surrealist comment on qualities of space and time, turning on some of the same basic feelings as distinguished Currier and Ives and Norman Rockwell.

Is the growing audience taking such surrealist expressions in precisely the terms that the early surrealists intended? I doubt it. But the ordinary man may be sensing factors here that the exploratory protesting artists were only partly aware of. He senses in surrealism a deep disturbance of the urban mind—denials of ordinary time, space, movement, identity—which took one form in rootless Parisians and another in New Yorkers. He may even sense that surrealist art may be the ordinary man's psychological therapist— doing inexpensively for him what the psychoanalyst of the "exclusives" charges a thousand dollars for, and permitting the ordinary man to take only as much of it as he needs. Until recently, ordinary people have not needed much of it, for they have not consciously faced the problem of the city. The older movie stereotypes have enabled them to retain contact with older remembered patterns of life. But more and more the movies themselves are making new patterns evident. And more and more ordinary people are coming to see parables in the spaciously ordered "irrationalities" of Dali and in the patterned distortions of Picasso.

All of which leads to one final question: May not mass audiences create out of works of art even greater works of art than their creators intended, in which the limited communication of the artist is turned into comprehensive communication by the people? I am sure this has been so in a semi-popular artist like Theodore Dreiser, who valued his books for their social rebels, while his readers have valued them for their presentation of the panorama against which the rebels rebelled. I suspect it is often true of both greater art and lesser art.

IX

COMMUNICATION IN PRACTICAL AFFAIRS

BY

LEO NEJELSKI

Along with other pursuits in business, the purpose of communication is to produce profits. Without profits, no business can either satisfy its owners or endure. So it is easy to understand why management directs its attention primarily to profits and only secondarily to the people who produce these earnings. This focus on money values in daily activities tends to dehumanize communication and thus to blunt its effectiveness.

Management is not alone responsible for this. Owners and stockholders who are not directly involved in operations tend to pressure managers to pay dividends regularly. They are focused almost entirely on money values. They may believe in the greater effectiveness of situations where human values are also considered in shaping business policies and in carrying out specific operations but when their returns are threatened they quickly swing to the more shortsighted columns. The effects of such attitudes are bound to influence management.

The Background of Business Communication

The depression jarred many business men into a realization that something was wrong with their viewpoint. Tending "strictly to profits" had dried up the sources of profits. Something was missing. Thinking business men began to wonder whether they had not overlooked important factors, whether concentrating on short range profit making might not undermine the business system as we have known it. Some had tried paternalistic methods and had failed.

143

Others began to realize that in a specialized, interdependent, changing and dynamic world people are not only interested in wages and money profits but in many instances even more importantly in such things as security, status, understanding, and continuity in a worthwhile activity. The business man discovered that the producer of profits was also a human being. He also discovered that his "business world" was only a small segment of an entire constellation of "worlds" that make up our culture; by overlooking the interrelationships of these "worlds" he had failed to recognize his own economic plight as we entered the low swing of the business cycle.

Following the depression, human values became increasingly important in business policy and planning. The human factors in business communication also emerged. It became clear that an evaluation of communication cannot be made unless, in addition to measuring the ultimate result, categories are established to determine *who* says *what* to *whom* through *what medium* and with *what objectives* in mind.

Long Range and Dynamic Considerations

Another trend which we should touch on is the increasing consideration given to longer range factors in business. We live in an economy characterized by cycles that seem to repeat themselves at more or less regular intervals of several years. Business cannot ignore the time cycle without failing to consider how the morale of the people affects and is affected by the heights of the booms and the depths of the depressions. During World War II, a group of business men founded the Committee for Economic Development with the long range survival of the business system in mind; the advertising business has set up an Advertising Council that is concerned with broad public problems. In such a climate, there is hope that business will give adequate thought to the influence of time on effective communication.

There is also hope that business men are becoming increasingly aware that methods of communication based on democratic principles (having due regard for the people involved) can obtain results far beyond those inspired by autocratic attitudes. Democratic methods are difficult because measures of deference and power are subjective and highly individualistic. These are not yet as tangible as money values and we will always encounter difficulties when we attempt to measure them in the world of practical affairs.

In spite of limitations we are already able to plot out ways of determining such values and of maximizing our skills in business communication. By scientific methods, the present footpath and faintly marked trails can be developed into a well defined road. Then those who wish may follow with confidence and even lead on to new goals of effectiveness.

The Belief in Word Magic

Business people, along with persons in other fields, very often overlook the psychological effects of a "business communication" and rely unduly on word magic to achieve their objectives. The mere economy of putting "instructions" into a memorandum does not guarantee that they will be read and understood by the person receiving it. Whether or not the instructions will be followed is still another question.

The writer of a memorandum finds it easy to convince himself that the mere act of committing instructions to paper will see that particular task through to completion. Yet, many things can happen to it. That memorandum may land on the recipient's desk at a time when he is swamped by other matters that he considers more urgent; after glancing at the memorandum he may place it in a folder for later attention. Or because the writer of the memorandum was irritated when he composed the instructions, the tone of the communication may be overcommanding and may generate hostility rather than interest. Or the writer may use general and ambiguous terms and attribute more specific knowledge to the recipient than he possesses. Or perhaps the beautiful clarity of the memorandum existed only in the writer's private world.

Business is dreamed of as a world of decision and action. Does an executive realize the number of steps between a decision and the completed action which finally puts a profit in his bank? Does he realize that a decision only initiated a series of actions—each of which created a new decision at a different level—but a decision nonetheless? Each step is dependent on communication between the people involved in producing the final result.

In small organizations, communication is less difficult than in large ones. But even in small companies the directing head responsible for translating policy decisions into practice may not be able to avoid the temptation to be autocratic and take the easy way out by issuing orders from his lofty perch. He may also have the illusion that the pressure of other demands makes it necessary for him to overlook the resistance and resentments of his people and order them to carry out instructions. The directing head may hope that word magic will work in such cases even though later experiences prove him wrong.

Reliance on word magic is most deceptive where changes of attitudes, habits and skills are involved. Changing people is still a most complex and difficult task. Business management has been prone to put detailed instructions into manuals and booklets, or moving pictures, and then to trust that people would modify their thoughts and activities accordingly. In recent years, we have had conclusive proof that a person does not acquire a new skill, or improve an old one, by reading about it or by seeing somebody else do it; although actually going through the new experience under expert supervision can greatly speed up learning. Modifying attitudes and habits call for even more expertness and patience. Persistent reliance on word magic in such instances can produce only minute modifications at best.

Business today faces the problem of changing the attitudes of fourteen million persons with military experience. It also faces the even more important problem of changing the attitudes of its executives accustomed to dealing with one purchaser, the United States Government. Word magic is proving of little practical value here.

In speaking of communication in practical affairs, I have in mind not the illusions of effective communication such as have been illustrated in the use of word magic, but the methods and skills of transmittal that produce desired and measurable results in one person under the direction of another. I refer not alone to written, spoken, acted or projected words and images but to any means of imparting to others the desired action or ideas. I am also assuming that each method has particular values and shortcomings, and that no one method can be applied to all people with equal effects at all times.

Business Communication is Human Communication in Personal Relations

Thus, we see that human factors cannot be eliminated from any serious considerations of communication in practical affairs. We must weigh who is communicating what for what purpose, and place on the scale all the considerations that add to our understanding of the personality, the motivations, the objectives and the capacities of the communicator, plus the esteem and regard held for him by those to whom he is addressing himself. We must consider the person receiving the communication. What is his attitude toward the communicator and the group he represents? These are only a few examples of the categories that must enter into our analysis.

The key person in business, next to the maker of policies, is the person doing the communicating. If he is secure and mature, he can concentrate his energies on his objective and on the most effective means of achieving it. He can also consider the motivations, capacities and interests of the persons involved, choose the means of communication that will make his multiple objectives possible, and utilize the best channels with skill. However, persons who possess such maturity and composure are rare.

The communicator is not always sure of his objectives and his resulting message may be vague and ineffective. Instead of one memorandum accomplishing a result, a long exchange of correspondence may be necessary. In every instance where more than one letter is necessary to obtain a result, the writer is not clear about what he wants to accomplish or has failed to clarify what action is desired.

You Think about Yourself as Others Do

The individual thinks primarily about himself. He also reveals himself in every word he puts on paper, in every manner and gesture. If he is uncertain of himself, he will spin a communication out until he is convinced that his own fears and apprehensions are satisfied. If he feels insecure, he may become a slave to an elaborate follow up system that annoys those with whom he has to deal. But even the most mature person feels tense and strange in new situations, and under such circumstances may temporarily convey an impression of an insecure and uncertain communicator.

The same communicator can be a many faceted personality at various times. I once knew a man who wrote dull, heavy, plodding letters on days when his wife nagged him and who rose to heights of mellowness and warmth whenever his boss praised him. He responded violently to the stimulation of other people and those who received frequent communications from him soon learned to guess the state of his particular world. Many persons do not reveal themselves this easily but their communicated attitudes cannot fail to shape decisions and actions. A young lady whose work was being studied observed that when she became frightened and tense she could not hear. Likewise, when she found herself in new and strange situations, her attention became self-focused. Anything addressed to her under these circumstances would not create understanding.

Likewise, the status of the communicator halos his communication. An order signed by the president of a company can galvanize his associates into action; the same order can create resentment and reluctant compliance at best if it is signed by his secretary.

The person doing the communicating may be insensitive to the wishes, interests and motivations of those to whom he is addressing himself. Unwittingly, he may stir up suspicions and resentments by choosing the wrong words and inept illustrations. Or his timing in releasing a bulletin may coincide with some activity that stirs up needless anxieties. This lack of sensitivity to others is very common and gives rise to many problems that cannot be solved except by modifying the personality of the communicator.

One failing that plagues most persons in business is to assume greater knowledge on the part of the person to whom a communication is directed than that person possesses. In technical businesses, the tendency is also strong to use specialized terms and to misjudge the capacity of the other person to understand. The mere fact that a person has investigated a subject sufficiently to understand it should loom up as a warning signal that the other person will have to look it up for himself unless this chore is saved him by the communicator, yet in many instances the warning goes unheeded.

Very few companies have studied their problems of communication to make the experiences of individuals available to the group. Since communication occupies so much time in business, even at the worker level, the evaluation of the communicator's role can yield untold benefits. Other phases of communication analysis will be touched on later.

We have seen very briefly that the person originating a communication is a complex set of variables. He may be mature or neurotic, clear about his objectives or confused. He may be insensitive to the wishes and needs of others, or may assume greater knowledge than the person to whom he is communicating possesses. These and the full range of human factors must be considered in evaluating the effectiveness of a communicator. And with that we will leave the person *who* does the saying.

What Is Said Has an End in View

Now we will turn our spotlight on *what* is said toward *what objectives*. We will look at the problems of content in business communications. Again we will have to rely on observations rather than on systematic analysis.

Recently, in working on a problem for one of our clients, we were interested to discover that the policy communications written to their field organization were factual and complete but that the home office executives made it necessary for their representatives to work out the applications by themselves. The men in the field had to work out successful applications of their own. Much of this waste motion could have been avoided if somebody in the home office had tested ways of putting the policy decisions into operation and had passed these on to the group.

So much has been said and written about the low comprehension levels of the masses that we tend to generalize too readily about the capacities of various audiences. I believe that if communication fails to take place, the blame must be placed squarely on the desk of the communicator. If *what* is said ignores the interests, capacities and motivations of the particular audience addressed, then no transmission can take place. Furthermore, even the so-called mass audience is mislabeled because mass groups are composed of many audiences. One of the first decisions that has to be made is how to delineate the audience to be addressed. Once that is clarified, what to say and how becomes a much more specific problem.

If It's "Technical" to You, What About the Next Line Interpreter?

We have already touched on the use of specialized terms and symbols in communications, but I will enlarge on this point here because of its importance in winning or losing particular business objectives. One company that deals in chemicals and medical products employed women to take orders over the telephone from retailers. These girls learned to spell and pronounce the difficult terms, but in instances where girls made frequent mistakes, it was found that the terms had no significance or meaning for them. These were "nonsense words." When the girls were allowed to see and handle the products, and to learn what they were used for, so that a meaningful content was created, errors dropped almost to zero.

There is no company or organization where any one person can encompass all that enters into the operation of that business. That is both the virtue and the shortcoming of specialization. What is communicated to any one person must be selected to fit in with his objectives within the company. The tendency in business is to play safe and to overburden the individual rather than to chance a slip up or a misunderstanding. This is particularly true in organizations where little latitude is allowed for individual judgment and decision.

Now let us turn to the person who is to receive the communication. As an individual he has separateness, personality, a history, and in general is a complex being. But if he is in an organization, his efforts must be coordinated with those of others on whom he is dependent and with whom he must be integrated. Since his activities must take an ordered form, he is directed and supervised. Along with his individual motivations and aspirations, he is subject to the drives and ambitions of his group. Certain work at the same levels carries more prestige than other jobs. All of these considerations are over and beyond the capacities of the person receiving the communication, beyond his education and experience.

Unionization, New Attitudes and New Language

Conditions that shape the receptivity of the individual change and affect his attitude toward the same communications. In many cases the attitudes of workers toward management are different after unionization than they were before. The worker who becomes a foreman finds himself facing not only toward the men in his department but also toward management. He sees communications with this dual view and the meaning of what he reads is richer and more complicated.

Changes in conditions and status affect communication greatly. Top management has a dual responsibility in the process of union-·ization: first, it must retrain its own attitudes as well as the thinking of its personnel officers; second, it must retrain all supervisory employees. The retraining aims at a new technique of communication using new status persons (shop stewards) and dealing with new symbols (union talk). As the unionization proceeds a new language, specified to new relationships, grows and matures to give wider understanding to both management and worker with new meaning to the responsibilities of both sides. Remember both sides, management and workers, have always existed, but they have now found a new method of communication.

The same observations apply to groups of people. When they are hostile or even suspicious, they select only what feeds their suspicions. On the other hand, when a group can put its attention on a plan or problem objectively, not only does more complete communication take place, but cooperation toward the objective is often enhanced.

Participation Heightens Interest

The extent to which individuals and groups participate in shaping the decisions that give rise to communication also affects receptivity, understanding, and the determination to see it through to completion. We resist change and when the direction of thinking, living, and working is changed abruptly, the individual may develop feelings of insecurity and aggression. This is particularly difficult for the autocratic executive to understand and he finds it easy to characterize those who work for him as dumb, selfish, and uninterested.

The problem of receptivity is complicated by the fact that in highly organized groups the communicator has little direct contact with those to whom he addresses himself. There is little provision made for communication back to the communicator so that he can better understand what is going on in the minds of his people. Techniques for acquiring such insights are beginning to emerge but only the first halting steps have been taken.

No Medium Is Best for Every Form of Communication

Let us go on to the media and methods of communication. The fact that one method works for one purpose does not mean that it can be used with equal success for all other objectives. During the war great progress was made in developing various skills. Showing moving pictures proved very useful in many training situations. Several manufacturers were impressed by the results and came to regard movies as the answer to all their training problems. The results did not measure up to their expectations because, excellent as films are for indoctrination, for imparting knowledge and for inspiring trainees, they cannot substitute for the actual practice in real life situations that alone makes for perfection.

Each method and mode of communication has its good points and its limitations. The interview, conference and lecture make up the range of interpersonal communication utilized in most business situations. There has been little innovation or even experimentation with other methods of communication, such as the seminar, guided discussion, the forum and other means.

Business has developed skills in communicating to large groups through printing and radio. The skills sharpened through the creation of advertising are now being utilized to improve more restricted communications. For example, some of the persons in public relations are busy making the policies and objectives of their companies understandable not only to their associates but also to groups outside their organizations.

With the perfection of television new skills in communication will be called for. Imagine the possibilities for hurdling distances when the boss can sit in his office and yet be heard and seen by every person in his offices and plants.

New Methods of Evaluation Are Needed

What are the effects of communication in practical affairs? Until the present, evaluations have centered on earnings, the presence or absence of unions and the avoidance of strikes, plus the number of readers and listeners. Obviously, these criteria are insufficient to provide a workable range. I am sure that progress will be made in this respect.

But, first of all, we must recognize that the methods of measuring subjective effects are still in the primitive stage. In advertising, we have reasonably effective, although crude, means of singling out readers and listeners but practically nothing is known about what enters into the formation of buying decisions, or how reading and listening fit in. In measuring attitudes, we have learned to draw out more or less spontaneous responses but only a start has been made in peeling off the top layers to get at the deeper conditioning and motivations.

Much of the waste in business communication can be minimized through more consistent pretesting of not only the content but also of the methods of presentation. Where a genuine attempt is made to duplicate the real situation, such pretesting is quite valid.

In interpersonal situations, evaluations are now possible through skillful interviewing procedures. The interviewer cannot be directly involved in the situation and must function as an objective sounding board. The interviewer cannot be in a position of having to alter the situation directly but on the basis of data can make recommendations to those in authority who can effect changes.

In these various methods of evaluation much progress needs to be made in relating more of the relevant factors to each other. Business today sees many facets of its problems and the progress it is making in meeting them. In many cases, however, the alternatives become confused because the various phases of research and analysis are not integrated into a large enough slice of reality to serve as a basis for decision.

When we take even this quick glance at the problems of communication in practical affairs we can see that word magic fails in its objectives fully as much as it does in any other field. When we deal with communication in business we must give due attention to all the human factors that enter into the ramified objectives of an enterprise. By doing this, we necessarily and realistically break up the main goal of producing a profit into all of the sub-goals that make continued profits possible. By perfecting the methods of communication in business we can inject new dynamism into a system that during the war gave a glimpse of promise that a business democracy can be the means whereby man can achieve the dignity toward which he aspires.

X

SCIENCE AND WRITING

BY

JAMES MITCHELL CLARKE

The value of standardized literary products to the owners of mass communication media has resulted in a shrewd and industrious study of the technology of writing. Formulae have been developed for achieving almost any kind of effect that will influence, or please, a wide public. But though many technicians have developed skill in using these formulae and it is now possible to diffuse information very widely among the public, the effectiveness of communication has not appreciably increased. The reason is that a formula is never fully effective unless the factors to be dealt with can be standardized. A cooking receipt or a formula for mixing paint works well because the quality and amount of the ingredients, and conditions of temperature, time, etc., can be controlled. The human factor is minimized. But the ingredients are never the same in any two pieces of writing; the human factor is critical, and writers are as variable as any organism yet discovered. Consequently, a writer who uses a formula is accepting a ready-made, passable method of communicating what he has to say, rather than devising the best method.

Realizing that the technologist must sacrifice the possibility of superior communication in exchange for certainty that his work will meet a commercial standard, "literary" writers have clung even more tenaciously than before to traditional methods and traditional beliefs. They have continued the ancient attempt to reproduce in their own work the characteristics found in reputable pieces of writing. Literary writing has therefore tended to be imitative, or else to run off into eccentricities spawned by the attempt to be original for originality's sake. The belief is still general that outstanding pieces of writing—which are always original in method as well as in content—are produced under a mysterious force called inspiration and that the genius is somewhat more than human.

The literary approach to writing therefore leads to a dead end. To hold that the working processes of the first-rate author are mysterious and superhuman is to block inquiry into the most important phases of writing. The person who wants to learn to write better is left with no alternative but to study the products of writers, rather than the processes of writing—or else to learn formulae so that he can be sure of turning out a standard and marketable commodity.

Science offers a way through all of these difficulties. Instead of formulae, which are effective only in dealing with one set of factors, science develops principles which are general enough to be applied to a wide variety of factors and can therefore be used in working out optimal solutions for many problems. It therefore does not suffer from the limitations of technology. Science is not limited in the same way as the literary approach because, in the first place, it furnishes methods for studying the processes of writing. It is by gaining greater control over these processes, rather than by reproducing the characteristics of respected works, that advances in writing are most likely to come. In the second place, science removes the ceiling from inquiry by holding the phenomenon called inspiration to be at least as knowable as the behavior of electrons, and the genius to be no more than an exceptionally well endowed human.

Though science is still groping toward an understanding of communication and many questions are yet unanswered, a great deal has been learned by psychologists, sociologists, anthropologists, and semanticists which promises to help writers to achieve greater control over their work and result in a higher percentage of successful efforts. Most of this scientific knowledge has been obtained in the course of the effort to add to the sum of knowledge, or in pursuit of some goal other than the improvement of writing. It remains to apply it to writing. This essay is an attempt to do so.

It is impossible to include here all of even my incomplete stock of scientific knowledge applicable to writing. Moreover, it would diffuse the discussion too much to talk about all kinds of writing. I will therefore confine myself to the kind of writing which is loosely called non-fiction, the communication of verifiable experience, as contrasted with the unverifiable fictions which are the principal subject matter of the imaginative writer. And I shall explore only those applications of science which seem most useful to the practicing author.

Writers Have Purposes

Every writer of non-fiction—except those who fraudulently present their fictions as facts—is trying to accomplish some change in human behavior, or prevent some change in behavior. One writes to be read, and the only reasons I can see for reading non-fiction are to gain the motive or the ability to do something different, or to get sanction for continuing to do as one has done before.

Of course, the range of things one can do with experience acquired by reading non-fiction is enormous. You can learn something which you would not have been able to learn had you not read a particular book or pamphlet; you can think new and different thoughts; you can perceive new and satisfying patterns in the world around you; you can build a rabbit hutch or save your life.

In every piece of non-fiction there are elements that let the reader know what he can do, or what he ought to do, or what the author wants him to do. For convenience, we can call these *instructive* elements. Then there are elements which make the reader better able to do something. We can call these *enabling* elements. There are also elements which *persuade* the reader to do what the author (or his employer) wants done.

I will bypass these persuasive elements and concentrate on the other two. Persuasion has been so valuable to those who seek wealth and power that it has been studied and talked about to the neglect of the instructive and enabling elements of writing, which are equally important. Moreover, a realistic consideration of the art and science

of persuasion leads into a thorn patch of ethical problems which are
beyond the scope of this essay.

The United States Treasury's War Savings campaign, in The
Second World War, is the clearest illustration I know of how persuasion compromises integrity. The larger part of the campaign was
deception on a grand scale, and many of us who were involved in
it found ourselves continually torn by inner conflicts. War Bonds
were intended to absorb the extra purchasing power that tempted
buyers and sellers to raise prices dangerously. But it was very difficult even to explain this reason to a public which, until the war,
had never heard the word "inflation." And even if we had made
clear the economic peril and the effectiveness of War Bond purchases
as a preventive, the public still might not have been sufficiently
moved. The real reason for buying bonds would have appeared
cold, remote, and materialistic.

We did explain the anti-inflationary purpose of the program to as
many groups as seemed likely to take the trouble to understand it,
and use their knowledge in making the decision to buy or not to
buy. But mainly we relied on our deception. We made people
believe that the government needed the money from War Bonds to
buy munitions and supplies; we did not scruple to let them think
that the GI's would go into the lines ragged and short of ammuni-
tion unless they invested ten per cent of their pay. We also attached
War Bond buying to the nebulous buy-exciting concept of patriotism.

It was true that War Bond money helped pay for necessities of
war; like most persuasive deceptions, this one was built on a partial
truth. What was not true was that the government needed to get
money in this way. It would have been far simpler and in the short
run cheaper to borrow all the required dollars from banks. But
bank borrowing is highly inflationary. The War Savings program,
then, was a highly inefficient way to raise money for war purposes,
but an effective check on inflation. Yet we persuaded people that
battles and lives depended on their bond purchases.

I do not cite this deception either to praise or to condemn. It is
an example of the sort of dilemma a writer may get into when he is

trying to serve either the public interest or his own by persuading people. In the practical world, the person who manipulates public behavior must often choose between truth and failure.

Lucidity, Comprehensibility, Appeal

In 1937 the American Association for Adult Education established at Teachers College a readability laboratory for research and experiment in the problem of humanizing knowledge. Lyman Bryson was the director. In the course of our experiments, we concluded that readable prose has three main characteristics. We called these: Lucidity, Comprehensibility and Appeal. These words are used strictly and somewhat arbitrarily and I will explain what I mean by them as I go along. A good many writers have found this way of approaching the problem effective.

Prose is Lucid when it says what the author means as accurately as possible.

This statement sounds simple minded, until you remember how very frequently prose does not represent what the author means with any accuracy whatsoever. When you say that a piece of writing is not clear, you are saying that you have to search for the author's meaning behind his inaccurate statement.

The process of writing lucidly has been worked on by many scientists and philosophers; notably by Schopenhauer, Havelock Ellis, and modern psychologists and semanticists. It seems primarily a psychological problem because, in order to say what you mean, you must find out what you mean. And this finding out happens in the mind.

To analyze the process of finding out what one means, we must go back to the basis of communication. The only thing that can be communicated is experience. We talk sometimes about a writer's material, or his subject, or the ideas he has taken from books, as if these somehow could be transferred to the page. Obviously, they cannot. It is the writer's experience which is transferred, his objective experience of sensory stimuli in the so-called real world, and his inner, subjective experience which modifies these stimuli and creates ideas. A writer's meanings, therefore, are the writer's experiences.

Naturally, the writer's experience need not be first hand. He can get experience from reading or listening. But experience of mere words will not suffice for communication. The writer must achieve for himself, in memory and imagination, the experience to which the language he reads refers, or he can communicate only a hollow distortion, an empty echo far less valuable than the source. An idea is a peculiarly complex experience. Ideas are previous experiences collected and organized into new wholes. When one gets an idea from a book, he re-creates the new whole out of experience fragments retained in the fabulous labyrinth of the brain. Words are merely stimuli which make this re-creation possible.

Writers Communicate Experiences

The writer's first step in communication is to identify and single out the experiences he wishes to communicate. At this point we come to a critical split in the concept of meaning. When we say that a statement has no meaning we may imply that there appear to be no experiences associated with the words. For instance, *The grapefruit is not a line, would you?* Or we may be saying that the statement makes no difference to us; that we cannot use it in any way, and that it is not worth communicating. *On the day Shakespeare finished Hamlet, the price of mackerel was very high in Barcelona.* In this statement the language refers to familiar experiences but the total is "meaningless" because it makes no difference to anyone. I think "meaning" is the right name to give the experience to which words or groups of words refer, that is, the right name for practical purposes. (Semanticists and semioticists have their own special purpose vocabulary.) "Significance" is a better term for the usefulness of experience, the quality of making a difference; the particular difference an experience makes is its significance.

Experiences which are worth passing on are characterized by their usefulness. A writer, then, must start by identifying a useful unit of experience. Next, he must identify and fit together its contributory parts. When he has done this, he has discovered what he means.

This identification at times seems instantaneous and easy and at times laborious and slow; it seems often to take place on the edge or beyond the edge of conscious thought. We do not know exactly what takes place. But some helpful evidence comes to light when we consider the accounts that writers give of their own working processes. Writers are sure of what they mean when they can trace an experience back to its sensory origins, or make some real world application of it. A physiologist is sure of what he means by "visual purple" because he remembers having watched its fluctuations in the eye. I am sure of what I mean by visual purple because I remember, among other things, clear diagrams of the fading and re-creation of this substance under varying conditions of light.

It takes a good deal of practice before one can identify experiences for communication surely and consistently. Few writers, if any, achieve absolute consistency; one of the functions of revision is to identify completely the experiences in soft spots which one has filled with words that merely sound as if they mean something, as a musician might play a few pleasant notes to fill out a passage he could not quite remember. It takes even more practice before one can make words communicate his experiences accurately. The student of language looking at a piece of writing says, "What do these words mean?" But the writer says, "How can I make words represent my meaning with fidelity?" He finds, of course, that no word by itself represents even the most fragmentary experience. He inevitably discovers that he must make an arrangement which not only has the total meaning he intends, but also gives appropriate meaning to each word making up the unit.

During the symposium from which these essays come, Professor Wendell Johnson said that a writer could give words any meaning he liked. Havelock Ellis says that the quality of a writer's prose depends upon the meanings he gives to words. Yet semanticists have spent great labor in counting the meanings of words. Apparently they believe, as do the makers of dictionaries, that the meanings each word may have are more or less restricted. How then can the writer give his own meanings to words and still use them in their accepted meanings?

Selecting Possible Meanings

I believe that this apparent conflict is unreal. I believe that the writer goes through the following steps: He chooses a word which by accepted usage sometimes refers to the area of experience he wants to communicate; he indicates this meaning area by context. Then, by further refinement of context he makes the word represent the exact fragment of experience he wishes to communicate. For example, I might have in mind a particular olfactory experience. The word "smell" indicates the general area, but I must say "smell of" something to indicate which of its several meanings I intend. So I might say, "smell of honeysuckle." But this is still far from communicating an experience, so I arrange my context more precisely and say, perhaps, "the too sweet smell of honeysuckle hanging in the breathless night air." Words are thus limited by custom in their general meanings, but unlimited in the number of particular meanings that authors may give them.

Of course, a writer in communicating a very particular experience may devise contexts which push words beyond their accepted meanings. Kipling speaks of "the little, wrinkled waves grieving along the shore." Obviously, waves do not grieve in any ordinary sense. In one of his eye-camera studies of reading ability, Buswell used a paragraph in which J. B. Priestley speaks of automobiles as being "ruthlessly comfortable." All but the most skillful readers stumbled over that combination. Yet I think the author was justified in using it because it communicates an important fraction of his experience of America's determination to be luxurious.

Very possibly Priestley's words would have been easier to read and understand if a much longer sample had been selected. The reader might then have been prepared for them by what had come before. This brings us to the greatly neglected fact that the meaning of individual words is affected by the entire context, that is, by the whole piece of writing. For a piece of writing is a design of contexts within contexts. In a way, it is like a mural where a nose is on a face, face is looking out of window, window is in a house, house is on a street, street is in a town and town is in a French valley. The nose has a unique effect because of its size, shape, color, etc. Its position not only enables it to have a further effect, but gives the nose certain characteristics. If placed elsewhere it would not contribute to the picture in the same way, nor would it look the same. Nevertheless, a nose is a nose is a nose is a nose is a . . .

It does not seem to me that a writer can be lucid unless he realizes the influence of large contexts upon the meaning of individual words and constellations of words. One of the most difficult feats in writing is the imaginative effort to hold in consciousness the whole web of meaning one is spinning and at the same time not lose sight of the particular meaning of the sentence being written.

These more remote influences on meaning actually begin with the author's relation to his audience. If a minister exclaims "God Almighty!" his hearers understand the meaning to be spiritual and reverent, if they know him to be a minister. If a bartender exclaims "God Almighty!" his meaning is taken to be blasphemous unless he is known as a religious man. The more an audience knows of a writer and what he stands for, the more surely his meanings will be grasped. A writer establishes meanings, moreover, by defining his areas of discourse and elucidating his point of view. The psychologist, for example, takes it for granted that his readers will derive the proper and highly technical meaning from the word *validity,* though he does not bother to say how he will use it. To the biologist, the word "man" means something quite different from what it means to the marriage counselor.

The particular devices by which an author achieves consistent lucidity are worth more space than is available. I would like, however, to mention two of them in passing. Definition, which is the usual tool for making one's meaning specific, is not sufficient by itself. The author is obliged to devise contexts which give words the same meaning as his definition. Only by doing so can he make himself consistently clear. To produce such contexts, the writer must make a determined effort to fix on the same experience each time. Writers often neglect to do so, with the result that the meanings of words which they at first carefully define become hazy and wavering.

A writer is obliged to supply many clues to meaning which are, in other situations, given by other signs. When the President of the United States speaks, he is not totally a stranger; you have a fair idea of what sort of person he is and what he is most likely to mean by what he tells you. A stranger's case—and most writers are strangers to their readers—is more difficult because they know virtually nothing about him. A public speaker has certain advantages denied the writer. His mere physical aspect gives some clues to his meanings; the audience can guess at the importance he gives to some statements and deduce attitudes which are likely to make him use words in certain meanings but not in others. He can clarify his meanings by inflections of voice and changes of loudness; he can make gestures with his face and body. None of these aids is available to the writer; he must devise word arrangements which take the place of these direct sensory clues. The inability to provide language clues which compensate for the absence of non-language aids in communication is one reason why good speakers often fail to write lucidly.

It is well known that people do not always want to be lucid. Both the writer's own personality and social pressure may put formidable obstacles in the way of saying what he means. This reach of the subject is extremely interesting and important but very complex. To explore it would take us farther into psychology, and social anthropology than is practical in this space.

Lucidity Is Not Comprehensibility

In many cases lucidity alone suffices to make communication effective. There are some writers whose meanings are perfectly comprehensible to their public, and all they need do is represent these meanings accurately. The case of Pepys is striking; he wrote his diary for himself, and in code, but managed to give profit and pleasure to hundreds of thousands of readers. There is also writing in which the lucid statement of an experience is the only objective, and this puts the burden of understanding upon the reader. Theoretically, scientists and scholars strive for complete lucidity and nothing more when writing for their colleagues, though many actually have the undeclared object of appearing erudite or original.

When a person writes for his professional colleagues, he has the right to assume that their background of experience is similar to his and that an accurate statement of new experience developed out of this background will be understood by them. They have the same vocabulary as he, the same general point of view and the same general attitude toward professional concerns. But when an erudite person writes for any audience except his professional colleagues, these assumptions are seldom warranted. It has been scientifically proved that a great many people are unable even to read material which communicates the experience of specialized vocations and professions in the usual vocabularies of those specialities. Such material is not likely to be read even by highly educated persons in vocations other than that of the communicator; if they are able to comprehend it at all, they are likely to find it too much work.

When people are free to read what they choose—as they are *not* when going to school or under pressure from occupational superiors —they tend to read only such materials as seem to them worth the trouble. It follows that the extent to which writing is read tends to increase with usefulness, and tends to decrease as difficulty rises. A good deal is known about what makes a piece of writing difficult or "unreadable." There are in use several systems for measuring "readability." In two of the more useful systems, the estimator obtains the average length of sentences and the average number of prepositional phrases in sample passages. In one, the Lorge system, the number of hard words is determined by reference to a list. In the other, the Flesch system, the number of prefixes and suffixes is counted. The Lorge system gives a score based on the reading capacity of school children. The Flesch scoring system is based on a magazine hierarchy in which *True Romances* represents the bottom stratum and *The Yale Review* the top.

A large amount of experimental evidence shows that the difficulty of the words, the length of the sentences, and the number of prepositional phrases are the main factors influencing readability. It is also quite certain that most of the writing intended for the general public can be made readable in this sense of being reasonably easy. The average adult has had about eight years of schooling, and his reading ability has regressed about one grade. When measured by the Lorge formula, magazines have a range from *The Yale Review,* at 8.5, to *True Romances,* at 5.9. The readability of *The Saturday Evening Post* is exactly seventh grade.

The measurement of readability is extremely useful. Many writers will find great profit in reading the explanations of their systems which Dr. Lorge and Dr. Flesch have furnished.[1] It is necessary, however, to bear in mind that their formulae are measuring instruments and not receipts for writing. With them you can describe a piece of prose accurately in terms of characteristics which critically affect difficulty. But this does not tell you how to achieve a piece of writing having those characteristics any more than the chemical analysis of a piece of steel tells you how to make it. These formulae are really partial measures of comprehensibility. To examine each of the factors used in measurement can therefore throw a good deal of light on the process of writing to be understood as well as read.

Pieces having a readability score near sixth grade usually contain sentences averaging about twenty words in length. This should not be taken as a prohibition against longer sentences; if you put in some very short ones, you can have sentences of fifty words or more and still come out with an average length of twenty. There are times when a long sentence is a great advantage; as when one is summarizing, or putting together a series of closely connected events which are none of them entitled to more than brief mention. Again, a long sentence may help to hold the elements of a unit of thought in their proper relation, keeping those that are subordinate in their place and showing the influence of one element upon another. Herodotus was a master of this kind of sentence. Moreover, changes in prose rhythm achieved by varying the length of sentences may help to give the proper emphasis.

A long, bad sentence is as confusing as a genuine misstatement. Most of these sentences seem the result of sloppy or inept thinking,

---

[1] "The Lorge Formula for Estimating Grade Placement of Reading Materials," *Teachers College Record,* March, 1944, pp. 404–19.

Rudolf Flesch, *The Art of Plain Talk,* Harper and Brothers, New York, 1946.

rather than unskillful writing. In some cases, writers are simply unable to distinguish one thought unit from the next, and string out sentences which run like Tennyson's brook. Other writers cannot resist the impulse to say everything at once, and turn out sentences with long and only vaguely relevant parentheses; the kind of sentence Schopenhauer likens to a stuffed goose. This tendency to say everything at once can be checked if the writer will keep his larger context in mind. By giving the reader the proper associations, that is, by suggesting what amount to cross references, he can use what has gone before to establish part of the meaning of each sentence. Each sentence should also prepare the reader to grasp the meaning of what is to follow.

Language Must Fit Experience

The process of writing in commonly understood language is more difficult than controlling the length and precision of sentences. To get at it, one must recall once again that experience is the thing to be communicated. No reader can understand the words representing an experience he has never had. You cannot, for instance, describe the color of a rose to a person blind from birth. To write comprehensibly a writer must therefore write entirely in terms of experiences his readers have already had.

On first hearing, this sounds like a denial that the writer can say anything new. But this is only another case of the deceptiveness of first appearances. If you analyze almost any dictionary definition, you find a new experience described in terms of experiences which readers presumably have had, or can get by cross examining the dictionary. Take, for example, "aardwolf." The dictionary says that this word refers to a hyena-like quadruped of South Africa; it feeds on insects and carrion. In other words, the dictionary gives us a collection of more or less familiar experiences which, in sum, approximate seeing an aardwolf.

An effective piece of writing builds a new and useful experience out of other, smaller experiences. Some of these will be familiar, some entirely outside the reader's ken. If the writer refers to the familiar experiences by words readers are used to associating with them, then the reader understands them, but one cannot grasp the new experiences unless the writer breaks them down into familiar components. Suppose a writer said: "Crossing the veldt we saw many aardwolves." Scarcely any American would understand him. But if he said: "Crossing the South African grasslands we saw a great many of those small, bushy tailed, hyena-like animals which the Boer farmers call aardwolves. They caught grasshoppers and grubs which they seemed to enjoy." Most people would understand the second telling well enough.

It is inevitable that a writer who builds new experiences out of familiar ones will tend to use simple, easily understood words. The easy words, the ones a child learns first, refer to those experiences that are common to all Americans. It is helpful to measure one's writing by either the Lorge or the Flesch method, then eliminate the hard words.[2] But a writer will save himself trouble and in the end communicate more effectively if, as he writes, he thinks in terms of experiences common both to himself and his audience.

In this connection it is helpful to remember one of Euclid's deceptively simple axioms; *things equal to the same things are equal to each other.* It is possible to have quite dissimilar experiences which are equivalent, or approximately so. For instance, you can experience the results of scientific ploughing by actually observing the run off along straightaway furrows as contrasted with run off across contours; or, you can make the same observations by putting dirt on a washboard and running water over it, first along the grooves, then across them. Science itself depends heavily on experience achieved under laboratory conditions which is, in critical respects, equivalent to experience in and of the world we live in. The operation is reversible. Comprehensible experiences of the world we live in can be equivalent, in critical respects, to laboratory or scholarly experiences which the reader may never enjoy.

The principle of equivalence holds also for language; words representing the same experiences are at least approximately equal to each other. I mention this because many people insist that in order

---

[2] Flesch believes that eliminating prefixes and suffixes is better than a direct attempt to remove words listed as "hard."

for a description to be useful or true, an experience must be represented by language approved by custom. This insistence is mainly due to the persistence of ritual in areas where it no longer has any place—if it ever did serve any useful function. It is probably a hold over from the time when words were supposed to have some effect of their own, even upon scientific processes such as the compounding of medicines. Language which is highly appropriate and useful in professional discourse may literally be abracadabra in popular communication.

The popularizer ought, also, to take advantage of the license to operate on various levels of precision which scientists grant to themselves. It is quite permissible, for instance, to make relief maps on which the height of the mountains is enormously exaggerated. In this case, the very lack of precision and fidelity is useful. The criterion by which distortions and simplifications should be judged, by both writers and critics, is usefulness; and the standard for estimating the appropriate degree of precision, is the use to which the communication will be put. If you are describing a room to a prospective tenant, you do not measure it in millimeters, but in feet; it is sufficient in describing a friend's home to say that his living room is large, middle sized or small. Inappropriate precision may, in fact, be a handicap to understanding and usefulness, for the important aspects of an experience may be the gross ones which can easily be obscured by too much qualification or refinement in description.

I believe that the criterion of use is helpful in determining just what experiences should be selected for communication. It is scarcely conceivable that the lay reader would find it useful to learn the chemical nature of bacterial toxins. On the other hand, he might be helped by knowing that many disease germs kill by the poisons they produce, and that there are antitoxins to combat these poisons. The lay reader's purpose is to protect his health, not to prepare or prescribe injections.

The writer who is careful to eliminate in advance the material which is not usable by the layman, however important it may be occupationally, will take a long step toward comprehensibility. Occupationally useful material is generally more precise, more studded with qualifications, and more detailed than that which serves the layman best. It must usually be stated in more difficult language. And it is built out of subsidiary experiences which are only to be acquired in specialist schools and on the job.

To use a great number of prepositional phrases per thousand words indicates that the writer has crowded a good many concepts into the space and has established complex arrangements among them. Lyman Bryson describes such writing as having great density, meaning that ideas are crowded close together as are the molecules in a piece of steel. To appreciate the difficulty of such writing, one needs only to examine the works of John Dewey, which are lucid, but for many ordinary readers, incomprehensible.

The Principle of Familiarity

The best way to avoid introducing this kind of difficulty is to hold fast to the principle of familiarity. Remember that every new experience, every new idea, has to be built by recalling old ones. If the new experience is simply constructed out of very familiar pieces, it requires no great labor on the reader's part to achieve it, and he can go on to the next experience immediately. But if the construction is complicated, or made of relatively unfamiliar pieces, or both as is often the case, achieving the experience is laborious.

Take for example Euclid's proposition that "the square of the hypotenuse of a right triangle is equal to the sum of the squares of the other two sides." To achieve this experience one has to remember what a hypotenuse is, and what a right triangle is, and recall what is meant by squaring a quantity; also what is meant by sum, and side. All these meanings are presumed to be previous experiences of any person who has gotten as far as this proposition. However, Euclid does not leave the statement bare. He follows it with a beautifully designed arrangement of the experiences of which it is made. This he calls a proof. But though it may be thought of as a set of experiences by means of which the reader can verify the proposition, it is equally useful in completing the communication, for it fills out the unit of experience and helps greatly in making it useful and easily remembered.

The reader needs time to fill out new ideas with a content of re-membered experience. The writer can help him by recalling to his mind familiar experiences arranged in the pattern that creates the useful unit. These contributory experiences should be as concrete as possible; they should be sensory stimuli out of which the useful unit was derived, or real world applications of the unit. Euclid's proofs are concrete in the sense that his graphic figures are sensory stimuli which can be manipulated. He invites you to give yourself a chalk talk, and thus acquire the experiences which create the whole.

Euclid's use of diagrams is a good illustration of the need for selecting the proper method of communication. Ideally, a writer should never use words to communicate something that can more effectively be communicated by a picture. There are large areas of experience in which graphic communication is essential. Mechanics is one such field. For example, it is literally impossible to commu-nicate the action and usefulness of a lever without models or pic-tures. (If you doubt this, try it!) A picture may be worth a thousand words, or a hundred thousand, if it communicates an experience that is literally beyond words. But some experiences—for example, pain—are beyond pictures or any other medium of communication except words. The nearer one can come to using the medium most ap-propriate to his material, the more comprehensible he is likely to be.

The view presented here of the art of writing comprehensibly rests on the principle that meanings are the essence of communica-tion. Language serves the same function in transmitting experience from writer to readers as radio waves serve in transmitting articulate sound from broadcasting station to home receivers. In writing, one puts the impress of his experience upon established language forms, and depends upon his readers to transform them into experiences as nearly identical with the originals as possible. Consequently, the place to make one's experiences intelligible to a particular audience is in the mind, not on the page. Unless experiences are reduced to their most familiar terms, and selected and arranged for the greatest comprehensibility, they are bound to be difficult to read and harder still to understand. It will be extremely difficult to state them in simple, "readable," language. If, on the other hand, the writer goes to the trouble of making his experiences comprehensible before, or during the act of writing them down, the easy words and constructions come naturally; sometimes they seem almost to come of themselves.

The formulae for measuring readability are an excellent guide; they can show you where you have failed to make your experiences comprehensible, and where you have written ineptly, choosing the first word that comes to mind even though it be unnecessarily difficult, and putting sentences together clumsily. But when a writer tries to write readably by formula, or to simplify writing that communicates experiences which have not been refined in terms of the needs of the audience, he is likely to come out with a bland procession of primer-like sentences from which his particular and individual meanings, which are often the most important meanings, have been lost. That kind of writing is like commercial bread made out of overrefined flour, lacking both body and nourishment.

In the face of the difficulties of being comprehensible, many writers, determined to be understood, reduce the experience content of their work to the barest minimum. It is as easy to communicate a slight amount of experience as to transport a bag of feathers. Commercial and propagandistic purposes are often well served by doing so. But the dissemination of knowledge, which in the long run is the most useful function non-fiction can perform, is not furthered. To accept the limitation on experience content which is imposed by the inadequacy of mere language devices to achieve comprehensibility is therefore to beg off from the most important part of the writer's job. To make one's experiences comprehensible to begin with is far more difficult than to use writing formulas, but the writer who does so can communicate almost anything that is useful for the public to know.

A Motive for Reading

Rex Stout, the mystery story writer, once stated the importance of appeal as concretely as it can be put. "Most government writers forget," he said, "that a pamphlet doesn't do any good if nobody reads it."

Textbooks and occupational literature are usually read to earn degrees or to win advancement or to help one do his job better. The rewards are so great and so evident that students and occupational readers will wade through almost any stretch of words, no matter how desolate. But books for laymen must be self-motivating; they themselves must supply most of the incentive for reading them.

The basis for this incentive is usefulness; people want, as they say, "to get something out of" a book or article. An important part of the process of achieving appeal is therefore to show the reader what reward he may get from using the experience one gives him. It is also necessary to make the usefulness of the work both explicit and emphatic. If the reader is led to expect to gain useful experience at a low cost in time and energy, the basic appeal of the writing is very great.

Mathematics for the Million is a striking case in point. The very title of this book promises the reader something he wants for small expenditure. It induced a great many people, who had thought mathematics too time consuming, or entirely beyond their capacities, to buy the volume. The charming and easily comprehended first chapter is a partial fulfillment of this promise, and many who had barely started the book induced their friends to buy it. The catch is that after the first chapter *Mathematics for the Million* presents an almost unbroken succession of new experiences, each of which is dependent upon the one preceding. I have been searching ever since the book came out for people who had read it through, and so far found only three; one is the science consultant to a broadcasting company, and the other two are psychologists who make mathematics a hobby.

A book that makes people WANT to read it offers an enticing promise. A book that people WILL read gives partial fulfillment of its promise all along its course, and contains besides a chain of smaller promises that lead the reader on. The ways of making, and keeping, these promises have been extensively studied, but they lie outside the scope of this essay. The relation between readers and author, and the author's attitudes, as appeal factors, demand attention.

It has been thought by some that a large proportion of personal pronouns heightens appeal. Some analysts have stated that personal pronouns help relate the communication to human beings, and that we ourselves and our fellows have more appeal than anything else in the universe. This may be true. The evidence is not conclusive. I only know that personal pronouns are not to be put in like salt; persons have to be made a genuine part of the experience communicated or the pronouns become extraneous decoration. Moreover, the writer must take pains to make the references of the pronouns clear or he will confuse his readers badly. And he must also take care that his personal pronouns establish a relation between himself and his readers which his readers will accept. Perhaps the most striking example of the importance of this relationship is the Protestant wedding ritual. In this situation the minister is permitted to say—"Dearly beloved, we are gathered together . . ." But in any other situation, "dearly beloved, we" would imply a relationship which would rouse an audience to violent objections.

To say that human beings are most interesting, implies that subject matter itself has intrinsic appeal. I doubt this. The appeal which often seems to reside in subject matter may actually be found in the emotional quality of the author's experience.

During the war we eagerly read the most shocking descriptions of death, carnage and torture, accepting these because the attitudes, the emotional reactions of the reporters, were compatible with our own feelings. John Hersey's account of Hiroshima during the atomic bombing was best seller. If he had shown amusement or gloating, readers would have turned away in disgust.

Making Yourself Known

A writer ought not to avoid communicating his attitudes and his feelings, even if it were possible to do so, for the emotional tone of a piece of writing is an important appeal factor. Feeling helps to give the step by step satisfaction which makes the reader anticipate satisfaction yet to come. Also, to communicate one's feelings is the best, in fact, the only way I know to make yourself known to your readers. One listens to and accepts information from acquaintances much more willingly than from strangers, whom it is natural to regard with either indifference or suspicion.

Communicating how one feels is not a matter of word choice, but of choosing the aspects of experience to which one has reacted with feeling. This is a very subtle process and is almost continuous during the act of writing. It is as if one turned every experience a little toward the light or a little toward the shadow.

One can, of course, have personality given to his work by passing it through the hands of editors such as those who process all that appears in the well known news magazines and digests. They will select and order experience so that the standardized attitudes and feelings of the magazine are communicated. Or, one can adopt the synthetic personality which is common to most feature writers and magazine article writers. Many of these writers believe that they have a set of tricks and devices which make their work appealing. But actually the slang, the clichés, the don't-let-it-awe-you-brother passages with which they interlard their work, communicate standard attitudes which have proved acceptable to the public. The author who does not actually hold these attitudes may adopt them, temporarily, for writing purposes. In doing so he assumes a standard personality, like a primitive actor putting on a symbolic mask. Every writer of non-fiction must decide (consciously or unconsciously) whether to assume a standard, synthetic personality, or risk trying to communicate his own in an attempt to produce a more valuable piece of work.

There is no blinking the fact that it is much harder to apply principles to writing than to use formulae. It is not likely that a scientific knowledge of the processes of communication will make writing a simpler or an easier task. The hope is that principles derived from scientific study, when intelligently applied, will give a larger number of writers a greater measure of control over their work, and thus make it possible to communicate a greater range and depth of knowledge to more people. Even though scientific knowledge accumulates rapidly and writers apply it faithfully, the results are bound to vary in effectiveness. Each piece of writing presents a different problem in application of principles and it must be solved by an individual person. It will therefore always be impossible to predict the outcome surely and precisely. But this does not mean that we must cling to a mystical conception of the writing process, and depend upon unseen powers to guide the author's hand. Medicine, which began as a pure art and will never cease to be an art, has achieved astonishing control over human health through the development of scientific principles, and a growing ability to apply them. In the years to come the art of writing may advance along the same road.

XI

RADIO

BY

CHARLES A. SIEPMANN

"The average person is surrounded today by ready made intellectual goods as he is by ready made foods, articles and all kinds of gadgets. He has not the personal share in making either intellectual or material goods that his pioneer ancestors had. Consequently they knew better what they themselves were about, though they knew infinitely less concerning what the world at large was doing." [1]

Radio for me has twofold interest, first as a powerful influence on thought, outlook and action, second as an institution reflecting, both in its history and its philosophy, current trends and tensions in our society.

We may gather something of its potential influence from a few sample facts. Consider first its range. It reaches virtually everywhere throughout our land. All but a tiny fraction of our population have radio sets. It is, moreover, the only medium of communication which can subject almost the entire population simultaneously to the influence of a single impression. Consider next its significance as this stems from the habits of its listening public. One measure, at least, of any given civilization is the amount of leisure that it offers and the use to which people put that leisure. In a sense the history of man is the record of his search for an escape from the hard struggle with nature for mere sustenance, the search for leisure and for the fruits of leisure. We in America have relatively more leisure than any country in the world. It is when we ask ourselves what use we

---

[1] John Dewey, *Freedom and Culture,* pp. 45–6, copyright 1939 by John Dewey, courtesy G. P. Putnam's Sons.

make of that leisure that the significance of radio's pervasive influence stands out for us in sharp relief.

Statistics tell us that the average American has his radio set tuned in some three and a half hours a day. This means that he, or she, devotes more time (if not attention) to the radio than to anything else but work and sleep. Thus peculiar interest attaches to radio audience statistics. Let me cite a few that seem suggestive. Radio listening increases as you descend the socio-economic scale; the poorer, the less educated a man is, the more he listens to the radio. Second, serious listening decreases as you descend the socio-economic scale. Third, radio is the preferred medium of the most suggestible.

What next of radio's second point of interest, its institutional significance, as this reflects prevailing trends and tensions in our society? How does it do so and how far may we hope that it will aid rather than obstruct the resolution of current conflicts in our minds and in our emotions? This, for me, is the central point of interest about it.

To raise the question is, I hope, to justify a brief examination of our current state of mind by way of preface to a bird's eye view of our specific subject field. Let me introduce the preface with a challenging hypothesis. It would seem to me that our society is sick— divided, irresolute, ill informed, anxious and confused about its destiny. Greatness has been thrust upon us. We recognize, while in a sense we deplore, the fact and with Hamlet we complain, "The time is out of joint. O cursed spite, that ever I was born to set it right." What is the occasion of this sickness in the soul, this doubt and confusion?

There is, of course, no single cause. Yet, if we can identify one major source of our troubles, it may put us on the road toward recovery. Of the many sources of our discontent, I should myself identify one as of particular significance, the more significant for being taboo at the conscious and articulate level of expression. The following incident may help to illustrate my meaning. On April 29, 1946, proceedings in the Senate were preluded by this prayer:

Oh heavenly Father, we meet at this hour in a world trembling on the edge of chaos, a world moving rapidly downward into the anarchy of a ghastly morrow that will sweep like a tidal wave *out of the impenitent evil of the old world to engulf our homes and burden the future of this blessed land with new tragedy and tyranny to curse the generations to come.* . . .

I do not know what the proceedings of the Senate were that day. Conceivably they dealt with the United Nations. Such a prayer, as prelude to such discussion, is surely revealingly incongruous. How representative of thought and outlook in our country was and is it? I should myself judge that it is more so than most of us care to acknowledge, for it bespeaks a sentiment, the roots of which delve deep into our history, the sentiment of isolationism. At the conscious level we have dismissed isolationism as inconsistent with our intellectual appraisal of the world situation today. Emotionally it cannot be so easily dismissed. To use (and I hope not to abuse) the jargon of psychiatry, we have repressed the emotion but it continues to operate at the subconscious level, inducing in us frustrations of which we may observe the symptoms on every hand.

It is as we trace the history of the influence of isolationism on us as a people that we can, perhaps, identify the occasion of much that seems schizophrenic in our attitudes today. It is not, I think, an abuse of language to suggest that it was the sentiment of isolationism that brought this nation into being. Our revolution was the affirmation of our independence, the deliberate severing of our ties with Britain. In succeeding decades it was this same sentiment that attracted fresh immigrants. They came to a "new world," to a continent where, isolated by the broad seas, men could realize the American dream of a civilization, unfettered by tradition and no longer subject to influences from which wave after wave of immigrants sought escape and isolation.

In origin, therefore, and throughout succeeding decades of our history, the spirit of isolationism functioned as a dynamic force which impelled us ever onward in the pursuit of happiness and in our devotion to progress. Imbued with this dynamic sentiment, we set about the conquest of a continent. We were a nation on the march, committed at the start to revolution and thereafter to progressive change, and always to bigger and better things. (It is of interest to note in passing that no nation has made such constant use in its language of the comparative.)

It is only in our day that the dynamic influence of isolationism has suffered a sea change. "There is a tide in the affairs of men." It has run fast and furious in our time. We must move forward with that tide or we move back. There is no standing still. To cling to the *status quo* is to deny the logic of events and the lesson of history. But some among us are unwilling to reckon with this truth. Part of the crisis of our time would seem to derive from this fact. The spirit of isolationism has in certain quarters changed from a dynamic to a reactionary force, to a fear of being committed to change, to a desire to stop the clock of our own destiny, to conceive of our democracy as static rather than emergent. The habit in such quarters, as with all men whose eyes are on the past, is to invoke in their support famous sayings by our forefathers and traditional symbols charged with high emotional significance. With a fine disregard for changed times and circumstances, Mr. Hearst cites Mr. Jefferson to the effect that the less government the better; big business harps on the theme of unfettered private enterprise and rugged individualism as hallowed aspects of Americanism. But neither recalls Jefferson's more timeless observation, "I know that laws and institutions must go hand in hand with the progress of the human mind. As new discoveries are made, new truths disclosed, and manners and opinions change with the change of circumstances, institutions must change also and keep pace with the times."

Repressed emotions tend to result in fear. Fear, in turn, tends to result in a state of mind which sees life's options in terms of black and white. "He that is not with me is against me." The fearful man thus poses to himself, and to others, false alternatives. Concerned to rally sentiment to his own side, he tends to associate with contrary opinions symbols of sinister significance. Fear thus tends to what I would call the "either, or" mentality, the association of one person's interests with the good and those of his opponents with evil. The prevalence of such a state of mind has particular danger in our time. But lest all this seem too remote from our specific subject matter, let me draw an illustration from the field of radio.

In March, 1946, a report was published by the Federal Communications Commission which drew attention to certain trends in radio, which the commission regarded as inimical to the public interest. The validity of the report is for our present purpose beside the point. Interest attaches to the reaction of the radio industry and the specific terms of that reaction. For succeeding months, Mr. Justin Miller, President of the National Association of Broadcasters, addressed audiences throughout the country describing the authors of the report, and those supporting it, as "intellectual smart alecs" and "stooges of the communists." The current repertoire of invective and innuendo proved, however, insufficient to his need. He was driven to coining a new phrase. He described his opponents as "stigmatic perverts."

That a man with a distinguished public record should campaign on an issue of vital public importance in such terms as these is perhaps the measure of declining standards in what I would call the good manners of communication. (I am thinking here of manners not in the limited sense of polite convention, but in that larger sense which William of Wykeham envisaged in his phrase "manners makyth man.") If we concede, as I think we must, a state of anxious perplexity among us regarding our future, such abuse of the good manners of communication assumes dangerous proportions as it aggravates a state of mind which, because rooted in fear, is peculiarly responsive to the "either, or" appeal. Moreover, to create fear and hatred, as such phrases are obviously intended to do, is dangerous not only because of people's susceptibility but because of the power of communication as an influence in our time.

This incident would have small interest but for the fact that it represents a tactic, as also a state of mind and point of view, more widely current than in the realm of radio alone. Other agencies and other individuals seem bent on forcing upon us the "either, or" mentality, a choice between false alternatives regarding the future of democracy. Herein lies the broader interest both of the incident and of the institutional significance of radio. It is as it reflects other more universal trends and conflicts that interest attaches to it as a field of study. Let me cite a few.

We are in a period of rapid social and cultural transition. We are seeking an adjustment of traditional patterns of thought and ways of living to new circumstances. If this transition is to be orderly, reasoned and without violence, we must reach agreement as to the nature and the pace of our adaptation to novel conditions. Implicit in this process is the need to define in modern terms: 1) the nature of the public interest, as this affects the unfettered freedom of individuals and groups (and by groups I have specifically in mind, business enterprises, large and small), 2) new consequent concepts of responsibility on the part of individuals and groups as these relate to public interest, 3) the role of government in relation to both private enterprise and public interest. The history of radio has, I think, something to tell us about desirable adjustments in the relations between the three major parties to that "social contract" which we think of as the democratic system—government, private industry and the general public. Let us briefly survey radio's history as it throws light upon this issue.

In establishing our system of broadcasting, Congress set a new precedent regarding that tripartite relationship of interest to which I have referred. It showed foresight in recognizing, albeit partially and dimly, the immense potential influence and power of a new medium of communication. Fearful of the abuse of such power, it made public interest the keystone of its legislation. The wave lengths of the air were deeded in perpetuity to the public. Radio's air waves were declared a public domain. Use of these wave lengths by private entrepreneurs was subject to their acceptance of a public trust. This notion of trusteeship marks a departure (though not, of course, the first of its kind) from traditional concepts of unfettered commercial competition. The tradition that in our society a man should be free to make money in competition with his fellows was subject to the *caveat* that his (the radio licensee's) desire for profit be subordinate to the public interest.

But what, you may ask, in the realm of radio constitutes public interest? The concept, as I think wisely, was not defined in narrow or specific terms, though as we read the hearings and discussions which preceded the Communications Act of 1943 we may gather a general impression of what the Congress was after. Radio services, for instance, were conceived as embracing adequate provision for education and the promotion of the interests of "non-profit organizations." It was indeed, only by a hair's breadth that we escaped provision in the law for specific reservations of time on the air for the reflection of such interests. The Congress, likewise, was aware of the dangers of excessive inroads by advertisers. We have become so accustomed to the dominant role of the advertiser in radio today that it is with a shock of surprise that we recall that in 1932 the Senate passed a resolution that brought us within an ace of operation under a different system. This resolution reads in part as follows:

Whereas there is growing dissatisfaction with the present use of radio facilities for purposes of commercial advertising, be it resolved that the Federal Radio Commission is hereby authorized and instructed. . . . to report . . . what plans might be adopted to reduce, to limit, to control and perhaps to eliminate the use of radio facilities for commercial advertising purposes and . . . whether it would be practical and satisfactory to permit only an announcement of programs by persons or corporations.

It is instructive to recall that only fifteen years ago advertising abuses and the public attitude thereto were such as to call in question the validity of the system we have adopted.

I have said that the Congress seemed to me wise in its reluctance to define too narrowly the nature of the public interest. It preferred (and again, in my judgment, wisely) to delegate responsibility to a regulatory agency of government which would use its discretion in interpreting the public interest as time and circumstances and unforeseeable public needs, relating to a medium still in its infancy, dictated. Here again it set a precedent, pregnant with significance as it relates to our adjustment to new conditions. It established an agency of government to function as guardian of the public and to set limits on the unfettered operation of free competitive enterprise. While not the first precedent of its kind, it marked a significant forward step in adjusting the balance of power as between government and private industry.

This adjustment of the power relationship between government and industry has been hotly disputed by the industry. It has claimed with increasing vehemence over the years that it should not be subject to any form of government control, apart from technical provision for allocating wave lengths to avoid interference between different station signals. This claim has been refuted by the courts and was finally disposed of by a Supreme Court decision that the FCC is "of necessity concerned with the composition of the traffic," *i.e.,* that the FCC, in granting and renewing licenses, is perforce concerned with the proposed program plans of applicants. That the industry is not only at variance with the courts but with the public on this matter was recently confirmed by the findings of a survey sponsored, ironically enough, by the National Association of Broadcasters.[2] Among a number of revealing disclosures was one which showed public opinion to be ahead even of the Congress in its concern for protection of the public interest in radio by the government. This survey shows that sixty-six per cent of a representative sample considered that government should have specific powers over radio stations to insure that news broadcasts are truthful; fifty-three per cent wished to concede like powers to government to insure that radio stations regularly carry programs giving both sides of public issues; forty per cent went the length of demanding that government insure that each station broadcast a certain number of educational programs. Here are definitions of the public interest far more specific than those provided in the Communications Act or as yet included among the regulations of the FCC. They seem to show that significant numbers of radio listeners are abreast of the times in their recognition of the need in our modern society for the protection of public interest by a responsible agency of government.

Our system of broadcasting thus reflects adjustments of outlook regarding the respective roles of free enterprise and of government as these relate to a concept, that of the public interest, which since the great depression has become a central preoccupation with our people. The days of cutthroat competition, at least in an area as vital to the public interest as radio, are past. We have instead a system involving a tripartite relationship in which government, industry and the

[2] Paul F. Lazarsfeld and Harry Field, *The People Look at Radio,* University of North Carolina Press, Chapel Hill, 1946.

public are each involved. The wave lengths of the air constitute a public domain. Private industry has conditional access to that domain and has been asked to accept responsibility for public service as the *quid pro quo* for the profits to be derived from that domain. How rich are its resources may be judged by the fact that the average profit of radio stations in the year 1945 was in excess of two hundred and twenty per cent of the depreciated value of all tangible capital assets. Such generous rewards for enterprise would seem to justify high expectations of the industry in the field of public service. How well has our system worked and what returns of public service have listeners received from an industry privileged to have access to so rich a kingdom?

There are two ways of answering this question. One would rest on evidence of the public's satisfaction with radio's services. The survey referred to above provides us with that evidence. Its findings, while seemingly contradictory at times, leave little room for doubt that the average listener is well satisfied with what he gets. Indeed an overwhelming majority of listeners express such general satisfaction. Discontent, even with advertising excesses, appears to be limited to a minority.

There is, however, another way in which the question can be answered. This would have reference to the hopes of radio conceived by the authors of the Communications Act, as also to the claims on radio as a means of information and cultural advancement dictated by the urgent necessities of our time. Greatness has been thrust upon us. To measure up to the world responsibility in which as a leading power we are involved we need, and quickly, to add a cubit to our stature. A public ignorant, ill informed, suggestible, is in our time an appalling, if not a fatal, liability. We are running a race against time. To win that race all the combined resources of education and enlightenment are needed to help us measure up to the new perplexing claims on our intelligence and emotional maturity. Radio is obviously one of our chief resources. Few, I think, can deny that, with reference to such claims upon its services and in such a context of need, radio has fallen far short of its potentialities.

In a sense, of course, radio's services are limited by the public's readiness to accept them. And certainly the heavy load of ignorance and seeming indifference, which as a people we still carry, cannot be blamed on the radio alone. It is our inheritance from the past, the liability we carry for the unfinished business of democracy. Nevertheless, there are those who feel (and there is evidence to support them) that radio has sacrificed public service to profits and to some extent is guilty of a sin which, in a democracy at least, is well nigh unpardonable. In adjusting its program services to our apparent needs, it has taken us for what we are and denied that which we have it in us to become. Having regard to radio's universal range, people's addiction to it, to say nothing of its psychological hold on the mind and imagination of its listeners, a great risk is here involved. There attaches to radio preeminently, as in a degree to other mass media of communication, the constant danger that it may impose a stereotype upon the culture, and that it may thus retard, if not stifle, that advancement of our understanding and that development of emotional maturity of which we stand in such dire need.

It was danger of this kind that was foreseen by the Federal Communications Commission when early in 1946 it published its report on "Public Service Responsibility of Broadcast Licensees." Defaults in program service to which this report called public attention included: failure of local stations to foster local talent and adequately to reflect local life and local issues; an alarming decrease in provision at convenient hours of "sustaining programs" (*i.e.,* unsponsored programs) devoted to subjects either inappropriate for sponsorship or scouted by sponsors; inadequate provision for the discussion of public issues, local, national and international; and lastly, the growth of advertising abuses on the air. This is not the place in which to discuss the merits of this report. I refer to it only as evidence that the agency of government entrusted with the definition and safeguarding of the public interest felt serious concern about certain current trends in radio's development. The system, as first conceived, was not working out well in practice. At whose door should the blame be laid?

Space does not permit of our exploring fully the answer to this question. In fairness I think we must say that the blame is divided. As we recall the hearings and discussions on which the Communications Act rested, we are forced to the conclusion that the FCC itself has been lax in the performance of its duty as guardian of the public interest. Twice only in thirteen years has it come to grips with central questions affecting radio's services. In 1940, in its "Chain Broadcasting Report" it grappled with the problem of monopoly. In its report of 1946 it tackled for the first time the central question of adequate program service in the public interest. For the rest its granting and renewal of licenses has been perfunctory and its record of supervision, timid and inadequate. The default of the industry itself is a matter for the reader's judgment by reference to such standards of performance as are implicit in the findings of the FCC report of 1946. What of the default of the public? In the final analysis it is the public which should and which will determine the nature and adequacy of radio's program services. It is we, the people, who likewise will determine the future of democracy. Thus, here again the subject of radio acquires a broader significance. As we identify the default of radio's listening public and as we can discover means by which to make good that default, we may discover also a partial clue to the future well being of our democratic system. Because of the momentous implications of this problem I plead exemption from detailed study of the default, either of government or of the radio industry. Let us concern ourselves exclusively with the default of the public and see what broader implications it has for each and all of us.

I have said that it is the public which should and will finally determine the nature of radio's program services. This is sound democratic theory. Its soundness, however, depends on the fulfillment of two conditions. Popular judgment must be informed. It is of little worth (indeed it may prove disastrous) if based on ignorance. There must, moreover, be means by which such judgment can be voiced with effect. In radio, as in other fields, there is great disparity between theory and practice respecting these two paramount conditions. Some indeed claim that the theory is being deliberately manipulated by selfish interests to confound and to confuse sound democratic practice.

These critics point to the fact that the apparent satisfaction of the radio public with what it gets rests upon total ignorance of what it might be getting if the program policy of networks and stations were different from what it is. The human palate is sensitive to an infinite variety of tastes. But it is only as we sample different flavors that we are capable of expressing preferences among them. By and large, it is claimed, radio has thus far limited the public's taste to a few crude and easily assimilated flavors. Ignorant of what they might be tasting, it is hardly surprising that they express satisfaction with what they get. Thus the public's verdict rests upon insufficient evidence.

If this argument is valid, it applies not only to satisfaction with radio's program fare but to public satisfaction with our system of broadcasting. For, according to our theory, not only programs but the system which makes them possible should be subject to popular consent. It is, therefore, disturbing to find on what slender knowledge the supposed consent of the people to the system that we have now rests. The same survey to which reference was made above discloses that only fifty-one per cent of the sample taken were so much as aware that government had anything to do with the operation of radio. Even more astonishing is the fact that only twenty-one per cent knew that our system differs in any way from that of the BBC in England! Appeal to public opinion, when this opinion rests on such dismal ignorance, surely has small validity and makes nonsense of democratic theory.

Ignorance and apathy is the one liability which a democracy cannot afford. The extent of our current liability may be judged by the fact that a recent poll disclosed that only twenty-one per cent of a sample interviewed were able to identify the Bill of Rights at all correctly. It is, then, hardly matter for surprise to find ignorance about our system of broadcasting so widely prevalent. And yet unless we dismiss radio as having no significance or reject the notion of a triangular relationship (between government, industry and the public) as the functioning basis of our system, knowledge must somehow be substituted for the prevailing ignorance. How can this be done?

I, for one, am skeptical of any quick or simple answer to the question. Indeed, I think that we should be on guard against those who are ready with a panacea. I would also part company with those who lay the whole blame on the radio industry for the disparity between the fare presently offered to the listener and that which any thinking person recognizes as a condition of healthy democratic life. Only by concerted effort, at different levels and by different agencies can we hope to alleviate the defectiveness inherent in any democratic society, by virtue of the burden of responsibility cast upon the people. I offer, then, only a few tentative suggestions for the amelioration, not for the cure, of our condition.

As far as ignorance of our system of broadcasting is concerned, radio itself can do something. The Columbia Broadcasting System has set a useful precedent in a series of weekly talks dealing with the system and the manner of its operation. While essentially defensive, and at times evasive, it has shed some light on the prevailing darkness of ignorance about this subject. By the inclusion of more critics (as well as advocates) of current practice and by supplementary discussions on various aspects of the system such service might prove even more useful. Local stations, in particular, might well make of application for renewal of their license occasion for rendering an account of their stewardship to the public they serve, and provide air time for many sided comment on their stewardship. Without regular and repeated provision for discussion of radio itself, there is small hope for increased interest in and fuller information about it. Public understanding of our system would also be better served if radio denied access to the microphone to those who, by special pleading and obfuscation of the issue, deliberately seek to throw dust in the public eye. Thus, Mr. Justin Miller, in his most recent utterance, for which the facilities of a network were freely granted, compares our radio system and its service to that of other countries only to write off the radio of the world outside America as "dull, lifeless dishwater . . . and great doses of government propaganda." The day, one hopes, will come when the conscience of our broadcasters is clear enough to admit of less irresponsible comparison of our services with those of other countries.

Radio likewise has primary responsibility and greatest opportunity to adjust the public palate to more varied and discriminating tastes.

We cannot, however, expect rapid adjustment. All we have the right to hope for is more definite concern among broadcasters with the real urgency of the problem, judged by standards of the public interest and the new and pressing demands now being made of us for informed and responsible judgement. The fact is, that at present there is no real "practical" incentive to such concern. So great is the appetite for entertainment and so limited are the hours during which the bulk of the population can enjoy it that four networks, with their affiliated stations, can hardly cope with it. As FM develops and more stations come on the air and as competition becomes keener, we may hope to see broadcasters angling for fish other than the omnivorous carp which, in its hunger for the bait of entertainment, now tends to drive smaller fry to the bottom of the pond. It is absurd to expect that we shall ever muster audiences for "serious" programs which compare in size with those for light and entertaining programs. It can hardly, however, be questioned that if radio applied the same techniques to the promotion of present minority interests as those which have been found effective in attracting audiences for lighter programs, more progress could be made. Popular audiences are attracted to programs by publicity, by continuity and ingenuity in the manner of their presentation. Audiences for serious programs could be vastly increased by the application of like techniques.

But if radio is to take the lead in this matter, it can hope for only small success unless its efforts are supported by those minorities whose interests it may one day seek to safeguard and promote with more zeal than is now displayed. "Intellectuals" and "serious" minorities do radio and themselves disservice by merely sniping at radio from the side lines. They would be better occupied in promoting audiences for the few programs currently offered to cater for their interest. Local, regional and national minorities (labor unions, the churches, social groups, women's organizations, etc.) can surely find associated interest, both in the promotion of audiences for worthwhile programs and in the specification of positive proposals for better programs touching upon interests which they have in common. Radio listeners' councils, within which and by which such groups can promote their associated interests, exist in a few communities. Extension of such councils is greatly desirable. They involve effort and time, but the only strength of a minority is its zeal and its energy.

There is one particular development which is already long over-due. If listeners are to enter into their birthright, if radio's wave lengths, in practice as well as in theory, are to belong to the people, there should be practicable means by which the people can safeguard their inheritance. When a local station is due for the renewal of its license, the community which it serves should be canvassed on the subject. It is then that groups in the community can and should take stock of the situation. Has the station really met its public service responsibilities? Its stewardship over the past three years should be reviewed. Just as at election times, public opinion should be brought into play. For it is only by the exercise of our rights that we become conversant with our rights. If democracy is to be more than a word, we need to become practitioners and not mere theorists about it.

Like action by interested groups is necessary not only at the local or regional level but at the national level, too. One recent illustration of current apathy about radio, particularly among leaders of thought, was the public response to the FCC's controversial "Bluebook" in 1946. True, many newspapers carried editorials and several journals of opinion gave it responsible consideration. But I am unaware of any concerted action on the part of those "non-profit organizations" (whose interests this report bespoke) to let the FCC know that it had any solid body of opinion behind it. At hearings before com-mittees of the Congress concerned with radio such organizations are generally conspicuous by their absence. In radio, at any rate, we have not yet learned to avail ourselves even of existing channels along which public opinion can find its way to those who, on the people's behalf, determine public policy.

Opinion can be mobilized also through the press. There were en-couraging developments in 1946 when an increasing number of dailies and some weeklies began to employ accredited critics of radio. The critic, if he is responsible, is important not only by virtue of the publicity he brings to the field he covers but of the standards of expectation to which he can rally public opinion. There are still few such critics outside of New York. Radio and the public can do with plenty more. Local papers, moreover, could do much to encourage the canvassing of public opinion within the community at the time of a station's license renewal application. It is here, too, that the FCC could function, at once to put the spotlight on radio as a relevant factor in community well being and to remove the sense of remoteness which now exists for the majority of listeners concerning its role as the people's guardian. If renewal hearings took place within the region in which stations are located and a commissioner were present, the role of this agency of government might become less remote and impersonal. Seeing that we cannot move the people to Washington, Washington might on occasion move to the people.

This is but a fragmentary list of possibilities. A huge job of social engineering has yet to be done before our democratic theory can be translated into practice. Radio here illustrates one of the most perplexing problems in democratic living, how in our modern society to restore to individuals and groups that sense of belonging which has progressively been lost as society has grown in size and complexity. For lack of exercise our democratic muscles are slack. Without eternal watchfulness, the whole system is in peril and watchfulness is not enough, unless, where we scent danger, we have ready means of action.

But of all agencies which might prove effective in disseminating knowledge about radio and in making more sensitive the palate of the listener I should choose one above the rest as having at once a golden opportunity and a peculiar responsibility for action, both because it is threatened and because its collective power might prove decisive in forcing radio better to meet the challenge of our time. I am thinking of the teaching profession. This, I believe, should be the spearhead of the attack on radio's default to date. When I say that the teaching profession is threatened by radio I refer to a development of which few teachers seem to be aware. Its origin and present consequences deserve special consideration.

In our lifetime there has been, I suggest, a significant shift in the center of gravity among cultural influences on our society. Teachers, with and like intellectuals, are discredited. Loyalties have been transferred. What, we may ask, is the occasion of this discredit? Has it not possibly something to do with that change in the center of gravity of cultural influences to which I have referred? As one looks back over the centuries, one might say that until comparatively recent times cultural standards—their formulation, refinement and dissemination—were the virtual monopoly of the churches and the schools. Allegiance in our time has shifted. The dominant influences of today, certainly in respect of the time they claim and possibly in terms of their formative influence on interests and values, are the mass media of communication; the press, the films, and, above all, the radio. Thus the balance of power has shifted. The voice of the teacher, as of the preacher, has, relatively speaking, shrunk in its significance and in the range of its appeal. Church and school are thus tending toward insulation from life in the sense of the relevance of their message to the environmental context of those whose outlook they seek to influence. Unless and until radio (and films) are related to the work of teachers and of preachers, as a convenient familiar frame of reference, until radio and films, at their best, are embraced as tools of education and, at their worst, are used as illustrations of crooked thinking and distorted values, their influence for good and for ill will run its separate course and the shifting of the loyalties of people will continue away from the schools and the churches to the media of mass communication.

Education for life can hardly disregard life. A child's listening to the radio at home is a part, and indeed a large part, of its experience of living. To disregard the experience and seek no relation between it and the experience offered in the classroom is to miss a golden opportunity. That opportunity, available to every teacher, is to find in radio a living and relevant context for those insights and explorations of value with which teaching is concerned. In my own judgment such use of radio has even higher potential value than the use of radio programs specifically designed for classroom use. It is for this reason that I, for one, do not greatly regret the transfer to out of school hours of the CBS School of the Air programs. They still provide material for inschool use. Because they do not conflict with the school curriculum, they are probably available to an even larger audience than before. By assignment they can certainly be made so.

But this is by no means all. Teachers, individually and collectively have wider scope than this for action. They, too, can play their part in mustering audiences for what is worthwhile on the air. No profession has daily access to, and potential influence on, more individuals. Concerted action by teachers (and this seems to me not so wild a dream) should eventually make possible the mustering of audiences which might even provide guaranteed markets which an advertiser could ill afford to disregard. The mechanics of such concerted action would be complex if conceived in nationwide terms. But until we consider the mechanics of this kind of social engineering we shall continue to drift in the direction of our thinking, as also of our action.

Extended research into radio and its manifold influences also falls naturally within the province of the teaching profession. At the university level I see such research developing hand in hand with courses designed to acquaint teachers with the relevance of the mass media of communication to their own activities. There are endless vistas open to research in the field of radio alone, though with it I should couple like inquiries into the influence of films.

Teachers' associations can be powerful, too, as pressure groups in the continual struggle for defining and refining developing concepts of what constitutes public interest respecting radio's services. Their present silence and inactivity at this level is as regrettable as it is marked. It is deplorable to think, for instance, that in the controversy over the FCC's Bluebook in 1946, the organized voice of education was unheard.

I have spoken again and again of the need for concerted action. Radio is everybody's business. I have spoken, too, of the danger which now exists, of our society being dragged, culturally speaking, in opposite directions. If the voice of radio and the voice of the teachers bespeak conflicting ideals and standards of value, we shall remain, as in part we are, a schizophrenic society. Only by the associated action of educators and of the mass media can we conceivably hope to win the race against time which we are running. Radio's default is great and it has still much to learn of what public interest constitutes. But the teaching profession is likewise in default and likewise has much to learn. Claiming air time, for instance, without regard to the effective use to which such precious time is put (*i.e.,* without regard to the limitations imposed on radio as a mass medium of communication and to the necessary skills by means of which to arrest and hold attention) is amateurism at its worst. Teachers and others concerned to raise levels of taste and interest would do well to recognize the proper division of labor as between themselves and radio's executives. For teachers, the formulation of priorities of need, of the strategy of advance along the whole cultural front. For teachers, too, the promotion of interest and the organization of a listening public. For radio, the adapting of such formulations to the peculiar requirements of microphone technique and the expenditure of skill and energy in the refinement of the art of radio related to such service.

The shift in the center of gravity among the cultural influences of our time is one of the central problems of our contemporary culture. Radio did not create it. It has merely aggravated a dilemma posed for us when we undertook the brave experiment of universal education. Latent in this experiment, from the very start, was the danger of diluting knowledge and the forfeiting of insights which are the final fruit of higher education. How in our culture can we maintain the supremacy of standards and values dependent on disciplines which mass education cannot impart except to a numerical minority?

Radio, in theory, is a heaven sent means of accelerating the acceptance of standards hitherto reserved for the privileged few. But, like other modern instruments of power, its potentialities are ambivalent. It can impose a stereotype upon our culture, based upon mass appeals and feeding on mass suggestibility, far more easily than it can wean us from ignorance and credulity. It is altogether too easy and too tempting for radio, taking us for what we are, to keep us where we are. Few of us are privileged to pursue occupations which provide more than a bare modicum of creative satisfaction. In this machine age millions are doomed to performance of tasks which are wholly uncreative in the satisfaction they offer. Indeed, they involve frustration rather than release. The best of us, moreover, develop insights and sensibilities which refine the art of living only as the result of long exposure and the diligent exercise of faculties that civilize human personality. Small wonder, then, that most of us prefer escape from, rather than concern with, reality. There is an indolence in each of us which is resistant both to growth and change. As radio indulges us in this respect it retards rather than advances our growth. Herein lies its danger. Radio's claim that it gives the public what it wants is a dangerous half truth. It can make of this potential instrument a drug rather than a stimulant. Radio has the responsibility to lead as well as to follow the opinion of its audiences. The concept of democratic living is meaningless if it excludes the concept of leadership. The rule of the people is doomed to disaster if it merely implies mob rule. It involves the survival, not of the fittest, but of the sickest.

An observer of our contemporary scene has well expressed the dilemma that we face and in which radio and our own system of radio are involved. "We cannot think if we have no time to read, or feel if we are emotionally exhausted, or out of cheap materials create what will last. We cannot coordinate what is not there." Our system of broadcasting and, who knows, the future of our culture depend on the extent to which we ponder the implications of this warning. "We cannot coordinate what is not there." How near to bankruptcy are we regarding the relevant coordinates of a life giving culture? It is with respect to such a question that radio is everybody's business.

XII

PROBLEMS OF FREEDOM

BY

ROBERT D. LEIGH [1]

I shall deal with the middle step in the three part process of communication. You have considered, at some length, the first part of the process, *i.e.*, the person initiating communication as speaker, writer, actor. Also you have become aware of the third part of the process, *i.e.*, the function of the listener, reader, audience.

I invite your examination of the machinery that connects the two, and particularly the mechanism of large scale communication which is especially characteristic of our time. The problem I pose is that of the relation of the principle of freedom of utterance, a basic value in our democratic theory, to our highly organized system of mass communication built on the model of modern business organization. The principle of free individual expression predates our industrial society. And it lives on in our industrial society as a vital concept. But does it continue to mean the same thing in the world of communication today characterized as it is by a *big* as well as a *free* press?

[1] Note: The talk on which this chapter is based was written just as I was emerging from two and a half years' work as director of the Commission on Freedom of the Press. During these years my own thought and expression on the subject of mass communication became hopelessly intertwined with the thought and discussions of the Commission. What appears below, therefore, bears close resemblance to, and at times identity with, the published reports of the Commission, especially the general report entitled *A Free and Responsible Press*, Chicago University Press, 1947. I am indebted to the Chicago University Press for permission to use the material from this book. On the other hand, the Commission is not in any sense responsible for the analysis or conclusions given here. Where I have used the Commission's terminology mostly by indirect quotation, I have been as conscientious as possible in using the language of my own memoranda presented for Commission consideration, some of which, often in condensed form, appeared in the published report. R. D. L.

What did a free press mean to the authors of our Bill of Rights when they took the novel step of embodying it as an enforceable legal right in the First and Fourteenth Amendments to the Federal Constitution and in similar clauses in state constitutions? These provisions state simply that no government, national, state or local, shall abridge the freedom of the press. Their framers were aiming at particular evils which had arisen in their own experience, *i.e.,* the suppression of publication, the intimidation and imprisonment of publishers at the hands of British colonial governors and their agents. They felt that transferring the power of government to people of their choice did not dissolve the danger. So they acted to prevent officials within their own elected government from taking any steps designed to interfere with free publication.

But theirs was not merely a specific approach based on immediate experience. The authors of our fundamental law were conscious heirs of the philosophy and tradition justifying the inherent right of the individual to have his say, a claim going far back in the history of Western civilization. Socrates paying with his life for the free investigation of ethical problems, the Roman Stoics developing a theory of natural law under which individual freedoms found sanction against unwise state action, the Church scholars asserting a unity of divine and secular sanction for a law superior to the commands of princes, the British philosophers and reformers including freedom of utterance from censorship by the state among the historic rights of Englishmen, the French apostles of the Enlightenment assuming either as a fact or as a useful myth an original state of nature where freedom of expression existed as a matter of course to be modified only by the perversions of artificial human institutions—all were known to the framers of the bills of rights. And it was in this larger background that they constructed their legal prohibition of governmental interference with free utterance.

The legal prohibition was not the sum of their application of the great tradition of a free press to the new constitutional system. The founders of our system were engaged in devising the governing machinery for a free society. They give clear evidence in their writing that they saw the importance of free communication not only as a press freed from government abridgment, but a press designed so that people should be adequately, not partially, informed. They knew that people uninformed or misinformed would be unable to govern themselves.

We can see recognition of this positive requirement in the writings and speeches of Washington, of Franklin, of Jefferson, all of whom declared that schools and newspapers, widely spread and available to all, were basic institutions of a free society.

This more positive requirement they took for granted as a complement to the legal prohibition of governmental interference, because they assumed the continuance of the easily expansible number of small, competing press units serving their contemporary society. The press they knew consisted of hand printed sheets issuing from dingy little printing shops regularly, as newspapers, or irregularly as broadsides, pamphlets or books. Presses were cheap and the journeyman printer could become a publisher-editor by borrowing the hundreds of dollars necessary to set up his shop, by engaging an assistant or two to help him gather local news and to clip items from other publications. He could also pick up foreign news from ship captains bringing mail and newspapers from abroad in their irregular arrival at port after a month or more at sea, and in these ways supply the community's printing and publishing needs.

With a limited number of people who could read, and with property qualifications for the suffrage—less than six per cent of the adult population voted for the conventions held to ratify the Constitution itself—there was no great discrepancy between the number of those who could read and vote and those who could command the financial resources to engage in publication. It was probably never expected that any considerable number of the citizens of the Republic would wish to take advantage of the freedom to publish their views to the world. But anyone with a continuing desire to say something and the ability to say it had a fair chance to set up a regular publication, and one with only an occasional message could print and distribute a pamphlet which would reach a fair proportion of the active voting citizens of the community.

No newspaper, it was thought, would represent all, or nearly all, of the conflicting viewpoints relating to a particular public controversy. Together, however, they would represent all the principal points of view so that the community would have an open choice between alternatives and eventually sort out the truth.

Not that many citizens would subscribe to all the local journals. It was more likely that the individual citizen would subscribe then as now only to the journal which would reinforce his prejudices. But in each village and town community, with its relatively simple social structure, and wealth of neighborly contacts, the various opinions would encounter each other in face to face meetings with a free field for competing ideas.

It was natural, therefore, for the men of the 1780's and 90's to assume that freedom of the press from government interference would furnish a solid guarantee of the widest possible dissemination of information from diverse and antagonistic sources, a condition held to be essential to the public welfare.

The idea of freedom of the press which grew naturally out of this earlier environment has survived to our present day. But the environment itself and the press itself have changed in size and character. The changes are not necessarily in the direction of less free individual utterance. Probably in the American community there is now more opportunity than in any earlier period for the person with something to say—no matter how bizarre—to put on paper and to distribute to those who will read it what he has in mind. Not only has government restriction remained at a minimum; the subtle voluntary censorships by religious and social groups are, if anything, less than in the earlier days.

Indeed, one of the difficulties of communication of ideas in our time is this very decline in institutional, social authorities with the homogeneity of thought and feeling they engendered. We do have, now as then, a common language, a common government and a common historical tradition. But in place of the easy interchange of ideas and opinions across occupational and neighborhood lines, there is a tendency in urbanized culture for personal association to form along specialized, occupational, nationalistic and religious lines. Such groupings become highly organized, but mutually insulated, sections of the community between which normal interchange dies out. The separate groups maintain an active life of internal discussion, but they each read separate media of communication presenting their own partial and colored versions of events. The result is that the different groups come to live in different worlds of fact and judgment.

In addition, we now have the task immediately before us in the international sphere of creating a universe of discourse based upon common cultural understandings, for which our own nation is only partially prepared. Thus the role that the press played in the simple homogeneous society has taken on a new character, because that society itself has become heterogeneous rather than homogeneous, and has developed insulation and division within itself. The communication of ideas on a large scale has become a job not only of free and varied expression, but also one of unifying expression, of interchange which lays the basis for common understanding.

More striking and easier to recognize than the change in the environment is the change in the size and character of the press itself. In place of the small scale, town newspaper there has emerged a large scale, costly press, including radio and motion pictures, organized so that a relatively small number of units carries the major position of the burden of communication on a large scale to large audiences.

I do not want to give a false or oversimplified picture of this technological communications revolution. We still have a small newspaper press very similar to the partisan sheets of a century and more ago. We have also a widely diversified and important partisan periodical press. With the coming of radio and motion pictures, moreover, there has been a growth in variety and in type of large scale communication. And with the emergence of FM radio, the broadcast facsimile newspaper and television, there promises to be still greater variety. But the most striking thing about the communications revolution which has given us the Big Press is the concentration of ownership in each medium so that in a locality three to a half dozen agencies carry the burden of mass communication and in the country as a whole four to a dozen units in each medium perform the major task of providing most people with current information and ideas. And between these major units in the different media there are interrelationships and interdependence for news sources, talent and some common owner-ship.

In the largest cities three to six newspapers, in smaller cities two or three, and in most smaller places one newspaper; three or four size-able newspaper chain ownerships and fifty odd smaller regional groups; three great press associations; a few big syndicates among, hundreds of smaller ones carrying the large volume of feature material and some of these few connected with the chief metropolitan news-papers and press associations; four principal radio networks, them-selves owning most of the powerful, clear channel stations and fur-nishing a large part of the day's radio programs for three fourths of the nation's radio stations; eight motion picture units together playing the major role in movie production and distribution and a strategic role in exhibition; a big five to ten in magazines and a big six to six-teen in book publishing, along with a large number of smaller units—this is the picture of the mass communications industry in the United States.

It is not a picture of monopoly or near monopoly: *i.e.,* a single ownership or control of what we read, hear and see. The nearest to single control is not on the national scale where it would be most dangerous, but in the smaller localities. In these smaller places the single newspaper press shares the function of political communica-tion with public meetings and informal contacts of all sorts. And it is at most a monopoly of local news only. In Stamford, Connecticut, for instance, the single local newspaper recently acquired control of the single local radio station. But actually seven or eight radio stations in near-by New York and three or four metropolitan newspapers have a larger audience and circulation in Stamford than the local radio station and newspaper. So also, Mr. Gannett by his ownership of the single newspaper plant and radio station in a number of New York State communities has an undoubted position of regional influence on account of that fact. But it does not mean that the people of upstate New York have to depend solely on Mr. Gannett's organization for their news.

Thus we still have today in mass communication, as we had a cen-tury and a half ago, a system of active, vigorous competition. But it is a competition between giants—for the most part, between like minded giants. These giants—how many in all?—I would estimate sixty to eighty—are in sharp, even ruthless competition, with each other. But they carry on their activities in a framework of incentives and compulsions so similar that they tend to an inevitable similarity of outlook and practice.

Let it be perfectly clear that I do not suggest in any way that the emergence of this Big Press is an unnatural or harmful development. Any nostalgia for return to the village press for our supply of news is as silly as a proposal to return to the village pump for our water supply. The Big Press is not only an accompaniment and effect of our more general industrial-commercial revolution; it is an essential factor in making possible the swift distribution of current intelligence necessary for the maintenance of an industrial, self-governing society on a continental scale. And it is an equally necessary instrument for the creation of an orderly, international society.

But the Big Press does create certain problems of free communication, and especially the problem of bigness. If we think of the basic idea underlying the bills of rights, the right of a man with something to say to have his say without hindrance in the press, that right still exists. Certainly he can talk to his neighbors, hire a hall, or issue a leaflet. But he cannot freely mount the platform of national public discussion and have his say without let or hindrance.

This is not a matter of will; it is a necessity for those who preside over the great public platforms. The relatively small number of major units of mass communication have an inevitable power of selection or censorship over those who use their facilities. In this sense it is they more than governments that today by their necessary controls and regulations have the power to abridge free and untrammeled expression. And we cannot re-create our earlier freedom of expression by an amendment of the First Amendment prohibiting the owners of the Big Press from abridging freedom of the press. Their selection and control are as necessary as our traffic regulations and our public control of communicable disease.

But as believers in free expression, it is our concern to see that the press controls are exercised responsibly, are exercised in such a way as to serve the major purposes of our historic concept of free expression and full communication: *i.e.,* freedom of the man with something to say to have his say and freedom of the citizen to be fully and fairly informed. It means that the Great Press shall be so directed and operated (1) that the day's events shall be accurately reported to all who care to read and listen and that the day's news shall include and emphasize with the greatest ingenuity possible the significant current events in their truthful setting; (2) that the individual citizen shall be given ready access to the principal conflicting ideas and opinions about major issues, that the individuals with something to say shall reach the public they deserve, and that this presentation of conflict, variety and balance of opinion and idea shall be within the Great Press itself acting more or less with the responsibility of common carriers of ideas and opinion; (3) that because they are the Big Press reaching wide audiences and bridging the gaps which separate occupational, geographical, religious and social groups, they shall perform the task through words, pictures and film of explaining the separate groups to each other, of projecting opinions and values across lines of prejudice; and (4) that especially the major values and goals and common understandings of our society shall through the Big Press be reiterated and illustrated and clarified for the whole of the population who read and listen and see the panorama of events provided in mass communication.

This is a great responsibility. It is a new and enlarged responsibility. It is a product of size and of heterogeneity. Needless to say, the press has not fully grown up to its position of strategic power and influence.

There are large and successful newspapers such as *The Chicago Tribune* which serve as the common carriers of the story of the days' events and controversy to hundreds of thousands of citizens, but which reject completely that major responsibility and interpret their function as that of partisan selection of news and of equally partisan advocacy.

There are radio executives at the head of major networks who have defined their function of selling time as "for one specific reason, and that is to sell goods."

There are motion picture producers who have fashioned their

product so as to avoid any controversy and have tailored it to yield to any and every pressure group that objects to being presented unfavorably.

There have been newspapers that have inflamed prejudice and intolerance toward groups and nations rather than promoted an understanding of them.

Just what members of the press and to what extent all members of the press act responsibly would be impossible to say with the small amount of quantitative knowledge of press performance within our possession. But we know there is both bad and good performance, responsible and irresponsible communication practice. It is important here only to note the directions which will seem most likely to promote the more responsible performance.

These directions can be summed up in the concept of professional self-discipline as opposed to the simpler pecuniary motives and standards characteristic of business undertakings. The owners of the Great Press are by definition big businessmen, large employers of labor with important connections with other large business. There is inevitable in this situation a tendency to limited view or bias. If this were the usual sort of business one would accept it as a normal part of our system of competing interests. One would not expect a steel maker, the head of an oil company, or of a national trade union, to be the arbitrator between ideas and interests in our economy. One would expect such a person to be properly representative of the interest of the enterprise for which he is responsible. But the large scale communications business is not a business of the usual sort. It is a business of a peculiar kind. Like teaching and the courts, its special function in society is to emancipate itself so far as possible from bias by recognition of its biases and by the adoption of institutional disciplines and methods which favor access to the varied points of views and diverse backgrounds of experience which clarify the major problems of public policy.

It is an interesting question in this connection as to whether this atmosphere of mediation and clarification is best promoted by present newspaper practice of appearing on the news pages as the strictly impartial reporter of the day's events and on the editorial page as the frankly partisan advocate of the interests of a political group, or by present prevailing radio network practice of seeking to hold the balance even between opposing viewpoints in presentation of news events, editorial discussion and argument. Either, however, is a sounder position than that of the motion picture industry which has maintained an elaborate system of self-regulation, the effect of which is neither to clarify nor to balance controversy but to avoid it.

The mass communications industries do not furnish an exact analogy with those older callings that are regarded strictly as professions. But they can wisely promote some of the same means for establishing standards and attitudes of professional responsibility and discipline. One means is the development of centers of training and independent criticism. Some of the better schools of journalism are developing as such centers. But they have a long way to go before they will become places where standards of conduct radiate out into the common practice of the profession, and where independent, severe, fearless criticism of unprofessional and irresponsible communications performance is felt as a disciplining influence in the industry as a whole. It is probable that journalism schools need to be moved significantly outward and upward; outward so that they become broadly schools of communication drawing together the newspapers, radio, film, magazines, books and those social science disciplines which are engaged in analyzing the processes of communication; upward so that they become graduate, or professional, schools on a par with those representing the other highly intellectual pursuits of our society. And coincident with this academic development there may well be the growth of freer internal and external criticism of practices and organization of mass communications in particular and in general.

Probably of as great importance in developing professional spirit and skill are the examples and influence of the pioneer communications units which operate successfully on a professional basis. We have such institutions and their influence for the improvement of mass communication is probably greater than all the schools of journalism put together. They may always continue to be the chief centers for the development of professional responsibility. Newspapers such as the *New York Times* and the *Christian Science Monitor,* magazines

such as *Harper's,* many of the activities of the major broadcast networks and of the press associations—these are the generating influences of the press as profession combined with the press as successful business.

A second promising direction which promises to lead toward a
more responsible and adequate performance in mass communication
is the supplementing of the commercial press, radio and film with non-
profit institutions of mass communication, both privately endowed
and supported by government funds.

A man from Mars looking at our system of communication in the
United States might be at a loss to explain what he sees. On the one
hand he would find that the major task of furnishing information and
ideas to the young is carried on almost entirely by government or by
endowed institutions. On the other he would see that the task of providing information and ideas to adults is reserved almost completely
for private profit making institutions with the government and endowed enterprises playing a very minor part. This is not to suggest
that we should revise this sharp division between the institutional
means of providing intelligence to people of different ages. It is to
suggest, however, that there are types and kinds of information which
might appropriately be furnished special adult audiences through
government and endowed agencies with more effectiveness and success than through commercial means. And it is to suggest that the
newer FM radio, the library of recorded radio programs, the factual
film, the attractively presented pamphlet, the facsimile broadcast,
radio and television, are mechanisms of communication which offer
a field for experimentation under the incentives, purposes and skills
of non-profit, endowed and governmental groups. Actually most of
the invention and significant achievement in the documentary film
has been carried out under government rather than private auspices.
Also, long distance (short wave) international broadcasting is almost
wholly a non-profit and largely a governmental undertaking. The
vigorous development of experimental, supplementary means of mass
communication other than commercial is likely to promote the standards, the attitudes and outlook of the profession as a whole. The communications expert, more and more, will engage in his proper task at

one time under commercial and at another under non-profit management. The result will be a gain for the profession.

These are some but not nearly all the means which will promote a free and an adequate press, adequate to the increased needs of our society. We will not promote either freedom or adequacy by breaking up the large scale units which have emerged as the principal media of current public communication. We will not promote freedom by the absolute negation of governmental regulation or participation in mass communication. We will not achieve adequacy or freedom by replacing business management of the press by government or eleemosynary institutions.

We can move in the direction of freedom and adequacy, it would seem, most surely by the slow process of professionalization of the communications occupation. We can advance on the road by nurturing in every way possible centers of training and criticism and centers of leadership in day to day operations. From them we may hope will come communications staffs and management with the skill and self-discipline adequate to provide the current intelligence necessary for a democracy occupying a vast continent which inescapably is assuming a role as leader in the search for a system of international order extending to all five continents and the seven seas.

XIII

A CASE HISTORY IN CROSS-NATIONAL COMMUNICATIONS [1]

BY

MARGARET MEAD

During the war anthropologists addressed themselves to various ways in which their discipline could be put at the direct service of their society, attempting to short cut the normal lag which obtains between the development of abstractions based upon laboratory and field research and their application to contemporary problems. One part of this anthropological effort concerned itself with delineating significant aspects of the national character, or culture pattern, of enemy peoples or peoples of occupied countries about whom our knowledge was wholly inadequate.[2]

[1] This research is part of the program of the Institute for Intercultural Studies. Large sections of this material were presented in a lecture before the New York Academy of Science, January, 1947, and are reprinted here through the courtesy of the New York Academy of Sciences, from their *Transactions,* Series 2, 9, February, 1947, 4.

[2] The most significant work was done on Japan and Germany, and references may be made particularly to:

Geoffrey Gorer, "Themes in Japanese Culture," *Transactions,* New York Academy of Sciences Series II, 5, March, 1943, 5, pp. 105–124.

Ruth Benedict, *The Chrysanthemum and the Sword,* Houghton Mifflin Company, Boston, 1947.

"Round Table on Germany after the War," *American Journal of Orthopsychiatry,* 15, July, 1946, 3, pp. 381–441.

Talcott Parsons, "The Problem of Controlled Institutional Change. An Essay in Applied Social Science," *Psychiatry,* 8, February, 1945, 1, pp. 79–101.

And to unpublished work by Gregory Bateson, Ruth Benedict, Geoffrey Gorer, Douglas Haring, Frederick Hulse, Clyde Kluckhohn, David Mandelbaum, Rhoda Metraux, Marian Smith, and others. Some of the general implications of this work are described in

A second use of anthropological techniques was the attempt to select salient aspects of our own cultures and describe them in such a way that they could be used for various sorts of rapid training or morale building.[3]

The use of anthropological knowledge in operations directed toward the enemy involved only a limited analysis of our own culture, except when a policy either had to be carried out by large numbers of Americans whom it was impossible to train in detail to act in any way antithetical to their usual behavior, or when, as in our formal treatment of the Japanese emperor, widespread public support of a national policy was necessary. The use of similar anthropological knowledge within the limits of our own culture raised all the problems we have been discussing, the ethical problems of the responsibility of leaders of a democratic society not to manipulate, but to appeal openly to existing and cherished strengths.

When an attempt is made to use anthropological methods to strengthen a relationship between peoples of two contemporary cultures, still different problems arise. Here the focus is not upon points of vulnerability, which may be breached, as with the enemy, or strengthened, as for members of occupied countries, nor upon traditional strengths and coherencies to be enhanced, and weaknesses and contradictions to be guarded against, as in work in own culture. Instead, our efforts have to be directed toward finding areas of agreement which can be used as a background for the acceptance of differences which are causing specific friction and tension. Research and resulting communications are focused upon a relationship, and the nodes selected for emphasis are defined in terms of that relation-

---

Margaret Mead, "Anthropological Techniques in War Psychology," *Bulletin of the Menninger Clinic*, 1943, 7, pp. 137–140.

Ruth Benedict, "The Study of Cultural Patterns in European Nations," *Transactions*, 8, June, 1946, 8, pp. 274–279.

[3] Gregory Bateson and Margaret Mead, "Principles of Morale Building," *Journal of Educational Society*, 15, December, 1941, 4, pp. 206–220.

"The Problem of Changing Food Habits," Report of the Committee on Food Habits 1941–43, *National Research Council Bulletin*, 108, October, 1943.

Rhoda Metraux, "Qualitative Attitude Analysis—A Technique for the Study of Verbal Behavior," *Bulletin of the National Research Council*, October, 1943, 108, pp. 86–95.

ship, not in terms of the emphasis within the whole culture pattern of each society. For instance, if foreign policy is to be discussed and the foreign policy of one culture is most congruent with upper class values, while in the other it is most congruent with middle class values, this asymmetry would be consciously explored, perhaps to the neglect of any exploration of the exactly corresponding class in the other country, because of its lack of immediate relevance to the problem in hand.

As illustrative material for such an operation, I shall draw upon my own experience in working on Anglo-American relations, and particularly use data upon the areas of friction and misunderstanding between American troops and British civilians in Britain in 1943. My own case is unusual because I had the opportunity to participate in framing the hypotheses with which I went to Britain, to combine field work on these hypotheses with lecturing all over Britain, under the auspices of the Ministry of Information, and later through the United States Office of War Information in London to prepare various sorts of materials, both as background and as immediate communication, for circulation to Americans and Britons. Thus activities which would more usually be divided among a large number of individuals with different skills—research, field work, analysis, interpretation, preparation of directives, writing, rewriting, broadcasting presentations, etc.—and which would be subject to all the hazards which attend communication within such a diversified group, were embodied in the work that I did. This is an accident which we have no reason to believe will be repeated often, and analysis of such an experience bears the same relationship to thinking about cooperative operations that an analysis of the functions of the vanishing general practitioner bears to an attempt to construct modern medical services in which many disciplines participate. It also provided a unique opportunity to explore some of the problems involved and to test our hypotheses on the spot.

I plan to discuss examples of a variety of the procedures and problems which arose so as to give as broad a picture as possible of the way in which anthropological methods may be applied to relationships between any pair of peoples, for the analysis of such binary relationships is a necessary step toward an understanding of more complicated patterns of relationship on which a world order will have to be built.

I have used the term *cross-national* deliberately, to indicate that I am dealing not with relationships between *nations,* self-maximating competitive national units, but between the peoples of different nations, whose effective communication is compromised both by differences in culture and the circumstance of different nationality which gives a special competitive coloring and significance to those differences. To the extent that local allegiance is an important ingredient of the picture of the own group, the acceptance of differences in culture will vary enormously according to whether any sort of boundary, even a state or county line, intervenes. In wartime, uniforms, and all the paraphernalia of nationalistic warfare exacerbate the sensitivities of the populations involved.

Application of General Theoretical Formulations to a Particular Case.

In the initial steps I depended upon the formulations of symmetrical and complementary schismogenesis, developed by Gregory Bateson,[4] in which the United States and Britain were both diagnosed as relying upon the stimulus provided by a greater strength in the opponent, (symmetrical pattern) rather than the stimulus provided by relative weakness (complementary pattern). With this approval of symmetrical relationships, shared by both the United States and Britain, was associated a common moral disapprobation of bullying, picking on someone who was smaller, throwing one's weight around, etc.

In addition to the original statement of this diagnosis, I had elaborated, before going to England, the American version of adequate provocation to attack, under the formulation of "the chip on the shoulder"[5] in which I stressed that the American boy, reared by

---

[4] Gregory Bateson, "Some Systematic Approaches to the Study of Culture and Personality," *Character and Personality,* 11, September, 1942, 1, pp. 76–84.

Gregory Bateson, *Civilian Morale,* 2nd yearbook of the Society for the Psychological Study of Social Issues, Houghton Mifflin Company, Boston, 1942, "Morale and National Character," pp. 71–91.

[5] Margaret Mead, *And Keep Your Powder Dry,* William Morrow and Company, New York, 1942, Chapter IX, "The Chip on the Shoulder," pp. 138–158.

women, was given a deep doubt of his essential aggressiveness, combined with a lack of pattern for exercising it, in contrast to the British boy, reared by older boys and men to combine a belief in his innate aggressiveness with an obligation never to use his full strength unless pushed into an extreme position in which he could turn at bay. The famous "backs to the wall" order of Haig in World War I to the British, and reported exhortations of General Patton to his men, emphasizing the difficulty of the task, but also the fact that the enemy was on the run and the United States Army had the best equipment in the world, are conspicuous examples of the way in which military leaders have intuitively relied upon these different patternings of a basically symmetrical schismogenic attitude. Phrased colloquially, the underlying similarity became, "Both British and Americans believe that the strong have an obligation not to abuse their strength. We both hate bullies, and conversely those who cringe to bullies."

The second theoretical formulation was the hypothesis of *end linkage*,[6] that the way in which parent-child relationships are patterned in respect to such behaviors as: succoring—dependence, dominance—submission and exhibitionism—spectatorship, provides a learning situation for the child which patterns his subsequent behavior in situations where these behaviors are involved. Specifically, in Anglo-American relationships, the exhibitionism is reversed, in Britain it is Father who exhibits to his children; he is the model for their future behavior. Father does the talking, provides the model, and before a very quiet and submissive audience, in accordance with the keen ethical disapproval of overuse of strength. Father underplays his strength, understates his position, speaks with a slight appearance of hesitation in his manner, but with the cool assurance of one who knows. In the United States this position is reversed, and at the American breakfast table, it is not Father, but Junior, who talks, exhibits his successes and skills, and demands parental spectatorship and applause, with an insistence that can be clamoring and assertive, because after all he is speaking from weakness to strength. The American background for this reversal was explored[7] and in the spring of 1943 we tried using the contrast in a radio program, in

[6] Bateson, *op. cit.*, pp. 71–91.
[7] Mead, *op. cit.*

which samples of parent-child behavior at the breakfast table were followed by excerpts from American and British public speeches.[8]

For lecturing in Britain, these two formulations, of symmetrical schismogenesis and end linkage provided both a theoretical background for understanding and material for interpreting one of the acute points of friction between British and Americans. This point was British repudiation of American "boasting" and American repudiation of British "arrogance." It lent itself particularly well to use on the lecture platform and over the radio, as tone of voice was the principal medium in the demonstration. By a little careful interviewing in each new area in Britain, I could get verbatim, and therefore acceptable statements of the British objections. "The trouble with the Americans is that when they are good at something they *say* so": "The trouble with the Americans is that they talk so much about what they are going to do; we don't talk, we just *do* it" (from the Scots). I could then rely upon the lecture situation, itself one in which the exhibitionistic role of the lecturer and the spectatorship role of the audience was defined, to provide me with additional illustrative material. I could quote from the chairman who in presenting me, putatively

[8] This program was given as part of the series, "Science at Work" of the American School of the Air of the Columbia Broadcasting System, published in *Education,* 65, December, 1944, 4, pp. 228–238. The two speeches ran as follows:

British Lecturer:

"Ladies and Gentlemen. . . . I have been asked to talk to you tonight about British war production. We have, of course, improved. Our over-all figures for the past year show a definite increase. But it is, I think, in planes that the picture is most striking. Our largest bombers, which incidentally carry four times the bomb load of yours, are now coming quite satisfactorily into production."

American Lecturer:

"Well, ladies and gentlemen. . . . I see I'm down on the program to talk to you tonight about Alaska. I can think of one good reason why I know something about that country. It's because I've had to make upwards of 20 to 30 trips there, Summer and Winter in the past fifteen years.

Two or three of these trips, I might add, were by dog sled, far off the beaten track. On at least one of them, I nearly lost my life. But the thing I want to tell you folks about tonight, is the change that's come over Alaska since our boys went in there. Yes sir . . . mass production methods and the Good Old American qualities of hard work and initiative are showing results up there these days. I predict that five years after this war finishes, we'll be spending Summer in Alaska the way we used to spend Winters down in Florida. That's a tip, folks."

in the parental role on a British stage, to a great tired audience who had come out in the blackout on a freezing Sunday night in Scotland, said; "Be as kind to the audience as you can, Dr. Mead"; or I could refer to the whole institution of the "vote of thanks," in which the British audience, after sitting, docile and respectful while the lecturer plays Father, reestablishes the balance by the paternalistic tone in which the proposer of the vote of thanks addresses the now seated lecturer.

Explanations of behavioral differences which stressed upbringing were easily acceptable to the British, because of the strong cultural emphasis upon "character" as something which is acquired in the course of the right education rather than an innate possession of any individual or class of individuals. It was possible to show that whenever an American spoke, he spoke as he had learned to speak when he was small and so would put that irritating overstatement into his voice which the British called "boasting." Whenever a Briton spoke, he spoke as he had heard his father and other elders speak, as the strong and assured, carefully pulling his punches with that irritating understatement in his voice, which the American, called "arrogance." It was possible to show how the words *understatement* applied to the British and *boasting* applied to the Americans, emphasized the virtues of British behavior and devalued American, while by using the parallel words *understatement* and *overstatement,* both British and American behavior could be put in a common frame, that of habits learned in childhood.

Exploration of a Friction Point

When I reached Britain, our troops were still pouring into the country, there were still many British troops in the country, and very few American girls had yet reached Britain. The relationships between American men and British girls were providing an acute point of misunderstanding among both nationalities.

The friction took many forms, which required quite different types of treatment. It was necessary to explain to British authorities that an American boy would have difficulty in judging the age and degree of discretion of a girl who told him she had been out of school and working for two years, and to try to construct ways in which the Americans could spend their disproportionately large pay on British girls without using up goods or creating new social problems. But there was the much more basic problem of the way in which disturbed heterosexual relationships were festering beneath the surface of Anglo-American relationships in general.

The problem was not primarily a police problem involving the reduction of illegitimate births, which seemed to be following a pretty similar curve whichever troops and whichever nationalities were involved, but rather to reduce the disorientation which expressed itself in the British statement that the American men were "immoral" and the American insistence that the British girls had "no morals." Accusations of this sort might have been, of course, mere expressions of symmetrical friction, in which case it would have been necessary to look elsewhere for more basic areas of discrepancy, but there is always a good possibility that under identical accusations there will be expressed some profound and unrealized difference, become the more dangerous because it is so completely masked.[9]

I set about to explore the relationships between American men and British girls. A key to the misunderstanding lay in the differences in the location of responsibility for sex advances and sex refusals, in fact for the whole modulation of sex behavior. The American girl is trained to look after herself, unchaperoned and without any insistence upon rules of etiquette which will insure her person immunity from physical advances. She is taught that her behavior is in her own keeping, and the boy learns to make advances and rely upon the girl to repulse them whenever they are inappropriate to the state of feeling between the pair. In Britain the situation is reversed; the girl is reared to depend upon a slight barrier of chilliness and frostiness which the boys learn to respect, and for the rest to

---

[9] Early in the war the British were frequently advised by American expatriates and Anglophiles to retaliate against American comments about India, by remarks about the treatment of Negro Americans in the United States. This *tu quoque* phrasing only increased the bitterness and intolerance on both sides, as the two cases were felt as basically dissimilar by the Americans, who equated Indian problems with American prerevolutionary problems as a country, and racial problems in the United States as equivalent to the slum problem inside Britain, a purely domestic matter.

rely upon the men to approach or advance, as warranted by the situation.

Both systems give about the degree of satisfaction which can be expected in any pattern which locates initiative formally in one sex, without reference to temperament. But in wartime Britain, it meant that American boys, taught to ask with a full expectation of being refused effectively most of the time, were confronted by British girls, taught to accede to every forceful invitation. Several characteristic patterns of response developed. Some British girls became even chillier and, repelling even American optimism, succeeded in keeping the Americans at arms length and sending them away to complain about everything in Britain. Some girls responded to the first stylized wisecrack with an impassioned surrender which was thoroughly disconcerting to the American in its intensity and implications. Some succeeded in maneuvering a middle course for a few hours until the Americans who seemed to be "serious" could be presented at home as future sons-in-law which annoyed a great many Americans very much. The interpretation of this difference to the men themselves, and to those who were charged with youth and protection programs, gave a working basis for improved relationships, and a phrasing under which the mutual accusations of immorality could be reduced.

Problems of Phrasing and Translation

The problem of communication in a language which was theoretically mutually intelligible, supposed to be "one language," presented a number of difficulties which could be partially resolved by reference to cultural differences. In all probability the greater the difference between the languages of the pair of cultures with which one is attempting to work, the more automatic warnings are provided to the translator. But between English and American, and between other cultures similarly related through a common tradition and a still somewhat intelligible pair of languages, language confuses rather than clarifies, and other sorts of clues are necessary.

Two systematic observations made it possible to communicate better. The first was analysis of the difference between the American and British sense of a scale of values. Americans tend to arrange objects on a single scale of value, from best to worst, biggest to smallest, cheapest to most expensive, and are able to express a preference among very complex objects on such a single scale. The question, "What is your favorite color?" so intelligible to an American, is meaningless in Britain, and such a question is countered by: "Favorite color for what? A flower? A necktie?" Each object is thought of as having a most complex set of qualities and color is merely a quality of an object, not something from a color chart on which one can make a choice which is transferable to a large number of different sorts of objects.

The American reduction of complexities to single scales is entirely comprehensible in terms of the great diversity of value systems which different immigrant groups brought to the American scene; some common denominator among the incommensurables was very much needed and oversimplification was almost inevitable.[10] But as a result, Americans think in terms of qualities which have unidimensional scales, while the British, when they think of a complex object or event, even if they reduce it to parts, think of each part as retaining all of the complexities of the whole. Americans subdivide the scale, the British subdivide the object. Americans are able to describe a room in terms of its "color scheme," where the British eye would retain a sense of some fifty elements involved in the whole interior pattern, even when speaking of a square inch of the rug. From this British insistence on complexity flows naturally enough, an insistence upon uniqueness and an unwillingness to make comparisons.

Discussions as to the relative merits of cities, which Americans make happily in terms of size, wealth, or some other common denominator, seem to the British either meaningless or as irrelevant boasting. In turn, the British refusal to provide statistics on the size or wealth of a city seemed to the Americans to be either obscurantist or unfriendly. In Anglo-American contacts of all sorts, committee meetings, teaching situations, etc., it was important to watch the misunderstandings which arose along these lines, as the British

10 Mead, *op. cit.,* chapter VII, "Brothers and Sisters and Success," pp. 54–70.

voted the Americans oversimplifying when they harped on some exact statement of a position on a numerical scale, and the Americans voted the British inaccurate, if not engaged in deliberate falsification, when they quoted the population of Bengal with an error of ten million, with the statement that "it doesn't matter," because they were concerned with the relative, not the absolute size of one Indian province.

Another sort of misunderstanding which influenced communication was the difference between the British and the American sense of the real world. The British see the world as something to which man adapts, the American as man controlled, a vast malleable space on which one builds what one wishes, from blueprints one has drawn, and when dissatisfied simply tears the structure down and starts anew.

The great sense of mechanical control of the environment, product at least in part of an empty continent and the machine age, extends to American attitudes toward crops and animals, which are again something to be planned for, streamlined, increased or decreased at will, and even to a certain degree, to human beings, who can be, if not completely molded by man made devices, at least sorted mechanically into simply defined pigeonholes. In contrast, the British see the world as a natural world to which man adapts, in which he assumes no control over the future, but only the experienced foresight of the husbandman or the gardener, who plants the best seed and watches carefully over the first green blades. Man is seen as the junior partner of God, expressed either in conventional or more contemporary forms, but still the junior partner of forces to which he can adapt but which he cannot control. He can "only handle one link in the chain of destiny at a time."

The humility of this phrasing has its own forms of arrogance, as in Milton's: "God is decreeing to begin some new and great period . . . what does He then but reveal Himself to His servants, and as His manner is, first to His English-men."

Vis-à-vis this state of mind, ordinary American figures of speech, implying control and mechanism, not only fail to communicate but actually establish barriers. It was necessary to drop the familiar figures of an America converting for full production, laying down blueprinted acres of factories, six months ahead of schedule, and streamlining labor-management relations, and use instead the figures of speech of horticulture, to speak of "planting the seed" in "carefully prepared ground," of an effort which even when skill and experience were used to their utmost, still depended in final outcome on forces with which man could cooperate but which he could not control.

Roads and buildings in Britain which have been there a long time, become part of the natural world, not something to be swept aside lightly for a new plan. This was difficult for Americans to understand, who often found that a badly bombed city, once the rubble had been cleared away, which was still a wounded landscape to the British, looked to them very much like any American city, in eternal process of rapid transformation, in which the old was torn down with hardly a sign of regret.

The very different sorts of self-consciousness about all social process had also to be analyzed and allowed for: the American's willingness to think about the immediate future and his unwillingness to think very far ahead; the British unwillingness to let too great a degree of self-consciousness interfere with the smooth flow of highly disciplined habitual behavior but their greater willingness to think ten years ahead; the sudden shift in British attention which permitted them to attribute to themselves, retrospectively, a degree of planfulness which they would have repudiated at the time as paralyzing. I was at first confused by these contradictions, by being told in one breath that to think about the next week's plan would be unthinkable, and that in some earlier operation of exactly the same nature "we were very clever," and infinitely cunning. Once the contrast was clear, it was possible to discuss the past, when any detailed dissection of motive and behavior was desired, and the far future if articulate goals came into question.

The Interpretation of British Behavior to Americans

My formal mandate in 1943 had included only the British side of the task and the work which I did in the United States was under various scattered auspices and not a part of the Office of War Information program. But during the next two years I did have occasion to lecture on Britain, to various types of professional and popular audiences, to write, and to teach selected groups of personnel destined for the Far East where they would come into frequent and friction laden contact with the British.

The problems of addressing members of one's own culture about their relations with members of another culture presented some distinct features, and led to formulations of significant differences which had not been pointed up during my British experience. These differences in insight are to be laid primarily, I think, to the inevitable shift in one's type of participation under the two circumstances. In Britain I was a friendly visitor, using my professional skill to facilitate relationships between two wartime allies. In the United States, particularly in my teaching role in the various outpost schools, I was concerned with the strengths and weaknesses of Americans for the tasks of cross cultural understanding which they were going to face. I had to find, if possible, approaches which, in clarifying their own cultural attitudes, would make it possible for them, not merely to be more understanding, but to act, in cross cultural situations. Furthermore one faces, in discussing one's own culture with fellow members, a different sort of cross fire of criticism, and is likely, occasionally, to abandon sympathetic impartiality for a note of urgency, if not astringency. In closed classes, designed for war purposes, there were no members of other nationalities, and it was sometimes difficult to convince the students that I would have used the same words and made the same points had there been British in the audience. In all work of this sort, it is essential to speak in terms which envelop the two or more peoples being discussed, and which represent the differences in ways acceptable to both, but this necessity is more vividly demonstrated if actual human beings of each group are present in the flesh.

Rapport difficulties

An American addressing an American audience about Britain is speaking to a people who have strong and partly unconscious attitudes about Britain which go very deep, much deeper than any attitudes which the British as a group had about America in 1943.

The American sense of national identity contains the earlier and severed relationship with Britain as an intrinsic part, while the British do not use the loss of America as a component of their sense of their national identity. Furthermore, the Anglophile position is traditionally associated in the United States with the position of the upper class, the conservative, the wealthy, and the more easterly part of our population, added to the circumstance that the bulk of American tourists before the war were women devoutly following the footsteps of one or another bard. The Anglophobe position contains a mass of assorted elements, Middle West against the East, European ancestry against the older Anglo-Saxon stock, the plain man against the would be aristocrat, etc. To discuss Britain dispassionately, it was necessary for the lecturer to face and deal with these strong currents of feeling, sometimes existing simultaneously in the same individual.

I finally solved this problem, satisfactorily for myself at least, by beginning a lecture with a caricature [11] of the pro-American British woman, who represents in a capsule form, a way of repudiating the snobbish note which over sweetened the voice of the Anglophile, and startling the Anglophobe into a provisionally British identification with the kind of Britons who would not like the type of Americanphile whom I presented. This produced a loosening of traditional identifications which permitted the clarification material to get a hearing.

A second difficulty arose from the inveterate American habit of asking about every piece of behavior, "Is it better or worse than ours?" This contrast with the British insistence on complexity and so on uniqueness has been discussed above, but it presented itself in a new form as I lectured on British wartime arrangements for community feeding, advising disoriented citizens through the Citizens' Advice Bureaus, or caring for the children of working mothers. Invariably the American audience wanted to know, "Is their system better or worse than ours?"

Behind this question were two unexpressed attitudes, one, the

[11] It should be noted that caricatures contain a strong hostile element, which has to be recognized whenever they are used.

hope that ours would be better, and second, the tacit acceptance of the obligation to copy theirs if ours was worse. As most of the audience vigorously resented any suggestion that they copy Britain, these presentations were always charged with rapport dangers. It was necessary to stress over and over again, that the British solution was different, not better or worse. While this point might be got over temporarily in a lecture, it usually did not survive in the next day's newspaper headlines, and actually represents one of the most serious hazards to any sort of comprehension of other peoples by Americans. A simple sense of either inferiority or superiority would be easier to deal with than this belief that all institutions can be placed on a single scale, and that it becomes the American's obligation to choose the best. The pleasure derived from the study of foreign behaviors which can be voted as inferior is alloyed by the discomfort of encountering those which are superior.

Attitude Toward Compromise

American audiences raised a question whose counterpart I never met in Britain and which illustrates how valuable each side of such a relationship is, in drawing attention to parts of the whole which the other side might neglect. "Why is it the British always insist on their own way in international affairs and we always lose?" "Why do the British always pull the wool over American eyes?" These were frequent questions. In comments upon our international negotiations the term, "the poor little United States," cropped up with amazing frequency.

In working out a clarification of these questions, of this American belief that we always lost, I again sought for a common element in the two cultures against which the differences would be highlighted. Americans share with the British a common tradition in regard to the appropriate behavior of the minorities that are minorities because they are in some way more right than the majority. Such minorities, best represented by the long line of dissident Protestant sects, but today also represented by the Roman Catholic minority in England, have been accorded, as part of our whole picture of our form of government, the right to differ and the duty to stand up for their positions. A virtuous minority in both countries is virtuous just because it does not compromise. But here the parallel ends because the British, speaking from strength, from the paternal position, do not identify governmental negotiations as made from a minority position. The government acts from strength and, being strong, can *include* some of the minorities' demands in any proposal. To compromise is the act of the strong and the entrenched, an act of graciousness, expediency, and a recognition that the heresies of today become the orthodoxies of tomorrow.

So in Britain the word *compromise* is a good word, and one may speak approvingly of any arrangement which has been a compromise, including very often one in which the other side has gained more than fifty per cent of the points at issue.

In the United States, the minority position is still the position from which everyone speaks: the President *versus* Congress, Congress *versus* the President, the state government *versus* the metropolis, and the metropolis *versus* the state government. This is congruent with the American doctrine of checks and balances, but it does not permit the word "compromise" to gain the same ethical halo which it has in Britain. Where in Britain to compromise means to work out a good solution, in America it usually means to work out a bad one, a solution in which all the points of importance, to both sides, are lost. Thus in negotiations between the United States and Britain, all of which had in the nature of the case to be compromises as two sovereignties were involved, the British could always speak approvingly and proudly of the result, the Americans had to emphasize their losses. Out of the same ethic, but a contrasting interpretation of one's own position, came these mutually reinforcing estimates of a document or treaty.

Closely related to this sense of being weak but on the side of the right, and therefore committed to demanding hundred per cent victories, is the American fear of being exploited by other groups, best summed up in the vernacular phrase, "Don't be a sucker." This is so deepseated and has been so heavily exploited in discussions of our relationship to other countries, both those who are believed to outwit us in the diplomatic game, and those who ask us for help, that it seemed important to analyze it.

First it was necessary to work out the interpersonal dynamics of the conception. In America, a "sucker," one who is not to be given an even break, is anyone who enters a game in which he does not have the skill or wit or strength to compete. Superficially, the American ethic that a sucker should be trimmed, seems discrepant with the ethic that it is wrong to bully. But seen against the way in which American boys are reared it becomes intelligible. Instead of the British father who supports the eldest son, as a surrogate of himself, against the competition of the younger sons, and at the same time exhorts the eldest to be gentle but firm, the American boy is reared by a mother who defends the younger against the elder, and continually uses the success of the younger to goad the elder toward achievement. The slightly younger brother, backed up by the mother, becomes a threat, especially to the boy whose games are continually subject to the intrusion of the younger.

This contemporary child rearing tradition combines with the frontier tradition in which the tenderfoot is a threat to the whole community. Older frontiersmen, alert to the dangers which one careless act may precipitate, and older brothers alert to the way in which the younger may spoil their games, both find refuge in the ethic, "Never give a sucker an even break," an ethic which is also honored by the admission of the American who loses, "I was a sucker, I asked for it." The extent to which this treatment of the sucker may justifiably be classified as a deeply rooted ethical attitude is illustrated by the report in *Time,* for November 6, 1944, in which Olendorf is pictured with the slogan "never give a sucker an even break," and his adherence to the slogan is then described as accounting for the way in which a successful ambush of Japanese ships was conducted. Stated for American consumption, the havoc was justifiably wrought among the Japanese because they had "asked for it."

At the same time the word sucker is used in another, and positively toned sense, to describe the man who is generous, enthusiastic, willing to give of his time and energy, as when a physician remarks in a public speech, "You know doctors always head the sucker list."

This is said with approval of the doctor's kind heart, and is tantamount to saying "We are admirably tenderhearted people." Or the student, cited in a psychological study as a normal, well adjusted young American, will remark on the offices which he has held in organizations and adds, "I'm a sucker for work."

This dual attitude toward the sucker position further complicates the American attitude toward other peoples, because it is just when Americans are behaving well that they are most likely to suspect that they are being made suckers against their will. Then the whole negative set of sanctions comes into play, and the ethic of never giving a sucker an even break is projected on to the other national group. The formula reads, "We are suckers in the international game, both when we compete and when we are generous. We aren't up to it, either way. We are playing a game we do not understand, therefore we will be trimmed." A perfect instance of this interpretation confronted by the British insistence on the assumption of an appearance of model, self-controlled parental behavior, was provided in an article by Senator Brewster.[12]

A number of different diplomatic commercial, and financial moves will be necessary if we are to hold our rightful place in world commerce, but one of the most important is this: We must stop being out-traded by our good friends the British, the world's greatest experts in economic diplomacy.

One day I was talking with Sir Gerald Campbell, Lord Halifax's right hand man in the British Embassy in Washington, and I told him I believed our statesmanship is so bad that in nearly every negotiation with the British we came out second best.

Sir Gerald smiled. "Of course, we put it over on you," he said. "But not half as often as we could! . . ."

This passage sums up the whole position, the American fear of being trimmed as suckers who do not know the game, the British failure to recognize the issue which is being raised, and their response first with a jocular acceptance of the stated inferiority, which from their point of view takes the sting out, coupled with a state-

[12] Owen Brewster, "Let's not be suckers again," *American Magazine*, January, 1945, pp. 24–26, 93–98.

ment of the high ethical behavior which all fathers, governors and persons in authority are supposed to display. The unpalatability of the British reply to the ordinary American can best be stated by referring to the Fijian form of insult in which most enemies were eaten but those who were to be most insulted were cooked and left uneaten. The jocular, Olympian assumption of restraint in the British answer simply exacerbates the American feeling of being treated negligently and condescendingly.

Another pretty example occurred in an article in the *Washington Star*, in 1945,[13] under the heading, "Critics air U.S.—British Views," in which Sir John Wardlaw Milne writes: "In this country we are thankful and *indeed proud* of the great United States, but we heartily dislike the tendency to suggest that America's intervention is a kind of act of grace from some superior beings who need not have engaged in the war at all." (The italics are mine.) And Senator Burton Wheeler writes, in the other column, "America wants no more deceptive slogans such as 'Give us the tools, we'll finish the job.' We are not going to tolerate any condescending attitude on the part of anyone that implies or assigns us the status of 'poor relations.'" Here we see the British tone of speaking from established position and discouraging any upstart claims, the American tone of maintaining their rights against those who would put them down.

The phrase *proud of*, so galling to American ears, was a British way of boasting on behalf of the Americans. The whole problem of how Americans should speak of British achievement and British of American was a particularly ticklish one all through the war. After repeated instances of the degree of misunderstanding which was generated by the way in which each ally spoke of its own allied efforts, Geoffrey Gorer and I worked out a phrasing in terms of the conceptions of partnership which provided a form of clarification suitable for lecturing and teaching.

All through the war the United States and Britain were spoken of as "partners," a word which is common to both languages. But the British associated the word when applied to international affairs,

[13] Burton K. Wheeler, "Critics air United States–British Views," *Washington Star*, January 14, 1945.

with a sports concept, with the tennis partner, who, for the duration of the game is treated as like oneself, whose successes one acclaims and whose failures one grieves over. It was possible to invoke from the memories of anyone who had played deck tennis with British partners the continuous, "Good shot, partner!" "Hard luck, partner!" which is an inseparable part of the verbal etiquette of the game.

The American, seeing international relationships primarily in a business context, associated the word "partner" with a business partnership, in which the relationship is conventionally asymmetrical; one partner putting up the funds, the other providing the brains or the entry, but neither committed to a social relationship with the other, with an expectation of the partnership lasting until it is disrupted by disagreement or death, and with no obligation on either to boast for or grieve for the other partner. So a careful British attempt to boast for their partners, as in the case of the great emphasis given to the American contribution to bringing down the buzz bombs, was met by the Americans, not by a little piece of symmetrical vicarious boasting, about, say the landing platforms, but instead by blowups in the American papers of what the British had said about the buzz bombs. This produced inevitable confusion, and even some abortive attempts on the part of the British to do their own boasting.

Conclusion

The methods described in this case history are anthropological methods, that is, they rely upon an understanding of the cultural patterns of the peoples involved, they invoke regularities for purposes of clarification. It is, however, important to recognize that clarification alone will not promote understanding, that it is still necessary to set some tone within which feeling may flow freely. In the presentations and teaching described in this case history, I relied on these methods which invoked feeling; first on emphasizing symmetries and when possible reducing what looked like complementary contrasts to symmetrical terms, second on giving a description of the other people's behavior in terms which made *identification* possible and third on arousing the kind of laughter which comes from the exactitude of the cultural statement.

Members of an audience invariably laughed hardest at the description of their own cultural behavior, not at that of the others. To obtain this effect, it is very important to avoid caricature, which is self-defeating. The device also fails if there are many expatriates in an audience, as expatriates already see their home culture with a degree of distortion which makes any exact description, which will invoke the laughter of recognition from others, seem to them a caricature, and usually a hostile caricature. The method failed, in other words, when it was used with those who were themselves very ambivalent about their own culture, and very overaccepting of the other culture. Significantly enough, attempts to give equally exact descriptions of German behavior have usually failed to evoke the same sort of recognition from Germans in this country, and it is possible that it is a method best suited to cultures and to situations in which ambivalence toward the own culture is least in evidence.

Undoubtedly, in other interpretative hands or in different media, other ways of evoking feeling would be more appropriate than the deliberate attempt to embody the clarifying statement in exact laughter producing verbatim vignettes. That the method is suitable for more than one culture is evidenced by the very similar response which I received from British and American audiences when I gave the same material, in the same way. But the evocation of pity, or eager purposive aspiration, may also be feeling states which might appropriately accompany the type of clarification which an initial objective anthropological analysis of cultural patterns provides. Evoking either fear or anger runs, I believe, into the danger of stirring up in the audience feelings which interfere with acceptance of the clarification. Strong identification is possible with an evocation of fear or anger, but the identification tends to be so strong as to interfere with the degree of distance which is necessary both for laughter and for an understanding of difference.

If we are to build a world in which a variety of cultures are orchestrated together so as to produce a viable social order, we need controlled exploration of the types of clarification and types of presentation which will increase understanding between pairs of cultural groups and then among more complicated groupings.

XIV

LEADERSHIP, SCIENCE, AND POLICY

BY

JOSEPH M. GOLDSEN

Even in this day of momentous decision there is inadequate scientific attention given to the problems of leadership. Here we live in an American society committed to the symbols, and to a significant extent, the practices of human freedom. We respect the common man, since from this mass rather than class population we expect our leaders to arise. Once existing leadership groups are empowered, we tend to support or criticize them, remove or retain them, and organize our collective influence accordingly. Seldom do we make concerted moves to heighten the understanding and skill of leadership in conducting the affairs of its office.

Our historical development saw the growth of mass production and mass marketing accompanied by mass education and mass communication. Heightened public enlightenment was valued, among other reasons, because it better prepared the citizenry for the responsibilities of democratic participation in the making and shaping of important decisions on public policy. Some attention was paid to the training of leaders, especially in the technical skills required. Professional schools of public administration, law, journalism, welfare and business administration are examples of educational response to evident needs. But in large measure we expect our leaders in politics, business and the communication services to sharpen their performance each in his own way. Trial and error, "experience," reliance on advisers, and self-study are among the characteristic avenues available to policy makers in the sincere effort to do the best possible job.

Many leadership groups have taken initiatives to inquire into the demands, habits, needs, information and opinion of the publics they serve. This knowledge has in turn been a more or less basis for modifying and guiding the thinking and decisions of leaders.

An important area open for vast scientific study is the analysis of the decision making process itself. More particularly, who in society makes what decisions on what basis? The purpose of such study is not only to increase our understanding of the leadership function, but to know how to improve the quality of decisions by leaders; to invent social institutions and communication methods for up grading the decision making apparatus and personnel.

From a necessary preoccupation with method between the two World Wars, the human sciences are now tending to inquire more actively into the critical questions of the day and the consequences for the morrow. The vanguard of this trend of inquiry has not forsaken "science" for "action." Rather, it has begun to apply the method of experimental science which says that we can learn a lot about a process by systematically trying to improve it. Further, we can contribute to both policy and science by grappling with the problems which confront practical men.

Although "policy scientists" apply varying procedures and theories, and specialize on different subject matter, there is a common focus on problems of human behavior, and a structuring of research in terms of the consequences of policy decisions. A number of terms are already in vogue to characterize current efforts to bridge the gaps that separate men of specialized knowledge from men of action: "action research," "operational research," "social engineering," "applied social science," etc. The term "policy sciences" may best describe the combined efforts of economists, psychologists, psychiatrists, anthropologists, sociologists, statisticians and natural scientists to increase our knowledge through scientific concern with social policy.

Problems of intergroup conflict, for example, are now being studied and worked out in live settings from the policy science perspective. The late Kurt Lewin was originally responsible for theoretical formulations and the training of specialists for integrated work on problems of group conflict and cooperation. Lewin's former students and others now at the Research Center for Group Dynamics at Massachusetts Institute of Technology have under way a number of projects involving community leadership, democratic group behavior, industrial conflict and race relations.[1]

In the field of mental hygiene, the Tavistock Institute in England, which made a major contribution to the war effort, has expanded its scope and is breaking new ground in many of the same fields which concern the M.I.T. group.[2]

Taking off from the pioneer work of Elton Mayo and his Harvard associates, a number of university centers and private organizations are active on human relations and leadership problems in industrial action settings. Burleigh Gardner and his colleagues in Chicago, the Management and Labor Center at Yale, and Nejelski & Company in New York are among the better known groups in America. For many years the National Institute of Industrial Psychology in England has been an important factor.[3]

In the public administration field,[4] policy oriented research has been highly productive in many government agencies. Perhaps the most striking example is the Bureau of Indian Affairs as it was

---

[1] Kurt Lewin, "Action Research and Minority Problems," *The Journal of Social Issues,* November, 1946. This entire issue is devoted to "Action and Research"; R. Lippitt and M. Radke, "New Trends in the Investigation of Prejudice," *The Annals of the American Academy of Political and Social Science,* March, 1946; see also vol. I, no. 1 of *Human Relations,* published jointly by the Tavistock Institute of Human Relations, London, and the Research Center for Group Dynamics, Cambridge, Massachusetts, 1947; also *The Journal of Social Issues* number on "Problems of Re-Education" edited by K. Lewin and P. Grabbe, August, 1945.

[2] *Human Relations, op. cit.; The Journal of Social Issues* number on "Social Therapy," edited by E. Jacques, Spring, 1947.

[3] Elton Mayo, *The Human Problems of an Industrial Civilization,* Macmillan Company, New York, 1933; F. J. Roethlisberger and W. J. Dickson, *Management and the Worker,* Harvard University Press, 1939; S. D. Hoslett, editor, *Human Factors in Management,* Park College Press, Parkville, Missouri, 1946; W. F. Whyte, editor, *Industry and Society,* McGraw-Hill, New York, 1946.

[4] John Collier, "United States Indian Administration as a Laboratory of Ethnic Relations," *Social Research,* September, 1945; H. A. C. Dobbs, *Operational Research and Action Research,* a pamphlet published by the Institute of Ethnic Affairs, Washington, 1947; Alexander H. Leighton, *The Governing of Men,* Princeton University Press, 1945; Harold D. Lasswell and Myres S. McDougal, "Legal Education and Public Policy: Professional Training in the Public Interest," *The Yale Law Journal,* March, 1943.

under the direction of John Collier. The Department of Agriculture's community participation studies should also be mentioned. The training of future public servants is now of special concern at the Yale University Law School and seminars are in progress on "law, science and policy."

All of this activity, and the list is far from exhaustive, points to practical methods for coping with, as well as understanding, important issues of our time. Many of the problems are of such deadly proportions as to warrant unorthodox approach on a scale never attempted before. Problems of such consequence, now confronting the leaders who are responsible for making policy decisions and for clarifying the public at large, demand the fullest application of combined intelligence and method.

Among the most urgent, is the problem of atomic policy. Here we have in its full enormousness the impact of science on society. The leaders of governments, educational and opinion forming agencies not only have to comprehend the basic technical facts, but make decisions that have immediate consequence on the lives of all whom they govern, teach, inform or inflame.

Can anything be done to increase the odds that their decisions will be the wiser, that their spreading of ideas will be the sounder? Perhaps, while there is still time, we can apply the policy sciences on the requisite scale. To that end, we follow with a brief outline of such a plan as might be used to meet this kind of situation. The description is deliberately hortatory in phrasing since its purpose is twofold: to describe such a mechanism, and to indicate the nature of a call for action such as might be used by those in the most favorable position to implement it if judged sound.

This is a plan to establish a "Leadership Training Institute on Atomic Policy." The objective is to indicate:

(1) Methods by which policy makers and opinion leaders can be informed and clarified.
(2) Methods by which these groups can be mobilized into action and aided in transmitting their insights and skills in such ways as to affect the course of public policy.

The detailed preparation and carrying through of this plan require the pooled skills of like willed specialists who are agreed on goals of security and freedom for the citizens of the world, and on minimum conditions for their attainment.

Several basic assumptions underlie the objectives of this plan:

(1) Worldwide social relations are the product of a pre-atomic age, and have not yet been adapted to control systems indicated by contemporary survival needs. Therefore, the present technological manipulation of atomic energy is a source of all pervasive danger.

(2) Danger generates anxiety with its stress toward action. Where dangers are realistically understood, they can be confronted more effectively. Fear of what is not known predisposes toward unpredictable, unpremeditated, and self-destructive acts.

(3) The threats to world existence let loose by the "mastery" over atomic energy are, therefore, overcomplicated and overintensified in the degree that real dangers are suspended in a welter of undifferentiated anxieties.

(4) Anxiety thus begets anxiety; personal insecurity and group tensions heighten. The alternatives for effective action become more difficult to extract, and the chances are lessened for rational behavior under conditions of stress.

(5) A responsive decision making apparatus still exists. Leaders are amenable to influence, and while some rigidity may be setting in, there are yet areas open for modifying trends, for action alternatives to get significant consideration, and for healthy improvisations of strategy.

Such a plan as this, therefore, would seek to funnel clarification through the still open bridgeheads for influence. It would take off from those toeholds of reason still accessible in the minds of influential citizens, and provide the means for first extending them in depth and then spreading out in scope. We shall describe it as an actual proposal.

For many reasons, a mass "public relations" or "public information" scheme is inappropriate as the starting point. Not the least of these reasons is the necessity for pinpoint economy in the use of the time and effort of the relatively few scientists qualified to advise and inform others on the basic problems. Their efforts should not be diffused in talking to the public at large and at sporadic intervals, advising publicists, advertisers, etc. Rather, their knowledge should be concentrated on enlightening those action leaders whose business it is to deal with segments of the public and with important decision makers.

The starting point, then, is with people in strategic social action positions, people who already are farthest along in understanding and responsibility. These people, whose business it is to mold opinion in public and bear influence in private, must be provided with keener insights, first; and then equipped to convert thought into action more effectively.

It is proposed that a selected group of reputable men of science and affairs organize an on-going institute; here tentatively designated as the LEADER-SHIP TRAINING INSTITUTE ON ATOMIC POLICY.

The Institute should be set up with such financial and prestige-ful backing as would attract as delegates, or students, the outstanding people in the country. Delegates could be recruited for attendance at the Institute from diverse fields, and membership would not necessarily be restricted to Americans. They could come from government (international, national, and local), from education, service professions, business, labor, science, the press, radio and film, from religion and public welfare. Scientific procedures have been tested for determining who is influential in these fields. The application of occupational, prestigeful, ethnic, territorial, and still other criteria can insure effective selection of influential leaders for attendance.

By manifesting its intensity of purpose and assemblage of outstanding experts, the Institute will probably find itself heavily petitioned for the privilege of attending. Screening procedures, established in advance, should be invoked to grant admittance only to those, regardless of citizenship, who are best equipped in influence potential, leadership skill and moral purpose.

The rigorous and intensive operation of the Institute should aim at:

Providing the delegates with *knowledge* necessary for reaching common understanding in so far as that is possible.

Providing the delegates with the *skill* for spreading this understanding to other opinion leaders, policy makers, and to wider segments of the public.

Motivating the delegates to take whatever action steps are found appropriate.

The development of a core of common understanding at the Institute would involve such subjects as:

A basic understanding of the scientific principles and implications of the release of atomic energy.

The objectives of atomic policy in relation to a total security program.

Analyzing the problems that are raised by formulating those objectives, and those problems that are involved in achieving the objectives. This means that the conditions that are to be controlled and the problems to be solved must be analyzed in terms of action alternatives rather than as principles for debate.

The operations of the global power process must be studied. The considerations of military, diplomatic, economic and ideological-psychological strategies in their global manifestations and interrelations are the broad categories.

The dynamics of social structure and personality formation should be indicated as basic equipment for evaluating policy possibilities and solving intermediary problems.

The Institute should serve as the delegates' "clearing house" at which they can exchange perspectives and reach consensus goals. Thus, the communication between delegates and staff should be a two-way affair.

All efforts should be directed to strip the delegates of irrelevant preconceptions, ideological deadweight, and fantasy-for-fact confusion about the intentions and expectations of power holders and peoples the world over.

Training for social action would involve:

The psychology of opinion formation and morale; the principles and techniques of exerting influence on policy makers, their advisers, and special purpose groups.

Concentrated skill training, as well as insight, can be given each delegate attending the Institute. This means direct practice in imparting newly acquired insights to others. The delegates are trained to become "trainers." Techniques for effective group action can be imparted. The efficacy of the community-team approach, in contrast to isolated individual effort, has been recently validated, for example.

The delegates can make group decisions on how best to implement programs in their regular course of activity, and do the actual planning at the Institute. These plans might be combined efforts integrating the educational efforts of a college president, such as special adult education courses; press and radio information campaigns; business policy proposals; as well as less public pressure on governmental personnel.

In this phase of the training, the stress is on stimulating and instructing the delegates actively to spread down, across and upward their understanding and influence.

The Institute should be in continuous operation, with each session running for as many consecutive days as the delegates can make available. Unbelievable learning speeds and retention spans were achieved by special military training schools during the war. Full use should be made of the most modern teaching methods, such as visual aids, supervised practise, problem solving clinics, etc. Instruction should be planned for groups small in size, so that the equipment of the delegates can be greatly enlarged in the learning-teaching process. Concise lectures, making use of demonstrations, films and other aids, would be one important instructional procedure. Conference and work sessions should be provided for dissents to be expressed and analyzed. Full advantage should be taken to have the group share in the special knowledge and experience of each delegate. Practise sessions might be held wherein the delegates are individually trained and counseled on how to act most effectively in their capacities as influential citizens. Supplementary training could be provided to those delegates who can engage in field development activity approximating the work of the Institute itself.

It is conceivable that more than one such Institute can be established after the original Institute has experienced its "shake down," and has demonstrated its value. Branches of the Institute might well be duplicated in other countries, as well as having "traveling" Institutes at home, which would move from region to region.

Appropriate procedures can be devised for periodic "refresher" and reinforcement purposes. Distribution might be made of relevant information materials. Confidential private communications tend to be more effective than such semi-public channels as journals. Selected delegates can be invited back to the Institute after they have spent some time at their regular activities. Such delegates can serve as advisers or special instructors at the Institute. Former delegates at the Institute should be periodically consulted by the Institute staff, preferably in person, to provide an assessment of field needs and to measure the effectiveness of the delegates' activities.

Action initiatives out in the field can be spearheaded and taken by delegates on the various problems.

Groups of delegates might take it upon themselves or be invited to draft statements of policy recommendations or analyses for the consideration of such groups as the United Nations Atomic Energy Commission, the United States Atomic Energy Commission, and scientific organizations. Business leaders might begin to organize the decentralization of plants and communities, if so indicated. Or, the delegates can serve as nuclear groups for implementing the layman's support for freedom of scientific inquiry. Wherever official bodies are slow to move in required directions, Institute trained leaders can generate unofficial voluntary action in their private capacities.

The panel of experts making up the staff of the Institute must be persons of unquestioned stature and authority in their fields, and who possess the required communication skill. The staff should include physical scientists, social scientists in the relevant subjects, and specialists from the new field of group action. Pressure can be brought to "draft" specialists for service on this panel despite present commitments. Because of heavy outside responsibilities already carried by most prospective staff members, it may be desirable to have a rotating roster so that each specialist spends a minimum time period on duty at the Institute.

Appropriate research and evaluation should be a part of the total operation. One function would be to provide current intelligence for the staff and delegates on opinion trends, and policy decisions and factors. A constant reevaluation of the problems dealt with by the Institute is an obvious necessity. Another research function would be to audit the work of the Institute itself: before and after studies of the delegates to measure the effect of attendance; evaluation of the training techniques to increase the effectiveness of the staff; and analyses of the action programs instigated by the delegates in the field.

To activate such an Institute, teams of highly skilled subject matter specialists, administrators, financial advisers, and liaison personnel are necessary. A spirit of top emergency should be instilled from the start, and should permeate through all stages of the Institute's development, from the planning group through the working staff and to every attending delegate. Ruthless speed must accompany all its activities: planning, teaching, learning, field development.

The Institute should operate by iron-like standards of scientific discipline and be closed to outside interference. Authority, prestige and conviction must unmistakably characterize it in order to fulfill its aim.

The basic approach in such a plan as I have here described is not uniquely applicable to "atomic policy." Its underlying conceptions are broadly adaptable to many policy issues and, as has already been noted, stems from work in progress in the policy sciences.[5] The plan does not offer specific "remedies" nor policy directives. Its stress is on training in ways of thinking and on skills of acting. The important first steps are to help people clarify goals and objectives; and to instill a problem solving attitude and technique for evaluating the alternative courses and consequences of action in relation to goals.

[5] In addition to works previously cited, the following are of particular importance on theory and application: Kurt Lewin and associates, *Studies in Topological and Vector Psychology,* University of Iowa Studies in Child Welfare; Harold D. Lasswell, "The Relation of Ideological Intelligence to Public Policy," *Ethics,* October, 1942; *World Politics and Personal Insecurity,* Whittlesey House, New York, 1935; and his *The Dynamics of Power and Personality* (forthcoming 1948); Gordon W. Allport, "The Psychology of Participation," *Psychological Review,* May, 1945.

The communication methods suggested rely heavily on the interaction among the laymen, among the experts, and between the two groups. These are not random meetings, but are planned to maximize the participation of all in the working out of a common task where each has something to give as well as take. The experts serve not only in the capacity of subject matter specialists, but also as discussion leaders, integrators and clarifiers.

If the experts do their job properly, and if their concurrent evaluation of the operation itself is intelligently designed and executed from the scientific point of view, they also will be contributing to our basic theoretical knowledge of social behavior. As John Collier put it: [6]

. . . this kind of research makes demands on the research worker that are far more severe than those made by the specialized and isolated kind. It requires of him a more advanced and manysided training, and in addition a type of mind and personality which can sustain, in suspension, complex wholes and which can entertain—yes, and be drawn and impelled by— human values and policy purposes while yet holding them disinterestedly far away.

The teaming up of diverse subject matter specialists on a problem framed in terms of action consequences does much to break down preoccupations with the separate disciplines. The psychologist gets an appreciation for the economics of a situation, the sociologist for the politics, and so on in a most constructive fashion. Each learns that the interplay of factors must be taken into account, since, in real life, the wholeness of a situation encompasses an array of considerations.

The leaders who gain a structural insight into their own roles, who are provided with a context as well as skill in shaping policies, are increased social assets. The function of leadership becomes that of decisions made on the basis of intimate collaboration between experts and policy personnel. As science and policy together probe the vast ground of mutual concern, we increase our chances of yet building a society befitting the dignity of man.

[6] *Op. cit.*, p. 300.

XV

ATTENTION STRUCTURE AND SOCIAL STRUCTURE

BY

HAROLD D. LASSWELL

When social scientists speak of social structure, they refer to the basic patterns according to which values are shaped and distributed in a community. The term value, in this context, is used in a purely descriptive sense to refer to a category of desired events. Power and wealth, respect and well being, for instance, are values. The determining and sharing of power, the production and distribution of wealth, the giving and sharing of respect, the fostering and sharing of physical and psychic health are all processes whose basic features constitute the social structure of community life.

Values

Power is participation in the making of important decisions, such as the declaring of war and the making of peace, the setting up and administration of the police force, the levying and collection of taxes. Wealth is income: Services of goods and persons accruing to the individual in any way whatsoever. Respect is the value of honor, recognition, prestige, the "glory" or "reputation" which Hobbes classes with gain and safety as one of the three fundamental human motivations. Well being is the health and safety of the organism. Besides these four values (power, wealth, respect, well being), we may list several more, such as skill, enlightenment, rectitude (the moral values—virtue, goodness, righteousness), and affection (love and friendship).[1]

[1] See Harold D. Lasswell and Myres S. McDougal, "Legal Education and Public

There is no doubt that the values named are sought after in our civilization, and that they are pursued in varying degrees in all known cultures. The list, let it be emphasized, is representative and not exhaustive. Note further that no assumptions are made about the relative importance of the values on the list in our, or any, community. The rank order is left to empirical determination. Indeed, we take it for granted that the relative intensity with which each category of value is sought can vary from culture to culture, from one part of a culture to another and from time to time in the same culture. One of the most interesting questions about the history of American civilization, for instance, is the relative significance from colonial days to the present of wealth, power, and other values. Perhaps it should be added that the list is not a biological inventory of "instincts" or "drives." The degree to which native biological equipment enters into the complex patterns of conduct now being discussed is an empirical question.

Institutions

When we examine the shaping and distribution of each value in a given community, it is usually—if not invariably—found that certain patterns are specialized to one value (or a limited set of values). These specializations are called institutions. Power institutions include legislatures, executives, administrative agencies, courts, political parties, and pressure groups, for example. The respect institutions include the honor conferring and the stigmatizing, discriminatory practices of society. The well being institutions embrace, among others, agencies concerned with the prevention and cure of disease. The wealth institutions are the industries and other economic patterns of the community. The rectitude institutions, like the church, are specialized to the defining and applying of moral standards. Among the enlightenment institutions come schools, colleges, universities, intelligence reporting services, and mass media of communication. To the skill institutions belong organized professional and occupational bodies.

Policy: Professional Training in the Public Interest," 52 *Yale Law Journal*, 1943, pp. 203–295. Reprinted in Lasswell, *The Analysis of Political Behavior; An Empirical Approach* (International Library of Sociology), Kegan Paul, London, 1948. A further systematic statement is in Harold D. Lasswell and A. Kaplan, *Power and Society* (forthcoming).

Although a given pattern is often highly specialized to one value (or a few values), every value is to some degree involved. For instance, a trade union or a trade association can be usefully explored in more frames of reference than the production and distribution of wealth, since unions and associations influence, or are influenced by, considerations of power, respect, and many other values.

Note further that what people say in casual conversation about an institution may be falsified by more exhaustive study. A power institution is often a striking example. In a given community the term "government" may be applied to certain officials and activities; but it would be a mistake to take this local usage as final evidence that such officials and activities do, in fact, constitute the main power institution of the community. Further investigation may reveal that important decisions are actually made by persons connected with institutions locally called "churches" or "fraternal societies" or "corporations" or "unions "

Each of the values referred to in our brief list has been the object of specialized investigation. This is notably true of wealth, the subject matter of economics. It applies also to power, the distinctive frame of reference of political science. The study of respect, though not the object of a distinctively named science, is a major topic of sociologists who deal with "social class" and "caste." The scientific study of education deals with some of the facts having to do with enlightenment. Well being is the frame of reference of specialists on public health. Certain sociologists concentrate upon the comparative investigation of morals (rectitude), skill (occupations, professions), and affection (*e.g.,* studies of the family and fraternities).

Value Distribution

When the members of a community are classified according to their position in relation to any value, it usually appears that values are unequally distributed. Lloyd Warner and his associates, who studied Newburyport, Massachusetts ("Yankeetown"), were concerned with social classes (respect classes).[2] Everyone was described according to

[2] W. Lloyd Warner and Paul S. Lunt, *The Social Life of a Modern Community,* Yale University Press, New Haven. The first volume of a series on "Yankeetown."

such criteria as club membership, availability for marriage, and for reciprocal dining invitations and the like. On this basis, the class (respect) structure was as follows: Upper Upper, 1.44%; Lower Upper, 1.56%; Upper Middle, 10.22%; Lower Middle, 28.12%; Upper Lower, 32.60%; Lower Lower, 25.22%; Unknown, 0.84%. In a southern community the cleavage between White and Negro results in a somewhat different structure; and it is obvious that mobility "upward" is severely restricted; hence social (respect) classes harden into "castes."

Studies of wealth and income distributions almost invariably show inequality. In 1935–36 there were over twenty-nine million family units in the United States. Four and a half million family units were on relief, and received a median income of $685. The 24.9 million non-relief families received a median income of $1,285. If comparisons are made according to such regional units as states, the differences are striking. In recent years 17.87% of the population of Connecticut is represented in Federal income tax returns, which is approximately 2% above the New England average of 15.74%. The corresponding figure for the South is 5.80%.[3]

Looking at the globe as a whole there are vast differences in average real production per head from country to country. During the period 1935–38, the figure for the United States and Great Britain was five times that for the U.S.S.R. and the Balkans.[4] In many countries the concentration of land ownership in a few hands has been noteworthy. Even after World War I, but 0.4% of the total number of landholdings in Germany comprised 20.2% of the arable land of the country (and this was 40% of the land east of the Elbe River): 59.4% of the total holdings of Germany accounted for only 6.2% of the arable land. In the United States the Senate's Temporary National Economic Committee reported in 1946 that three family groups—the du Ponts, the Mellons, and the Rockefellers—have shareholdings valued at nearly $1,400,000,000 which directly or indirectly give control over fifteen of the two hundred largest non-financial cor-

---

[3] A convenient compendium is Simon Kuznets, *National Income; A Summary of Findings*, National Bureau of Economic Research, New York, 1946.

[4] See Colin Clark, *The Economics of 1960*, Macmillan, London, 1944.

porations in the country with aggregate assets of over $8,000,000,000 (or more than eleven per cent of the total assets of these corporations.) [5]

Differences in the degree of power sharing are obvious enough: Remember the restricted franchise and the insignificant role of legislative institutions in Nazi Germany, Fascist Italy, or Imperial Japan. With such instances may be contrasted the comparatively broad franchises and powerful legislatures of Great Britain, the Scandinavian countries, Canada, Australia, New Zealand, and, of course, ourselves.

Consider the distribution of enlightenment. In non-industrialized countries illiteracy rates of above forty per cent have not been uncommon. India still has an enormous percentage of illiteracy; and yet some of the most distinguished scientists and scholars, to say nothing of well informed politicians and journalists, are East Indian.

Attention

Without pursuing this point of inequality any further, we may turn directly to the interconnections between social structure and the structure of attention. That such connections exist need occasion no surprise. Common experience provides us with many examples: It seems obvious that the President, the Cabinet, the chairmen of the important committees in the Senate and the House, the leading men in the political parties will have access to a different (and presumably more comprehensive) picture of political developments than less influential leaders, to say nothing of the ordinary voter. It also seems obvious that the managers, owners and regulators of giant corporations in banking, mining, industry, commerce, transportation and communication will have a more inclusive set of economic reports brought to their attention than are available to smaller and less influential businessmen and consumers. No one doubts that the daily concerns of the upper-upper social (respect) class differ in several particulars from the attention frame of other classes. And the

[5] Monograph No. 29, *The Distribution of Ownership in the 200 Largest Non-financial Corporations*, 1940.

same remark applies to those who hold an elite, mid-elite, or rank and file position in the distribution of any value.

This is not to affirm, however, that we have enough knowledge about these interrelationships to answer the questions raised by scientific curiosity or by considerations of public policy. Look at the matter, for a moment, from the standpoint of the policy of a democratic community. One maxim of democratic doctrine is that the effective functioning of democracy depends upon an enlightened public opinion, not merely upon the statutes that prescribe a broad franchise. And it is clear that enlightened public opinion depends upon access to a stream of news and comment on the basis of which rational judgments can be based. It follows, therefore, that the success of democracy depends in part upon whether the mass media, such as the press, radio and film, do in fact reach public attention with the news and comment called for by democratic theory.

No doubt every man (expert or layman) has an answer, and I have no doubt that a poll of readers would disclose that many of you are dissatisfied with the press. But have we thought (or done) anything about it? Have we clarified the criteria to be applied in evaluating the performance of the press? Do we have qualified persons engaged in applying these standards to typical situations and making the results generally available? And do we have qualified persons probing into the factors that account for performance (or nonperformance)? The fact is that our civilization does not, at present, possess a body of specialists who define their criteria and apply them objectively to the content of press, radio, film and lecture. And we do not have many specialists devoting themselves to describing the frame of attention of persons who occupy various positions in the world social structure.[6]

Observational Procedures

However, several methods of describing the structure of attention have been devised and demonstrated in exploratory and cir-

---

[6] Recommendations along this line are outlined in the Report of the Commission on Freedom of the Press, *A Free and Responsible Press,* University of Chicago Press, Chicago, 1947.

cumscribed studies.[7] One method is to induce representative groups to make a voluntary record of what they read, see and hear. Another method is participant observation, in the course of which the investigator unobtrusively keeps a record of the activity cycle of representative persons, noting the position in the social structure of other persons met, corresponded with, and so on; and keeping track of the time spent in exposure to mass media. A great many studies have been made for the purpose of finding who pays attention to specific channels of communication. Some radios, for instance, are geared to gadgets that report when the instrument is turned on, and to which wave band. A commercial reporting service telephones to individuals, who are supposed to be representative samples of various brackets of income, and asks whether the radio is tuned in, and what is being listened to.

In order to ascertain the attention getting function of different parts of newspapers and magazines, interviewers have been trained to ask sample groups whether they recall having read various items. In this way estimates are made of how many readers in a hundred (divided by sex, age, income, etc.) pay attention to headlines, editorials, comics and other departments; how many look at advertisements located in different positions (which page, which column and area of each page); and how many read advertisements with or without photographs, diagrams, cartoons, color and the like. Counts are made of persons who stop to look at window displays, outdoor advertising signs and posters; and of attendance at theaters, churches, lectures, and similar gatherings. Readers and listeners are invited to send fan mail, or to send in a coupon and get something in return—all for the purpose of discovering who exposes himself to what.

Libraries keep circulation cards, and by special studies it is possible to determine the reading habits of age, sex, and other groups. Investigations are made of the arrangement of exhibits at museums and the effect on "museum fatigue." By examining curricula, textbooks and study aids, it is possible to find what children are exposed to

[7] For more detail consult the introductory articles and references in Bruce L. Smith, Harold D. Lasswell, Ralph D. Casey, *Propaganda, Communication and Public Opinion; A Comprehensive Reference Guide,* Princeton University Press, Princeton, 1946.

at school. Research can also show the type of desk and lighting arrangement that helps the child to keep at his work without developing eyestrain and postural tensions and becoming distracted. In the same way auditoriums for musical performances, lectures, theatricals and other presentations can be investigated with a view to disclosing the psychophysical factors affecting attention. Industrial engineers apply comparable procedures to the work bench in the factory, the clerk's station in the office or store, and the boss's office. The interiors of dwellings, planes, buses, automobiles, and other vehicles are examined from the same point of view. The packaging of goods and the packaging of people (clothing, cosmetic aids) are examined with an eye to the effect of the packaged object upon the human environment.

Many studies describe the content of what is brought to the focus of audience attention. A rough and ready way to describe the press is to conduct a clipping bureau and to select all items bearing on a given topic. A more elaborate and refined method is to use a system of content analysis categories. In relation to political content, for instance, a list of key symbols or statements is drawn up, and a count made of the frequency with which each item on the list is mentioned. The key symbols may include the names of countries, parties, and leading personalities, together with the key words invoked in systems of political doctrine ("democracy," "freedom," "socialism," "capitalism"). A record can be made of the number of times the word, or a full statement of doctrine, is presented favorably or unfavorably. Clerks can readily be trained to apply such procedures with little inconsistency. For routine items agreement is more than ninety-nine in one hundred. The same basic procedure is also applied to motion picture scripts when they are read to note the occurrence of unpermitted words or scenes; and also when the final product is complete. Radio broadcasts, lectures, street corner conversations, letters, parliamentary debates, and the like, are all capable of being summed up this way.

Researches on attention have usually been carried on in close conjunction with the study of communication effects. Effect analysis appraises the impact of a given channel or content upon audience response. The key questions are: How much attention does the audience give? How much comprehension is there? How much enjoyment? How much impact on valuations? How much effect on action?

It is, of course, necessary to distinguish between what we have called the frame or focus of attention, on the one hand, and attention effect, on the other. The effect is the response by an audience *beyond* the minimum necessary to bring the object of reference into the frame of attention. A radio broadcast that is made inaudible by static is not in the attention frame. But if a minimum level of response (set at some convenient point by the investigator) is attained, the program has come into the attention frame of the listening audience. If you are studying the national radio audience, you may specify that one receiving set in a thousand must receive a broadcast clearly (for instance), and all sets above this (which keep tuned in for a specified interval) are attention "effect."

It is perhaps apparent from what has been said above that much of the effort devoted to the study of attention has been by business, notably in connection with merchandising, and especially advertising. However, it need not be overlooked that wealth is not the only value whose pursuit has led to the gathering of attention data: power institutions (governments) have made extensive use of such information, during a war period particularly. In World War II, enemy radio was monitored for the purpose of guessing where the enemy next expected to strike, and in order to evaluate the state of morale. Broadcasts and other publications clearly revealed the propaganda line of the enemy; and attention studies of broadcasts and publications at home, in allied and neutral countries, not infrequently established a strong presumption that a given radio station, editor or producer was controlled by, or in sympathy with, the enemy.[8]

Many values besides wealth and power can be fostered by objective descriptions of attention. In order to improve the level of public

---

[8] See especially Ernst Kris, Hans Speier and others, *German Radio Propaganda: Report on Home Broadcasts During the War,* Oxford University Press, New York, 1944; H. L. Childs and J. B. Whitton, editors, *Propaganda by Short Wave,* Princeton University Press, Princeton, 1942.

health (well being) we need to know what health advice is given
to the layman, with a view to correcting whatever misconceptions
exist. In the interest of morality (rectitude), it is evident that we
cannot afford to ignore what is disseminated through the media of
communication.

Milieu and Surroundings

It is, however, from the scientific (enlightenment) point of view
that I want to consider the systematic study of attention structure.
All hypotheses about human response require attention data for
their confirmation or disconfirmation. After all, response is determined by two sets of interacting factors, environmental and predispositional; and the immediate impact of environment is upon
attention. The part of the environment which gets into the frame of
attention during a definite period we call the *milieu*. Although the
non-milieu part of the environment, the *surroundings,* does not act
directly upon response, the milieu may nevertheless be indirectly
affected.

In historical and comparative analysis it often is taken for granted
—hence not demonstrated—that an invariant relationship exists between a certain set of surroundings and the milieu. But serious
errors can arise when this invariancy is assumed or blurred. Furthermore, when the attention structure is not clearly described, the
treatment of attention effects, and of certain closely related responses,
such as comprehension and evaluation, are left in an ambiguous
state.

I shall choose two or three examples from the field of economics
and political science to document this criticism. No doubt every
scholar agrees that innovations in the technique of production are
likely to inaugurate profound changes in the way people feel and
think. Certainly no one is surprised to find that you cannot introduce factory methods of production without setting up a set of
significant social results. Now one of the most conspicuous features
of modern history has been, not only astonishing changes in technology, but evidence of discontent among workers exposed to new
work situations.

One of the most conspicuous features of the "material" environment of the worker—namely, the repetitiveness of the machine—has been seized upon as one of the major factors which explain the worker's dissatisfaction. It is alleged that the repetitiveness of the machine induces fatigue, which accounts for the varying degrees of latent or overt hostility on the part of the workers. I do not need to remind you how much repetition has been given to this interpretation by social historians and industrial psychologists, to say nothing of propagandists.[9]

And yet, in recent years, evidence has been piling up that operations, even when repetitive, can give rise to harmonious rather than hostile attitudes when the environment provides the worker with friendly and considerate treatment.[10] Where hostile attitudes are found, the explanation may lie, not in exposure to the gadget, but to an environment which is disrespectful of human dignity and unfriendly—in our terminology, if the environment deprives rather than indulges the worker in the values of respect and affection.

Armed with these insights, we turn to the social histories in quest of descriptions of the attention structure of workers at successive stages of their exposure to machinery. We want to know whether the milieu of the worker included, besides machines, friendly and considerate greetings from fellow workers, foremen and other "bosses," or whether, on the contrary, they were subjected to a continuous flow of abuse, contempt, and surly disregard. Unhappily, when we look into social history, we find a minimum of systematic reporting along these lines. Because of this lack of attention to the frame of attention, our own attention has been taken up with what may very well prove to be false, and to be a falsification which has had socially pernicious consequences.

The machine has been held culpable for what men themselves

---

[9] The vogue of the "fatigue" concept is indicated by the title of the British Commission, "Industrial Fatigue Board."

[10] The most significant American studies have been initiated by Elton Mayo; see especially, Elton Mayo, *The Human Problems of an Industrial Civilization*, New York, 1933; F. T. Roethlisberger and W. G. Dickson, *Management and the Worker*, Harvard University Press, Cambridge, 1939. A recent critical review is by Georges Friedmann, *Problèmes humains du machinisme industriel*, Gallimard, Paris, 1946.

may be directly responsible for—namely, the human context in which machines and men were introduced to one another. In short, because the "material" features of the environment have been so obvious, they have become part of the milieu of the scholar, who has exaggerated the role they played at the focus of attention of the workers. This has come from disregarding the non-machine features of the environment and the milieu of the working force.

I might go on to suggest that the same exaggeration applies to other features of the "material" environment, *viz.,* wages. And the importance of another value in fostering discontent has quite probably been seriously underestimated, namely, power. Modern research has found factory situations in which the presence or absence of consultation between management and worker appears to be the critical factor in eliciting positive or negative responses. And here again the historical data frequently fail to present a total context, a comprehensive account of the environment and the milieu of representative (and atypical) work situations.

An example of the failure to discriminate clearly between the frame of attention and effect is to be found in the account of "expectations" given by John Maynard Keynes in *The General Theory of Employment, Interest and Money.* Classical economic theory was built on a speculative model which postulated that the bargainers in a market had full foreknowledge of the impact of their acts upon market relations (supply and demand at a price). In a memorable chapter Keynes modified this postulate in an eloquent and penetrating account of the changing structure of expectations of bargainers in a market.[11] Yet even this account does not at all points distinguish between "expectations" in the sense of what is available at the focus of attention, and what is valuation on the basis of such exposure.

This ambiguity continues to hold back the progress of economic theory, and the study of economic institutions. For instance, we do not have institutional studies of the actual focus of attention of representative businessmen or consumers on the basic of which they arrive at economic judgments. We have no realistic and systematic account of what typical (and atypical) producers and consumers

[11] Chapters V and XII deal expressly with "expectations."

were told about recent and forecasted technical innovations, changes in legal regulation, shifts of consumer taste, attitudes of labor, changes in the severity of competition—to name only a few factors entering into economic choices.[12]

Another example of neglect is from political science. It is difficult to find studies which systematically describe what is brought to the focus of attention of decision makers, and on the basis of which policies are crystallized. I speak, in this connection, of the neglect of research on the intelligence function, which is the function of providing facts and interpretations on the basis of which the best available rational judgment of policy can be made. I have already referred to the public intelligence function, to the nature of the news and comment reaching various levels of the body politic. A noteworthy exception to the general neglect of research on the attention structure is the study by Lazarsfeld and associates of the whole stream of communication reaching the voters of Erie county in the presidential campaign of 1936.[13]

The General Theory of Attention

As an aid to further research it is useful to systematize our hypotheses about the interrelations of attention and social structure. Under what conditions do the members of social classes increase or decrease the amount of attention given to one another, relative to the amount given to the members of other social classes? It will be remembered that the term social class refers to position in the upper, middle, or lower distribution of power, wealth, respect and other values. The present question includes the problem of when the members of the upper class give attention to the middle and lower classes; when the middle classes are concerned with themselves rather than the upper and lower classes; and when the lower classes pay attention to the middle and upper classes. Looking at the social structure of the world as a whole, such problems as these arise: When do the power elites of the world shift from one another to bestowing more

[12] It may be that the present situation will be somewhat improved when the results are available of the interviews conducted in the investigation of credit by the National Bureau of Economic Research.

[13] *The People's Choice*, Duell, Sloan and Pearce, New York, 1945.

attention upon the "masses"? When do the wealth elites withdraw attention from one another and focus upon the middle and lower income elements? And so for each class of each value.

As a working tool, let us set up a speculative model. Assume first that *the members of a given position in the social structure are more identified with one another than with the members of other social classes*. This means that the personality structure of the members of a social class includes the members of the class in the self, even though the members of other classes may be excluded. This means that primary ego symbols, the "I" and "me," are bracketed with symbols of all the members of the social class, thus delimiting the boundaries of the self.

Another postulate is that *the class value is the object of demand*, at least to the extent of maintaining value position, at most in striving for the maximum realization of values.

Another postulate is that *the class value is in more demand for the members of the class than for other classes*. Thus it is assumed that the members of a power class are more concerned in maintaining or extending the power of their own class than in preserving the power of another.

A further postulate is that *expectations are shared about the characteristics of a situation which constitute the class value, and which favor or endanger the realization of the value*. This means that there are shared assumptions about what is to be recognized as wealth, for instance, and what is to be construed as a threat or opportunity related to wealth.

The speculative model thus conceived lends itself to the derivation of many hypotheses, of which the following are examples:

1. Attention varies directly with deprivation (loss, blocked gain).

a. An elite increases its attention to non-elite when the non-elite menaces or obstructs the elite.

Consistent with this is the growing preoccupation of a ruling group with revolutionists who challenge the right of the established order to continue, and attack and obstruct it. Consistent, also, is the concentration of attention upon the most threatened or blocked part of the self. When revolutionary hostility is aimed at certain institutions or doctrines or persons, these parts of the self are brought to the center of attention. An assassinated ruler, a captured garrison, a challenged doctrine (such as the "divine right of kings") are at once brought into self-attention.

If threats external to the class subside, relatively more attention is given to members of the same class—when there is rivalry among members of the class for control over values. Consistent with this is the preoccupation of the elites of power with one another, the mutual surveillance that characterizes the top elites of the states of world politics.

b. A non-elite class increases its attention to the elite when the elite menaces or obstructs the non-elite.

In harmony with this is the attention given the big corporations by smaller businessmen or ex-businessmen when business is "going to the chains."

2. Attention varies directly with indulgence (gain, blocked loss).

a. An elite increases its attention to non-elite when the non-elite affords opportunities to improve the value position of the elite or to avoid loss.

When the elite of wealth sees an opportunity to improve its position by adding to the skill of the working force through such measures as education, housing and medical care, the elite pays more attention to the non-elite elements of the community. A power elite, fearful of losing to a rival elite, may seek the loyalty of the rank and file, thus directing its attention toward non-elite elements with the expectation of avoiding loss. (If the power elites as a whole felt endangered by this turning to the non-elite, it would not happen.)

b. A non-elite increases its attention to elite when the elite affords opportunities to improve its position or to avoid loss.

When the elite is increasingly viewed as a source of indulgence in the form of more wages, more power, more respect, or more of any other value, the non-elite gives attention to the elite. In the same way when there is increased expectation that the elite will protect the non-elite against loss (whether of income, respect, or any other value), the attention given to the elite will rise.

Any subsection of the non-elite is exposed to indulgences and deprivations from sections above and below, and acts according to the most favorable expected result. Although the members of middle classes, for instance, are rivalrous with one another, they can often be unified against the "proletariat," or the "monopolists."

The Attention Control Response

The general theory of attention can usefully include the theory of the control response, the effort to control the attention of those whose conduct is expected to affect the value position of the controller. On the basis of our model, we can formulate the hypothesis that:

3. Attempts to control attention vary with the expected margin of indulgence over deprivation.

It is consistent with this when the elite typically uses symbols rather than violence to influence the response of the non-elite. As political analysts have long pointed out, symbols are cheaper and surer than violence as means of maintaining an established order.[14] Hence, even if power is for a brief moment naked power resting purely on control over the instruments of violence, rulers soon evoke an ideology to consolidate power and to economize the means by which the new system is perpetuated. The ideology includes political *doctrines,* the political *formula,* and political *miranda (cf. Chapter IV, p. 44)*. The doctrinal statements are the fundamental justifications of authority. The formula includes the statements prescribing the organization of authority and the detailed prescriptions to be followed as applications of the doctrine. The miranda are the legends and rituals.

Intermediate between the full statement of a proposition that occupies an important place in the ideology and the single word or key symbol, is the slogan. The slogan is a phrase or synoptic statement addressed to the masses as a guide for action. When we undertake to examine the symbols brought to the attention of the community by elites we begin with the distinctions just drawn.

---

[14] Rousseau wrote: "The strongest man is never strong enough to be always master, unless he transforms his power into right and obedience into duty." Hobbes made the point more concisely: "Even the tyrant must sleep."

In world surveys of political attention during the war, key doctrines, slogans and symbols were described according to their frequency of mention and position of prominence in broadcasts, newspapers and other media of communication available to the attention of various elements of the social structure. Trends were described in the use of various symbols in media at home and abroad under the control of each elite, in this way providing data on the basis of which the relative weight of different factors affecting attention could be assessed.

For instance, the elites played down doctrinal symbols that they expected might alienate allies and played up those they expected to hold allied support. The newspapers of the Soviet Union de-emphasized attacks on "fascism" during the pact period with Germany. The Soviet press played down "communism" and other world revolutionary symbols during the whole war, a period of expected support from certain foreign governments. The Italians adopted racism after aligning themselves openly on the side of the Nazis when France fell.

The procedures described above are applicable to the control responses of the elite as well as the non-elite. In particular, it is important to examine the symbols antithetical to the ideology (the "counter ideology" or "Utopia") which may be clandestinely circulated until revolutionary action reaches a high level of intensity.[15]

Homogeneity and Heterogeneity of Attention

The hypotheses previously stated indicate why one of the most revealing topics of investigation is the homogeneity or heterogeneity of the attention structure of each social class. Consider the attention frame of the elite of power. When rulers expect that disclosure will endanger their position, rulers will attempt to prevent public (non-elite) disclosure, and do what they can to maintain this heterogeneity of attention. During the Battle of France the government tried to conceal the true state of affairs, realizing that public knowledge would precipitate vehement demands for change in the government. A sample of the French press shows that the newspapers actually pre-

[15] Reference is made to the researches of The Experimental Division for the Study of Wartime Communications, The Library of Congress, Washington, D.C. (H. D. Lasswell, Director; Paul Lewis, Joseph M. Goldsen, Research Directors.)

sented the situation of France in a favorable light from the day the Low Countries were invaded (May 10, 1940) until May 27.[16] From May 28 to June 10, there was more realism, but even after the evacuation of Dunkirk the situation was presented almost as favorably as at the beginning. In the sample favorable statements always outnumbered the unfavorable by more than two to one. The British press, on the other hand, dealt more realistically with the Battle of Britain.

In this connection it is worth considering the ways by which the stream of communication permitted to reach the public can present a deviant picture. One device, obviously, is omission; but another is compensation, which consists in accompanying unfavorable statements with favorable ones. *Direct compensation* occurs when unfavorable statements touching on a certain feature of the self are counteracted by statements related to the same features. The Paris press, for example, when it did allude to loss of territory to the Germans, usually accompanied such statements by denials, or admissions that "explained away" the loss as of no consequence, or made claims of successful counterattacks.

Indirect compensation consists in shifting unfavorable presentations of the self to a less serious category, or the balancing of adverse statements by favorable presentations in another category. Instead of reporting the loss of strategic territory, for instance, the press may admit the loss of equipment; and even this may be counterbalanced in the day's budget of news by reports of great success in the "battle of production." A further means of buffering reality is to refer to ambiguous features of the self, since statements of this type are less open to disproof. Instead of dwelling on battle successes the emphasis may be on "our rising morale," or our "masterly (secret) battle plan." When things are going badly, compensation can be sought in the use of normative themes, such as the barbarity of the enemy (a favorite Nazi theme concerning the Russians), and the moral discipline of our own troops and civilians. It is also convenient to direct attention toward the future, and to discuss war aims and the prospects of permanent peace.

---

[16] The material on the French press is from a manuscript by N. C. Leites and others prepared for The Experimental Division for the Study of Wartime Communications.

Attention can also be deflected from a disagreeable present by dwelling upon past glory, and especially upon the successes that followed previous tribulations.

Discrepancies between the elite's picture and what the rank and file is permitted to see is not always in the direction of covering up the unfavorable. The ruling group may calculate that a shock will stimulate greater effort on the part of the public; hence bad news may be released without putting it in what, from the point of view of the best informed, is a more encouraging perspective.

Spatial Distribution of Attention Patterns

On the basis of the hypotheses formulated thus far we can consider how patterns of attention are distributed in space. In world politics the power elites of each state tend to keep a wary and watchful eye on one another because of the expectation of violence which is the expectation that, whether one approves of it or not, many serious differences will probably continue to be settled by war or threat of war. The states of the world thus tend to align themselves in diplomatic blocs or fighting associations, and these alignments constitute the "balancing of power" pattern of a given historical period. It is consistent with our hypotheses that attention is directed toward the greatest enemy (the expected sources of deprivation) and the greatest ally (the greatest sources of external indulgence). In World War II there were interesting contrasts in the comparative amount of attention given to Allies. Germany and Italy gave relatively little notice to Japan; Britain and the United States paid more attention to China. At the start, the Germans expected to win with a minimum of aid from the Japanese; and the Italians were dependent on the Germans. Our top strategists recognized the great importance to us of China.

In general the structure of attention in world politics conforms to the general pattern of power. Today, when Russia and the United States are the powers in relation to which all powers orient themselves, the world attention pattern tends toward a bipolar structure, in which those paying favorable attention to Russia are grouped together, and those favorable to the United States are also grouped. Before the recent war the world political pattern was polypolar, as there were more major powers; and the attention pattern had the same polypolar form.[17]

When the elite is apprehensive of the loyalty of the non-elite members of the country, a process of segregation begins which tends to bring together the persons who share the same expectations of indulgence and deprivation. Thus the civil struggle in the United States was preceded by a movement North or South of sympathizers with the Northern or Southern cause. When revolutionary tension develops along economic class lines, the low income, working quarters of cities are typically aligned against the upper income residential areas. The general point may be formulated in these terms:

4. Crisis concentrates attention; non-crisis disperses it.

The conception of crisis is of a situation in which there is great stress toward action, toward the resolution of conflict. Under such circumstances the alternatives become limited in number, and attention is narrowly focused in relation to them. When the situation is less critical, individuals are free to concern themselves with conflicts of lesser scope. This means that the part of the total self which includes cooperation and solidarity with a great many others is active in collective crisis, while, at other times, more circumscribed parts of the self are involved. In relation to the larger self, attention is turned inward (internalized)—the well known tendency of people at the end of wartime sacrifices for the national self to become preoccupied with private affairs.

The Realism of Attention

We have said nothing up to this point about the realism of the elite or any other class. Yet it is of no little consequence to explore the conditions under which groups make false choices. The postulates laid down when we set up our speculative attention model include the possibility of mistakes. We have not followed the precedent of that form of classical economic theory which postulated omniscience on the part of all bargainers in a market. Our postulate is that the members of a class share expectations about the characteristics of a situa-

[17] On tripolarity, consult W. T. R. Fox, *The Super-Powers*, Harcourt, Brace and Company, New York, 1944; on bipolarity, Harold D. Lasswell, *World Politics Faces Economics*, McGraw-Hill, New York, 1945.

tion which constitutes the class value, and which favors or endangers the realization of the value. Although expectations are shared, they are not necessarily correct. That false policies can be followed by the members of a social class is abundantly demonstrated by the ruling groups who have undermined and extinguished themselves. Looking back, the analytic historian can often discern the seams that eventually widened and cracked the structure. Perhaps the consequences of introducing money and credit were not foreseen, and if foreseen, were not counter balanced by the invention of new practices by means of which the elite could perpetuate itself. Perhaps the practice of resenting bad news, and of making the bearer of unfavorable intelligence afraid for his job, brought about estrangement from the facts. (Certainly this appears to be a major factor in the downfall of Nazi Germany.)

When we do not have the benefit of knowledge after the event, we can nevertheless make explicit assumptions about the factors that do, in fact, affect the survival and expansion of a given class; and we can describe the degree to which a group entertains these expectations. Willingness to listen to qualified persons report on bad as well as good news can be one criterion, for example.

In exploring the factors affecting realism, it is necessary to look into the whole process through which a class arrives at common expectations, and to give particular attention to the points at which deviations from reality first arise. Concretely, this calls for research on the intelligence function which serves the choices made by the members of the group. The intelligence function (which means organizing the focus of attention of the chooser) is carried on in many ways, particularly by the specialized media of communication.

Communication contributes to three processes: surveillance of the environment of the members of the class, locating actual and potential indulgences and deprivations; correlating the internal responses of the class to the environment; transmitting the experience of the class to its incoming members (education).[18] The powerful, for instance, may have police spies and other specialists scrutinizing the

---

[18] See Chapter IV, p. 40. Also Harold D. Lasswell and Joseph M. Goldsen, "Public Attention and Public Opinion," in *The International Journal of Opinion and Attitude Research*, Mexico City (forthcoming).

non-elite. The wealthy may have reporters devoted to the task of describing the general economic situation, and estimating the factors affecting it. Both the powerful and the wealthy carry on educational activities of varying degrees of elaborateness. And what applies to the elite applies to many non-elites, and to subsections of each class. The power elite of a given country uses diplomats, attachés and other correspondents to report on the political environment abroad.

The specialized media of communication transmit in two directions, toward and away from centers and subcenters. Incoming reports from abroad typically reach the chief executives of the government or of the news agencies, and later may be relayed to larger audiences. Each relay point is a potential modification point: there may be omissions, additions, distortions. And research on the communication net will focus upon these relay links, beginning at the point of origin with an analysis of the focus of attention and the communication response of the first observer-communicator in the chain.

In investigating a community as a whole, it is not only necessary to consider each value separately, but the relative importance of each value in relation to all values. For the elite or non-elite of power, for example, what is the relative importance of power in relation to wealth, respect, and other values? In gathering the data to answer this question we develop an inventory of how the self of every individual in the community is identified with other sectors of the community, what values are demanded with that intensity, and what expectations are current about the characteristics of a situation that constitute values, and also the factors that affect their realization.[19]

It is evident that the focus of attention, and the specialized media of communication, perform for social classes (and indeed for all human groups) an equivalent function to that which is performed by comparable structures in the social life of animals, and in the individual organism. A general theory of life will one day bring all the phenomena together which are connected at any level with the surveillance of the environment, the correlation of response, and the

[19] On basic conceptions of "self" and "communication," consult George Herbert Mead, *Mind, Self and Society,* University of Chicago Press, Chicago, 1934; Charles Morris, *Signs, Language and Behavior,* Prentice-Hall, New York, 1946.

transmission of experience. In common with other responses, the focus of attention appears to conform to the general postulate of behavior (the postulate of maximizing total indulgence over deprivation). The attention of the members of a social class, whether directed within the class or outside it, is an instrument for maintaining or advancing the position of the class in relation to the class value. Hence the structure of attention is in perpetual interaction with social structure in the total processes of society; and research on attention structure offers some hope of illuminating many of the interactions in society which, in the past, have been obscure or obscured.

Brief World Survey of Political Doctrine: 1939

The following is a brief summary of key doctrines and symbols which were distributed around the globe and invoked by elites with varying degrees of intensity and effect on the eve of war in 1939. I give a doctrinal statement and one quotation from an authoritative elite source. These sources are not necessarily close to the year 1939 since many doctrines received authoritative expression years before the global war.

We will quickly pass by the familiar doctrines of liberal democracy and the key symbols of "freedom," "equality" and "individual rights," coupled with the slogans ("all men are created equal"). A few reminders:

1. Our moral authority rests upon the consent of the governed.

Governments (derive) their just Powers from the Consent of the Governed.
—*Declaration of Independence*, 1776

2. In respect of rights, all men are created free and equal.

. . . all Men are created equal . . . they are endowed by their Creator with certain unalienable Rights . . . among these are Life, Liberty, and the Pursuit of Happiness.
—*Declaration of Independence*, 1776

3. The function of government is to secure these rights.

. . . to secure these Rights, Governments are instituted among Men . . .
—*Declaration of Independence*, 1776

4. The proper method of government is the balancing of functions among various agencies of the state and society.

(5) That the legislative and executive powers of the state should be separate and distinct from the judiciary; and that the members of the two first may be restrained from oppression, by feeling and participating the burdens of the people, they should, at fixed periods, be reduced to a private station, return into that body from which they were originally taken, and the vacancies be supplied by frequent, certain, and regular elections, in which all, or any part of the former members to be again eligible or ineligible, as the laws shall direct.

—Virginia Bill of Rights, 1776

5. Our ideas are self-evident.

We hold these Truths to be self-evident . . .

—Declaration of Independence, 1776

The Communist doctrine was the most lively challenge to elites exercising authority in the name of the people. The Communists did not deny the moral ideal of popular rule. They said that it was unrealizable save where private property in the instruments of production is abolished. The Russian elite asserted:

1. Our moral authority is superior to any in the world.

The Soviet system is more impregnated with democracy than any other system.

—V. M. Molotov, 1936

2. Our superior morality is determined by the collective ownership of the means of production.

Article IV. The economic foundation of the U.S.S.R. consists of the socialist economic system and the socialist ownership of the tools and the means of production, firmly established as the result of the liquidation of the capitalist economic system, the abolition of private ownership and tools of the means of production, and the abolition of the exploitation of man by man.

—The Constitution of the U.S.S.R., 1936

3. Other regimes, including modern capitalism, are morally inferior.

Hitherto, every form of society has been based, as we have already seen, on the antagonism of oppressing and oppressed classes.

>—Karl Marx and Friedrich Engels, *Manifesto
>of the Communist Party,* 1848

4. The immorality of other regimes depends upon the means of production and ownership.

. . . the modern bourgeoisie is itself the product of a series of revolutions in the modes of production and its change.

>—Karl Marx and Friedrich Engels, *Manifesto
>of the Communist Party,* 1848

5. The collapse of capitalism is inevitable.

What the bourgeoisie therefore produces, above all, are its own grave-diggers. Its fall and the victory of the proletariat are equally inevitable.

>—Karl Marx and Friedrich Engels, *Manifesto
>of the Communist Party,* 1848

6. Revolutionary violence against the bourgeoisie is justified.

In order to be able to build the new society in our country, a society without the exploitation of man by man, the workers, in alliance with the peasantry, had to overthrow the capitalists and landlords by means of revolution and establish their own power—the power of the Soviets, the proletarian dictatorship. History provided no other way of emancipation from capitalism, and, as you know, it provides no other way now.

>—V. M. Molotov, 1936

7. Our ideas are true; they are determined by material conditions.

The theoretical conclusions of the Communists . . . merely express, in general terms, actual relations springing from an existing class struggle.

>—Karl Marx and Friedrich Engels, *Manifesto
>of the Communist Party,* 1848

Without limiting ourselves to foregoing citations, but to material of similar authenticity, it is evident that certain symbols invariably receive a negative connotation:

> Bourgeoisie
> Capitalism (capitalist, capital)
> Imperialism
> God (religion, church)

> Plutocracy
> Idealism (subjectivism)
> Anarchism
> Syndicalism

Certain terms are given a positive meaning:

> Communism (Communist Party, Communist International)
> Proletariat
> World revolution
> Dialectical materialism
> Dictatorship of the proletariat
> Collectivism (collective ownership)
> Classless society (of the future)
> Class struggle
> Masses
> People

For various reasons some terms are employed in both senses, positive and negative. The love of "socialism," for example, does not exclude vehement rejection of "socialist parties." (According to the Communist line of the 1928–35 period they are "social fascists.") "Democracy" in general is positive; yet "bourgeois democracy" is dismissed as a hypocritical device of the bourgeoisie to retain power and befuddle the workers. The "middle classes" are usually treated with contempt as "counter revolutionary" influences. Yet in many situations an effort is made to maintain a united program with them.

The first conspicuous post World War I example of a political doctrine calling itself new, and challenging both Communism and Liberal Democracy, was Italian Fascism. Whereas the Communist seizure of power came after nearly three quarters of a century of theoretical analysis and practical action, Mussolini and the Italian Fascists took over control in Italy after a brief agitational period and gave very little attention to the systematic exposition of a doctrine. In fact it was not until Mussolini's article in the *Fascist Encyclopedia,* on "the doctrine of Fascism," almost ten years after the seizure of power, that it was possible to find a relatively succinct and coherent official formulation. Even this brief article proceeds with a minimum of system and is chiefly notable for the number of positive and negative symbols that it compresses into a few pages. It is rather the product of a rhetorician than a theoretician. Possibly the doctrinal ideas can be at least partially summarized as follows:

1. Our superior morality comes from success in struggle.

(Fascism) conceives of life as a struggle.

—B. Mussolini
The Doctrine of Fascism, 1932

2. The state is the supreme unit of life and morals.

. . . everything is in the state, and nothing human or spiritual exists, much less has validity, outside the state.

—B. Mussolini
The Doctrine of Fascism, 1932

3. Our goal is the expansion of the state.

. . . the state is organization and expansion.

—B. Mussolini
The Doctrine of Fascism, 1932

4. We repudiate equality.

Fascism . . . affirms the irremediable, fruitful and beneficent inequality of men.

—B. Mussolini
The Doctrine of Fascism, 1932

5. The Fascist state defends religion.

The Fascist state does not remain indifferent to the fact of religion in general and to that particular positive religion which is Italian Catholicism. The state has no theology, but it has an ethic. In the Fascist state religion is looked upon as one of the deepest manifestations of the spirit; it is, therefore, not only respected, but defended and protected.

—B. Mussolini
The Doctrine of Fascism, 1932

6. Our doctrine is true.

The doctrine itself, therefore, must be, not words, but an act of life. Hence, the pragmatic veins in Fascism, its will to power, its will to be, its attitude in the face of the fact of "violence" and of its own courage.

—B. Mussolini
The Doctrine of Fascism, 1932

7. The future is with us.

If the nineteenth was the century of the individual (liberalism meaning individualism) it may be expected that this one may be the century of "collectivism" and therefore the century of the state.

—B. Mussolini
The Doctrine of Fascism, 1932

8. The leader is always to be obeyed.

Mussolini is always right.

—*The Fascist Decalogue*, 1934

In Mussolini's statements a number of terms are given very contrasting plus and minus meaning. On the affirmative side:

Fascism	Will
State	Activism
Totalitarian	Nationalism
Corporations	Collectivism
(corporative system)	Positive
Struggle	Anti-positivism
God	Pragmatism
Italian Catholicism	Discipline
Soul	Leadership
Faith	Order
Inequality	Universality
Empire	Tradition of Rome

Among the negatives:

Scepticism	Liberal
Agnosticism	Masonic
Pessimism	Historical materialism
Passive optimism	Anarchism
The "comfortable" life	Indifferentism
Materialism	Absolutist state
"Happiness" on earth	Tyrannical state

Classical liberalism	Police state
Socialism	Monarchical absolutism
Bolshevism	Feudal privileges
Class struggle	Castes
Class syndicalism	Progress (myth of indefinite)

Certain key symbols appeared in opposite contexts. "Democracy," in the sense of majority rule, is vilified, but in the "purest" sense supported. For example, Fascism is defined as "organized, centralized, authoritarian democracy." In the same way, "individualism" and "individualistic abstractions" are rejected; yet we are told that "the individual is not suppressed, but rather multiplied."

National Socialism, of course, was the doctrine of the most dynamic movement opposed to liberal democracy and Communism. The most influential Nazi writings resembled Fascism in looseness of structure. Some of the foremost propositions may be stated as follows:

1. Our moral authority is derived from the fact of biological superiority.

All that is not race in this world is trash.

—Adolf Hitler,
Mein Kampf, 1925 (p. 406)

2. Our first aim is to prevent racial impurity.

Just as little as Nature desires a mating between weaker individuals and stronger ones, far less she desires the mixing of a higher race with a lower one, as in this case her entire work of higher breeding, which has perhaps taken hundreds of thousands of years, would tumble at one blow.

—Adolf Hitler,
Mein Kampf, 1925 (p. 392)

3. The greatest menace to all races comes from the inferior race, the Jews.

No, the Jew possesses no culture-creating energy whatsoever, as the idealism, without which there can never exist a genuine development of man towards a higher level, does not and never did exist in him.

—Adolf Hitler,
Mein Kampf, 1925 (p. 418)

4. The Jewish method is to encourage weakness by fostering dis-unity and immorality.

For example, "First he uses the *bourgeoisie* as the battle ram against the feudal world, then the worker against the *bourgeois* world. Just as at one time he knew how to gain by sneaking the civil rights for himself in the shadow of the *bourgeoisie,* thus he hopes now that in the worker's fight for his existence, he will find the way towards a leadership of his own."

—Adolf Hitler,
Mein Kampf, 1925 (p. 440)

5. The state is the instrument of the race.

. . . the "folkist" view . . . sees in the State only a means to an end, and as its end it considers the preservation of the racial existence of men.

—Adolf Hitler,
Mein Kampf, 1927 (p. 579)

6. The organization of the state is a natural hierarchy.

The principle . . . of our whole State constitution: authority of every leader towards below and responsibility towards above.

—Adolf Hitler,
Mein Kampf, 1927 (p. 670)

7. The exploitation of any part of the race by other parts of the race, or by other races, is intolerable.

For example, "10. It must be the first duty of every citizen of the State to work with his mind or with his body. The activities of the individual must not clash with the interests of the whole, but must be pursued within the framework of the national activity and must be for the general good. 11. We demand, therefore, the abolition of incomes unearned by work, and emancipation from a slavery of interest charges."

—*The 25 Points Program of the National
Socialist German Workers Party,*
24 February, 1920

8. Our doctrine is true; it is a creation of genius.

. . . for humanity blessing has never lain in the masses, but in its creative heads who therefore in reality have to be looked upon as the benefactors of mankind. It is in the interest of all to safeguard their most decisive influence and to facilitate their activity. Certainly, this interest is not satisfied and is not served by the rule of the masses who are either unable to think or are inefficient, in any case not inspired, but solely by the leadership of those whom Nature has endowed with special gifts.

The selection of these heads is carried out above all . . . by the hard struggle for life.

—Adolf Hitler,
Mein Kampf, 1927 (p. 665)

The following is a brief selection of some of the plus and minus symbols in Nazi doctrine:

Positive	*Negative*
Race	Jew
Blood	Marxism
Folkish	Free Masonry
Führer	Pacifism
Idealism	Materialism
Positive Christianity	Interest Slavery
God	Usurers
Inequality	Majority Rule
	Bourgeois Democrats

National Socialist doctrine employs the term "parliament" to talk about institutions of government that it endorses; at the same time it rejects "liberal and bourgeois and plutocratic parliamentarism." The term "socialist" figures in the very name of the Party, yet it is found in many adverse connotations, such as "social democrat." The term "party" is also included in the designation of the Nazi organization, though "bourgeois" and "revolutionary parties" are stigmatized.

During the prewar period more and more regimes in the West justified their authority in the name of God as interpreted in Roman Catholicism. Hence the political doctrines of Rome have become increasingly important, notably in Ireland, pre-Anschluss Austria, Spain, Portugal, middle and South America. In recent years the Pope has restated the doctrines of the church in a series of official communications, chiefly encyclicals. Some of the basic doctrines of Catholic civil authority may be formulated thus:

1. Our authority is from God.

. . . there can be no public power except from God.
—*Encyclical Immortale Dei,* 1885

2. Our "rule . . . must be just."

The right of rule, however, is not necessarily joined with any special form of government: it may assume either one form or another, provided that it be such as to insure the general welfare.
—*Encyclical Immortale Dei,* 1885

3. . . . Among rulers the Name of God must be holy; and one of their first duties must be to favor religion, to protect it, and to cover it with the authority of the laws, and not to institute or decree anything incompatible with its security.
—*Encyclical Immortale Dei,* 1885

4. God has divided the charge of the human race between two powers, the ecclesiastical and the civil, the one being set over divine and the other over human subjects.
—*Encyclical Immortale Dei,* 1885

5. There are limitations upon the authority of the state.

No human law can abolish the natural and original right of marriage, nor in any way limit the chief and principal purpose of marriage ordained by God's authority from the beginning: increase and multiply.
—*Encyclical Rerum Novarum,* 1891

6. These propositions are true by direct revelation of God's Will and indirectly by the exercise of reason and observation.

And I say to thee: That thou are Peter; and upon this rock I will build my church, and the gates of hell shall not prevail against it.
Matthew, 16:18,
New Testament (Douay).

A very brief list of key symbols is:

Plus

God	Spirit
Pope	Authority
Catholic Church	Private property
Revelation	Family
Soul	Private associations

Minus

Materialism	Revolution
Agnosticism	Totalitarianism
Atheism	

Certain terms acquire a double meaning. Although "liberalism" is usually a negative word; it is also employed in its "true sense." "Democracy" is another term with a double function.

Among the major powers the authority with the most outspoken religious doctrine is Japan. The basic tenets may be surmised as follows:

1. Our authority is from the gods.

We solemnly announce: The Heavenly Deities and the Great Ancestress (Amaterasu Omikami) established the throne and made the succession secure. The line of Emperors in unbroken succession entered into possession thereof and handed it on. Religious ceremonies and government were one and the same (*saisei itchi*) and the innumerable subjects were united.

Imperial Rescript, 1870

2. Our divine mission is to endure forever and to rule the world.

This Reed-plain Land of Fifteen Thousand Autumns of Fair Rice-ears is the country over which my descendants shall be lords. Do thou, my August Grandchild, proceed thither and rule over it. Go! and may prosperity attend thy dynasty, and it shall, like Heaven and Earth, endure forever.

Nihongi

3. Our military power is decisive.

The military might of Japan is always a "divine soldiery that is sent to bring life to all things."

Magota and Hara, "Commentary on the Fundamental Principles of the National Structure," Tokyo, 1940, p. 100

4. Our authority is by revelation.
   (See above.)

Marxist emphasis upon the problems of the low and middle classes in modern society, coupled with objective changes in social structure, led to modifications in traditional liberalism by the incorporation of the doctrine of social security as a recognized individual right. An effort to integrate modern currents of political theory found expression in the *San Min Chu I, The Three Principles of the People,* by Sun Yat-sen, the chief political treatise of the Chinese Republic.

1. We endorse the people's nationalism (*Min-ts'u*).

We must espouse nationalism and in the first instance attain our own unity, then we can consider others and help the weaker, smaller peoples to unite in a common struggle against the two hundred fifty millions (of the powerful European states).

Sun Yat-sen, February 10, 1924

2. We endorse the people's sovereignty (*Min-ch'uan*).

. . . we must distinguish between sovereignty and ability. The foundation of the government of a nation must be built upon the rights of the people, but the administration of government must be entrusted to experts. We must not look upon these experts as stately and grand presidents and ministers, but simply as our chauffeurs, as guards at the gate, as cooks, physicians, carpenters or tailors.

Sun Yat-sen, March 16, 1924

3. We endorse the people's livelihood (*Min sheng*).

Livelihood is the center of government, the center of economics, the center of all historical movements. (Peaceful methods: social and economic reform; nationalization of transportation and communications; direct taxation or the income tax; and socialized distribution or cooperative societies.)

Sun Yat-sen, August 3, 1924

XVI

POPULAR ART

BY

LYMAN BRYSON [1]

When modern critics talk about "popular" art it is often difficult to discover precisely what they are talking about. They show signs of obscure trouble because the ghost of Plato and the ghost of Aristotle stand at their elbows and give them shadowy bad advice. It is out of the ancient tradition that we have derived our canons of judgment and we try to apply them today without much concern for the changes made by modern conditions. Technological change has drastically affected all forms of art. Plato and Aristotle would have been interested in these changes; they could not prophesy them.

By popular art, I mean something different from what has been talked about in the books on esthetics. It is an element in our culture of considerable importance and not to be dismissed, I think, because it happens not to be the sort of thing that critics have been trained to admire. We can begin by distinguishing the popular from the other kinds. I would suggest that there are three categories of which popular art is one. The other two are fine art and folk art.

The definitions are for working purposes and cannot claim to satisfy everybody. But let *fine art* be the name we give to the art in which the creator conveys emotion by means of design. He will do other things also, of course, but that is his purely esthetic purpose, the creation of "beauty." The secondary and sociological characteristics of this kind will include these: That the creator will concede little to his audience, expecting appreciation to come to him. That

[1] The substance of this chapter was published in *The Saturday Review of Literature,* 30, May, 1947, 19.

his patterns whether in color, form, sound, plot, character, or any other element of design will be his own invention. That authorship generally will be single and claimed as an honor. That the artist's purpose will be primarily in creation itself.

By *folk art,* for our purposes here, we mean the kind of creative activity that develops in local, partly self-conscious cultures. The patterns are conventional; variation is slight. Authorship may be impersonal. The skills called for are common although their high development is necessarily rare. The purposes are ritualistic, as in altar embroideries; social, as in improvised ballads; utilitarian, as in pots.

By *popular art* we mean creative work that measures success by the size of its audience and the profit it brings to its makers. The patterns are likely to be conventional although they use varying content and escape routine. Authorship is notorious and is kept as public as possible for the sake of gain. The skills needed may be fairly common, as in folk art, but their high development is rare.

It is not possible to get rid of the problem of popular art by concluding that whatever has neither the beauty of fine art, nor the dignity and human meaning of folk art, has therefore no value at all. Nor can we escape the problem by saying that popular art is important only in so far as it contains, even by accident, the elements of beauty. The fact remains that great numbers of people in our culture spend hours of their time in consuming these delights. If it is not a question of esthetics it is still sociology and (here Plato's ghost rears his head) it may be morals.

Sociologically speaking, popular art is a product of the machine age. It was not possible until we had cheap print and the cinema and broadcasting, each one of these means of mass communication coming along in turn. Their effect was cumulative. They made it possible for millions upon millions to enjoy vicarious living. They cost so much and were produced on such a scale that they had to appeal to huge audiences which meant that they found low common denominators of interest and taste. Above all, and this was crucially decisive in setting their character, they used up invented material so fast that no possible supply of "artistic" talent could keep up with the demand. What is quickly done is likely to go quickly; popular songs are short-lived and when they are broadcast they are snow on the desert's face. A new song is always needed and a new story; if possible a new idea, although it almost never is really a new idea.

This voraciousness of the mass media will help to explain in part the qualities of popular art. But this art has another more important characteristic. In order to get its mass audience, popular art in any medium must always tell a story. It must be fiction. In more technical terms, it must be representational. As far as the evidence goes, we can be quite sure that any art that did not have a large element of explicit representation could not be popular.

So this kind of art offers the consumer a chance to identify himself with characters in the story. The enjoyment of it is day dreaming, by a plot more logical than a sleepy passive mind could devise. It is day dreaming with a trusted guide. And a good many limitations on this kind of art are the result of this full representation. Ironies are dangerous if not impossible. I once asked the shrewd editor of a cheap magazine the first element of success in his kind of merchandizing and he replied, "Always be serious." For much the same reason, fantasy is tiresome unless it has a realistic accoutrement. The fairy tale set in a place that looks like the corner drug store and with characters that look like neighborhood people is acceptable while a realistic tale of Burma or Siberia might not be. What is wanted is a plausible drama in which the consumer can imagine himself taking part and it must have a plot that does not, in its denouement at least, offend his moral taste.

If, in addition to an explicit and concluded day dream, the consumer can get some of the elements more properly called "fine," no harm is done. He may even enjoy the broadcast serial, or the movie, or the magazine tale, a little more for the emotion that comes of meeting beauty. There are natural instincts for this kind of happiness, no doubt, in all of us, although they seem not to count for much unless they are trained. I am not speaking now of the insertion of something beautiful into a piece of popular art, as when Iturbi breaks into the pattern of a movie with a few moments of music. That is something different and may be good for other reasons. Nor do I mean to forget that some men who have created successful popular art can also be great artists by the strict conventional canons. There are examples like Gershwin and Walt Disney and many more. These considerations do not change the principle that the essential elements of popular art, as I am now using the word to describe something real and important and distinguishable in our present culture, lie in its presentation of a tale with a moral by which anyone can get outside himself for a time and expand his experience for his own virtuous self-understanding.

To get back to the difficulty of the critic who tries to judge this phenomenon, peculiar to our times, by canons of another stage in cultural development, we can imagine Plato and Aristotle in a modern movie theater. We can imagine them, disguised by darkness, watching a vividly photographed and competently acted modern story. It makes little difference what the story is. They would both be wondering what was happening to hundreds of men and women and boys and girls who sat together in that magic darkness seeing themselves do deeds of courage and cleverness, sweeping up rewards of honor and romance. Plato, I think, would be wondering if it was good experience. Aristotle would be wondering if it was good art. Since we judge everything else that we call art by the traditional versions of their attitudes we can at least understand our own judgments on popular art better if we try to guess what they would be thinking and why.

We can be aware of the fact that as time goes on it is harder, not easier, to say just what the ancients thought about any question because the more study we have, the more different interpretations. Aristotle apparently did believe in an effect he called purgation, and after a good deal of esthetic theorizing it has become evident, I think, that Aristotle did not, in talking about purgation, mean to abandon his essential position that art is for art's sake or for beauty's sake. The truth of his idea of purgation then would lie not in one's imaginary bearing of all the suffering laid upon a tragic hero but rather in one's much more subtle response to the artist's presentation. This is probably another way of saying that while we respond to great tragedy both emotionally and intellectually, our response is not mere vicarious experience nor sympathy for the pitiable spectacle of a human being in distress; it is response to beauty in the design. Our own emotions and recognitions are possibly part of the design to which we respond. Purgation comes on the esthetic level and not in the grosser and more obvious elements of sympathetic feeling. A great tragedy proves its greatness by the exaltation that lifts us out of ourselves, and out of all ordinary existence, and transcends the suffering we have shared with the protagonist. On the level of vicarious experience alone, no such exaltation would seem to be possible.

So Aristotle in the movie theater would be looking for a work of fine art. He would be judging the movie by its logical consistencies; the balance of character elements. He would be seeking something to respond to emotionally but it would not be to the obvious vicissitudes of the heroine. Out of that he would not be getting much purgation. The esthetic elements in the movie are probably pretty thin. There is not much logic. The design is carelessly tied up at the end. The issues are not significant; the action is not of a certain "size." The emotions are those that can be aroused by a quick appeal to the ludicrous or the pathetic. One can be reasonably sure that Aristotle would not consider the laughter and tears of his companions the kind of purgation that makes art a noble experience.

Plato, being an older and sadder and quite possibly a wiser man, is unhappy for a different reason. He takes it for granted that the imaginary life that is enjoyed with tears and laughter by the people around him is precisely the purpose of the whole institution. People have come to the theater to be absorbed for a time in the affairs of imaginary persons and they are quite properly letting themselves be swept on by the story. Plato's unhappiness would be because he would, as he listened and looked, pass judgment on all the moral implications in what was happening on the screen. He would look for some profound or noble concept of life's purposes, exemplified in the chief characters, and he would probably fail to find them. He would look for attitudes of heroic devotion to the institutions and the ideals of the culture, exemplified and praised and rewarded in the fable, and all that would seldom happen. He would look for examples of high-mindedness and unselfishness and civic understand-

ing and they would be mostly missing. So Aristotle would be unhappy in a mediocre movie because it was bad art; Plato would be
unhappy because it was bad teaching.

There appears to be no other way of judging popular art. The
true esthetes, of course, would like to banish all but fine art and folk
art. They would allow only masterpieces or unpretentious routine
products. They talk and write about getting "back" to a time when
popular taste was simple and "sound." By that they mean they
would prefer to have no one ever express an opinion about beauty
or the imagination who was not a trained appreciator. The rest of
the "folk" could get along with pots and jingles in their own quaint
fashion.

The people, however, continue to enjoy their own popular tastes,
and they do have standards of excellence. Their kind of art is possible only because modern technology has produced mass communication. As has been said, all forms of mass communication are
monstrously voracious; they use up material at such a rate that
standards of excellence, in the fine art sense, cannot be maintained.
Where then do standards come from! If there was anything like
popular art in the "folk" days it was probably in neighborhood
gossip.

The appetite for moral tales, for romancing, for imagining the
texture of the lives of other people, on other levels of comfort or
conduct, is not itself a result of modern conditions. It must have
been indulged somehow in older and simpler times. Men and
women, perhaps especially the women, had to have the fun of talking about the neighbors, or the rich people who lived on the hill in
the big castle, or the boys who had gone to the wars. There was
folk art also in those days, of course. The fairy tales were fun to
recall and to tell to the children; the myths were awesome or reassuring. The tales of the saints were inspiring. But they all had the
same quality of convention, of routine and of repetition. It was the
talk of the men in the tap room or of the women at the spinning
wheels that provided something like the popular art of today, vicarious living in freshly told stories, all on old patterns, made up
of moral problems solved without moral struggle, of malice toward

the rich and condescension toward the poor, of naïve surrender to the delight of living in someone else's life where problems are simpler and grief is less wearing and love is real. This is the *poesis* of common life.

That the sources of today's popular art lie in yesterday's gossip is no more, at present, than a guess. The important point is that today's popular art did not come out of yesterday's fine art. It is not a degenerate form of yesterday's fine art as the esthetes fear it is, nor is it degeneration of yesterday's folk art. It is something developed out of natural social habits and needs by the machine. It exploits something in the lives of the common people that was there before the machine came but was then of much less extent and power.

Whatever it comes out of, the substance of popular art is always fiction and it always has a moral. It is easier, in other words, to change it to satisfy Plato's objections than it would be to meet the criticisms of Aristotle. There will always be difficulties. Loose thinking is easier than rigorous thinking. Cheap emotions are easier to arouse than fine ones. Crude attacks on the attention of the general public are the first to succeed even if they do not last. What appeals to many, and appeals easily, is not likely to be delicate or oblique or ironic or reticent. And these are difficulties from Plato's point of view as well as when the work is judged by the canons of beauty because they make necessary a dangerous breadth and force and may lead the artist into sacrificing meaning for effect. But the objections that Plato might make to a modern example of popular art would be objections that the consumer of that kind of art would understand. I am afraid he would not know what Aristotle was talking about.

We have high authority then for the principle that a piece of modern popular art is to be judged by what it says about life as a moral struggle, by what it teaches. It may often fail but we can at least be good enough critics to judge it by what it tries to do and not by something else.

We may say in passing that it is not from our ancient canons that we would get any depreciation of these stories on the ground that they were escape. They are escape, of course. That is one of their chief purposes. To be quite realistic, psychologically speaking, we probably ought to arrange our movie goers along a continuum, in the order of the degree of attention that they give to the entertainment. There are some, no doubt, who want to be surrounded by a vacuum of indifference and they find it easier to be indifferent inside a theater than on a park bench or in bed. They mark the bottom of the scale. They are not really carried out of themselves; they only want a temporary Lethe. At the other end are the passionate appreciators who brood for hours afterward on the fate of the wicked and glow with borrowed happiness for the happy ending. In between, somewhere, go the sapling minds that are not much concerned with the story but are lost in love of the actors. They are a different problem, also pedagogical no doubt, but not to be threshed out here.

As for the appreciators, they are the ones who send wedding cakes, real wedding cakes and often very good ones, into a radio station when they hear on the air that some daytime serial heroine is going at last to be married. They know well enough that the girl is a character in a play but they have to express somehow their intense absorption in the unrolling of her fate. And no doubt there is also in their minds a confused or ambivalent interest in the actress who plays the part and likes pastry. The intensity of the experience and the depth of response is, we see, a response to realistic representation and a gratitude for vicarious expansion of one's own life. Escape on any level is a natural and honorable way of living a part of one's life. There may be neurotic escape; just as there may be neurotic effort. But within healthy limits, it is the quality of the world escaped into that counts. What the moralists and the philosophers, following Plato, have insisted on is that escape should be into a world of the imagination where the dreamer can get refreshment, pleasure, release, and not only these things which he seeks but also some new understanding even if it be no more than a restored wholesome love of commonplace friends and ordinary things.

It should be quite clear by now that I am not talking about the popularizing of art that is great or fine. However, since we acknowledge that the strictly defined esthetic experiences are possible in greater or less degree to all men, it must be that fine art can be made more popular if the right devices can be found. It would remain something different from popular art. The strategy for this pedagogical task, which is no more than applying in mass communication what is used to train the individual, even a member of the elite, in his artistic perceptions, may be found in studying the popular response to those great ones who are both creators of beauty and friends of the crowd. They mix representation, and vicarious moral experience, in with patterns of beauty.

Is it possible to mix patterns of beauty into what is offered the crowd as a story? I spoke previously of a bit of Chopin played by Iturbi in the midst of a rather silly tale produced as conventional Hollywood popular art. If we take the long view it might well be that Mr. Iturbi is doing more for wider appreciation of music, music as a fine art, that is, by putting Chopin into this unexpected place than he would be by giving a concert in Carnegie Hall. This is not said in any ironic comment on Mr. Iturbi's piano playing. I admire it. In fact, it is because it is still manly, appreciative and skillful playing that it is useful for pedagogical purposes in a movie. The device is to hold and satisfy the customers with the real thing they came for, a story, and to expose them to music.

The reason for the device is that fine art, even in music, is made rather formidable, these days, by the paraphernalia of the appreciators and by the pageantry of its presentation. A great many people do not know whether or not they like good music because they have never really heard any. It is cruel nonsense, of course, to say they do not like it when in fact they have never had a chance. But if they are exposed, especially in these brief and painless bits, tney can and often do discover quite unsuspected responses in themselves. The whole modern development of good music is a proof of that fact. Making fine art popular may, therefore, be an enterprise in adult education that is helped by the judicious use of popular art as a vehicle. This is, I repeat, very different from the effort to make popular art into something esthetically fine. That attempt is dangerous; the pseudo-fine is the worst of all the art varieties. But it is well not to forget that taste is not a ladder but an escalator. Wherever you get on you move upward—provided the escalator is going up—because it is natural to like better and better things as your experience is expanded and you are exposed to better and better things.

What I have been saying can be summed up in this: that we cannot judge popular art as if it were trying to be something else. All parties concerned are basically satisfied to have it judged by its moral lessons. Some of the creators may occasionally retreat into a quite shallow art for art's sake defense if they are accused of corrupting the young; the consumers always know what the game is all about and the creators will boast of their moral influence if they dare. If we have to follow either of the main stems of European thought about such matters we can at a respectful distance follow Plato, the moralist. "Shall we make a law?" says the Athenian in *The Laws,* "that the poet shall compose nothing contrary to the ideas of the lawful, or just, or beautiful, or good, which are allowed in the state?"

Most of the consumers of popular art would answer, "No, not a law. We don't like laws about such things." But they would approve the principle nevertheless, and would enforce it by their patronage. We can develop our canons in good Platonic fashion out of that.

CONTRIBUTORS TO
"THE COMMUNICATION OF IDEAS"

LYMAN BRYSON, LL.D. (Occidental), *Professor of Education, Teachers College, Columbia University; Counsellor on Public Affairs, Columbia Broadcasting System.*

JAMES M. CLARKE, B.A. (Pomona), *Editor-in-Charge Readability Laboratory*

JOSEPH M. GOLDSEN, B.B.A. (College of the City of New York), *Vice President, Nejelski & Company, Inc.*

LENNOX GREY, PH.D (Chicago), *Professor of English and Head, Department of the Teaching of English and Foreign Languages, Teachers College, Columbia University.*

WENDELL JOHNSON, PH.D (Iowa), *Professor of Psychology and Speech Pathology; Director, Speech Clinic, State University of Iowa.*

HAROLD D. LASSWELL, PH.D. (Chicago), *Professor of Law, The Law School, Yale University.*

PAUL F. LAZARSFELD, PH.D. (Vienna), *Professor of Sociology, Columbia University; Director, Bureau of Applied Social Research.*

ROBERT D. LEIGH, PH.D. (Columbia), *Director, Commission on Freedom of the Press; Visiting Professor of Political Science, University of Chicago.*

IRVING LORGE, PH.D. (Columbia), *Professor of Education and Executive Officer, Institute of Psychological Research, Teachers College, Columbia University.*

MARGARET MEAD, PH.D. (Columbia), *Associate Curator of Ethnology, American Museum of Natural History.*

ROBERT K. MERTON, PH.D. (Harvard), *Professor of Sociology, Columbia University; Associate Director, Bureau of Applied Social Research.*

LEO NEJELSKI, B.A. (Michigan), *President, Nejelski & Company, Inc.*

WHITNEY J. OATES, PH.D. (Princeton), *Ewing Professor of Greek; Chairman, Department of Classics; Chairman, Divisional Program in the Humanities, Princeton University.*

CHARLES A. SIEPMANN, B.A. (Oxford), *Professor of Education; Director of the Film Library; Chairman, Department of Communications in Education, New York University.*

INDEX

Abstractions, high and low orders of, 70ff.

Action, stimulus to, 16f.; *see also* Reaction

Adult education, media for, 207

Advertising, use of prestige symbols, 20f., 102; and responsibility, 22; deference to social norms, 114f.

Afferent-efferent impulses, 41f.

Allee, Warder C., *Animal Aggregations,* 39n; *The Social Life of Animals,* 39n

American Association for Adult Education, 159

Anglo-American relations, techniques in the communication of ideas, 211ff.; sources of friction, 215ff.

Anthropology, analytical techniques in mass communication, 209ff.

Anxiety, and speech defects, 59

Arapesh, 10ff.; contrasted with Manus, 13f.

Architecture, 129ff.

Aristotle, vs. modern art forms, 277ff.

Art forms, standards for mass media, 111; for the public, 119ff., 277ff.; purity of, 122ff.; "the literary taint" in, 125ff.; conditions of popular acceptance, 128f.; functional usefulness, 130, 134; need of new social esthetic, 132ff.; mass production, 133ff.

Atomic research, policy orientation, 234f.; proposed institute for, 236ff.

Attention, structure of, and the social structure, 247f.; studies of, 247ff.; and environment, 252ff.; general theory, 255ff.

"Attention frames," 40f.

Audience, vast size of American, 99

Automobile, social effect of, 99

Bali, 14ff.

Ballad, function in communication, 40

Barzun, Jacques, *Of Human Freedom,* 119, 121

Basic English, 93

Bateson, Gregory, "Bali," 14n; *Civilian Morale,* 212n; "Social Planning and the Concept of Deutero-Learning," 20n; "Some Systematic Approaches to the Study of Culture and Personality," 212n

—— and Margaret Mead, "Principles of Morale Building," 210n

Behavior, as reaction to environmental stimuli, 38f.; speech frustration and, 53ff.; affected by the enforcement of social norms, 102ff.; in response to varied stimuli, 148; the writer's purpose to effect changes in, 157; emotional reactions, 180; evaluation of contrasts in, 222f.; parent-child relationship in England and America, 213f.

Belo, J., "A Study of Customs Pertaining to Twins in Bali," 15n

Benedict, Ruth, *The Chrysanthemum and the Sword,* 209n; "The Study of Cultural Patterns in European Nations," 210n

Bigness, an American criterion of value, 218

Bill of Rights, on freedom of the press, 198

Boasting vs. understatement, 214f.

Brewster, Owen, quoted, 226

Broadcasting, *see* Radio broadcasting

Bryce, James, *The American Commonwealth,* 104n; quoted, 110n

Bryson, Lyman, 28, 159; radio program, 107f.

289

Bullying, Anglo-American attitude toward, 212f.
Burke, Kenneth, *Attitudes toward History,* quoted, 114
Business, use of mass propaganda, 143 ff.; and the public interest, 182ff.

Calendar, Balinese, 15
Canalization of advertising, 114f.
Catholic Church, *see* Roman Catholic Church
Censorship, 198; *see also* Press, freedom of the
Characteristics, physical, adverse effect of, 61f.
Children, parent-child relationship, 213f.
Childs, H. L., and J. B. Whitton, eds., *Propaganda by Short Wave,* 251n
Christian Science Monitor, 206
Churchill, Winston, quoted, 18
Clark, Colin, *The Economics of 1960,* 246n
Class names, unreflective use of, 69f.
Classical education, value of, 28f.
Collier, John, "United States Indian Administration . . . ," 233n
Columbia Broadcasting System, 189
Commission on Freedom of the Press, 197n; report: *A Free and Responsible Press,* 248n
Communication, social and personal importance of, 2f.; media of, 28, 42 (*see also* Mass media); process of, *diagram,* 56; hindered by societal groupings, 200f.
Communications Act (1943), 182f., 185
Communicator, the, 41, 48; necessary qualities, 147; effect of status of, 148; choice of experiences to be communicated, 160f.; *see also* Speaker, the
Communism, doctrine of, 266ff.
Competition, in communication media, 202f.
Comprehensibility, in writing, 159ff.
Comprehension, test of, 80ff., 87ff.
Compromise, attitude toward, 223f.
Content, analysis of, 38ff., 250
Cooper, Gary, 136

Coughlin, Father, 115
"Crusades," *see* Reform movements
Cultural exchanges, 42; difficulties of, 4f.
Cultural institutions, 244ff.; class groups, 256f.
Cultural standards, changing locus of responsibility for, 192f.
Currier and Ives, 135

Dali, Salvador, 141
Darwin, Charles, *re* Greek and Latin, 2
Definition of terms, limitations of, 55f.
Democracy, doctrines of, 265f.
Democratic principles, as basis of mass propaganda, 144f.; ignorance and apathy vs., 187f.; and enlightened public opinion, 248
Deutero learning, 20
Dewey, John, 170; *Art as Experience,* quoted, 132; *Freedom and Culture,* quoted, 177
Disney, Walt, 133f.
Dobbs, H. A. C., *Operational Research and Action Research,* 233n
Documentary films, 207
Dos Passos, John, *Manhattan Transfer,* quoted, 139f.

Eaton, Helen, "Semantic Frequency List for English, French, German, and Spanish," 92
Economic theory, 254f.
Education, and cultural standards, 192f.
Efficiency, in communication, 46ff.; in staging, 62
Emotional reactions, 180; in primitive societies, 11ff.
Empson, William, quoted, 95f.
England, control of radio, 106; parent-child relationship contrasted with American, 213ff.
English language, 66
Enlightenment, principle of equivalent, 50f.; public, 231; distribution of, 247; and the suppression of bad news, 263
Environment, behavior in reaction to, 38ff., 43f.; specialization of response

to, 38ff.; mechanical control of, 219; attention analysis and, 252ff.

Euclid, 170f.

Equivalencies in communication, 38f., 41ff.

Espionage, 45

Evaluation, affected by identification and projection, 72ff.; need for new methods of, 153f.; of radio programs, 187f.; American vs. British criteria, 214f., 218; of contrasting behavior, 222f.

Experience, choice of apt words to express, 167ff.

Experimental Division for the Study of Wartime Communications, 259

Fairbanks, Helen, "The Quantitative Differentiation of Samples of Spoken Language," 66

Familiarity, 134; effect of, 128; use of the principle of, 170ff.

Fascism, doctrines of, 268ff.

Fatigue, and attention, 253f.

Fear, effect of, 180

Federal Communications Commission, 184f.; report (1946), 181, 186f.; "Bluebook" (1946), 191, 194; "Chain Broadcasting Report" (1940), 187; "Public Service Responsibility of Broadcast Licensees," 186

Fiji Islands, form of insult, 227

Fine arts, vs. popular art, 120f.; as language, 124ff.; American attitude toward, 132

Fisk University, 18n

FitzGibbon, Constantin, "The Man of Fear," 25n

Flesch, Rudolf, *The Art of Plain Talk,* 65, 165f.

Folk art, 277ff.

"Food Habits, The Problem of Changing," 210n

Fortune, R. F., "Arapesch," 10n

—— "Manus Religion," 13n

Foster, Stephen, 136

Fox, W. T. R., *The Super-Powers,* 262

Freedom of the press, 197ff.; objectives, 204; methods of promoting, 206ff.;

A Free and Responsible Press, 248n

Freedom of speech, and mass communication, 197ff.

Freshman, university, language analysis of, 66

Friedmann, Georges, *Problèmes humain du mechanisme industriel,* 253n

Game (word), meanings, 92

Gannett, Lewis, 202

Gardner, Burleigh, 233

Georgias (Plato), 29; quoted, 31f.

Germany, "Round Table on Germany after the War," 209n; land ownership, 246; *see also* National Socialism

Gershwin, George, 136

Girls, sex behavior, Anglo-American differences in, 216f.

Gorer, Geoffrey, 227; "Themes in Japanese Culture," 209n

Government, role in private enterprise and public interest, 182

Great Britain, real production, 246

Greek, educational value of, 2

Greenleaf, Floyd, 61

Harper's, 207

Hayakawa, S. I., *Language in Action,* 68n

Hitler, Adolf, 96

Hobbes, 258n

Homer, Winslow, 135

Human factors, in business communication, 144, 147f.

Humanities, the, 125

Ideas, Plato's theory of, 29f.

Identification, undue, as a disorder in communication, 69ff.

Ideologies, societal, 44f.

Ignorance, a barrier to effective communication, 47; disturbances due to, 67f.; and popular judgment, 187

Illiteracy, 247

Indian Affairs, Bureau of, 233f.

Individual, the, responsibility of, for appropriate action, 16ff.; verbalization of tensions, 64f.; projection of experience, 71ff.; effect of speech disorders, 76ff.;

Individual (*continued*)
  personal concern of, 148f.; appeal to, in the personal pronoun, 174; freedom of speech, 203f.
Industrial uses of mass propaganda, 143ff.
Industry, concentration of shareholdings, 246f.; worker responses to propaganda, 252ff.
Institute for Cultural Studies, 209n
Institute on Atomic Policy, proposed, 234ff.
Institutions, cultural, 244ff.
Instructive elements, the, in writing propaganda, 157ff.
Insult, Fijian form of, 227
Intellectual reaction, vs. emotional, 14; as a criterion of effectiveness, 46f.
Interest, as a factor in understanding, 86
International relationships, anthropological techniques in propaganda *re*, 209ff.
Isolationism, 179f.
Iturbi, José, 285

Jacques, E., ed., "Social Therapy," 233n
Japan, religious doctrines of, 275f.
Jefferson, Thomas, quoted, 180
Johnson, Charles S., ed., *Education and the Cultural Process*, 18n
Johnson, Wendell, 161; *People in Quandaries*, 56n, 68n

Kaplan, Abraham, 44n
Keynes, John Maynard, *The General Theory of Employment, Interest and Money*, 254
Knowledge, the instructive elements in propaganda, 157; the communicator's assumption of, on the part of the listener, 165; increase of, through scientific concern with social policy, 232ff.; *see also* Enlightenment
Korzybski, Alfred, *Science and Sanity*, 68f.
Kris, Ernest, "Some Problems of War Propaganda," 18n
—— Hans Speier, *et al.*, *German Radio Propaganda*, 251
Kuznets, Simon, *National Income*, 246n

Land ownership, concentration of, 246
Langer, Susanne K., *Philosophy in a New Key*, quoted, 126f.
Language, teaching of, 2; as a communal symbol, 3; Anglo-American problems, 217ff.
Lasswell, Harold D., 44n; *World Politics Faces Economics*, 262n
—— and A. Kaplan, *The Science of Politics*, 244n
—— and Myres S. McDougal, "Legal Education and Public Policy," 233n, 243n
Latin, educational value of, 2
Lazarsfeld, Paul F., and Harry Field, *The People Look at Radio*, 24n, 184n
Lazarsfeld, Paul F., *et al.*, *The People's Choice*, 255
Lee, Irving J., *Language Habits in Human Affairs*, 68n
Leighton, Alexander H., *The Governing of Men*, 233n
Leisure, use of, 100, 177f.
Leites, N. C., 260n
Lewin, Kurt, 232f.; "Action Research and Minority Problems," 233n
—— and P. Grabbe, eds., "Problems of Re-Education," 233n
Lippitt, R., and M. Radke, "New Trends in the Investigations of Prejudice," 233n
Listener, the, distorted interpretations by, 56ff.; evaluation of the speaker, 73; assumption of the knowledge of, 84f., 149f., 165; conditions of receptivity, 150f.; responsibility for radio standards, 187f.
Literature, American novels, 138ff.
Longfellow, Henry Wadsworth, *Divina Commedia*, quoted, 129
Long-range objectives, 144f.
Lorge and Thorndike, Semantic Count, 93
Lorge system, 165
Lowell, Lawrence, 104
Lucidity, 164f.

MacKenzie, Helen F., *Understanding Picasso*, 123

Malinowski, 102
Mannheim, Karl, 44n
Manus, 13f.
Mass communication, 6f., 9ff., 36, 42, 95ff.; sentiment groups, 49f.; definition of, 80; social concern with, 95ff.; objectives, 149; narcotizing effect, 105; deference to social norms, 107; supplementation through face to face contacts, 115; responsibility to the public, 204f.
Mass media, ownership and operation, 106f.; self-established standards, 206; and public attention, 247f.; analysis of listener exposure to, 249; attention-getting functions, 249
Massachusetts Institute of Technology, 233
Mathematics for the Million, 173
Mayo, Elton, 233; *The Human Problems of an Industrial Civilization,* 233n, 254n
Mead, George Herbert, *Mind, Self and Society,* 264n; quoted, 122, 126
Mead, Margaret, "Administrative Contributions to Democratic Character Formation at the Adolescent Level," 15n; *And Keep Your Powder Dry,* 212n; "Anthropological Techniques in War Psychology," 210n; *Growing Up in New Guinea,* 13n; "Kinship in the Admiralties," 13n; "Our Educational Emphasis in Primitive Perspective," 18n; *Sex and Temperament among Three Primitive Societies,* 10n; "The Mountain Arapesh," 10n
—— ed., *Cooperation and Competition among Primitive Peoples,* 10n, 13n
Meaning, choice of words for, 160ff.
Media, suitability of, 152f.
"Men of Distinction," 102
Merriam, Charles F., 44n
Metraux, Rhoda, "Qualitative Attitude Analysis," 210n
Miller, Justin, 181, 189
Milne, Sir John Wardlaw, quoted, 227
Milton, John, quoted, 219
Minorities, 233n; and radio, 190f.; appropriate behavior toward, 223f.

Misinterpretation, 79ff.
Misunderstanding, 67f.; Anglo-American, 215f.
Monopolization, of public interest, 113
Morris, Charles, *Signs, Language and Behavior,* 264n; quoted, 127
Mosca, Gaetano, 44n
Moving pictures, characters as symbols, 136ff.; and music, 140; concentration of ownership, 202; self-regulation within, 206; as art forms, 281f.
Mumford, Lewis, *The Culture of Cities,* 120n
Murphy, Donald R., tests of readability, 86ff.
Murray, Henry A., and Clyde K. Kluckhohn, *Personality in Nature, Society and Culture,* 15n
Music, symbolic nature of, 126f.; mass communication of, 136; and moving pictures, 140

Narcotizing dysfunction of mass media, 105f.
Nast, Thomas, 104
National Association of Broadcasters, 181, 184
National Economic Committee, U.S. Senate, 246
National Institute of Industrial Psychology (England), 233
National Nutrition Program, 22f.
National Socialists, doctrines of, 271ff.; control by monopolization of mass media, 113
Nejelski and Company, 233
Nervous system, effect of impaired transmission, 75
New Guinea, communication among primitive tribes, 11ff.
Newspapers, prestige values, 101; concentration of ownership, 201f.; attention-getting functions analyzed, 249; *see also* Freedom of the press; Press
New York Academy of Sciences, 209n
New York *Times,* 206; prestige value, 101; and the Tweed Ring, 104

Nightingale, Florence, as a value symbol, 20f.
Novels, American, 138f.

Oratory, use of, among the Manus, 14
Ownership, of media, concentration of, 201f.; land, concentration of, 246

Parent-child relationships, 213f.
Park, Robert E., *Masse und Publikum*, 49n
Parsons, Talcott, "The Problem of Controlled Institutional Change," 209n
Pepys, 164
Personal contact, to supplement mass propaganda, 116f.
Personal pronouns, 174
Personality, *see* Individual
Persuasion, 157f.
Phaedras (Plato), 29, 32ff.; quoted, 34f.
Picasso, 123, 142
Plato, theory of communication, 27ff.; *re,* the sculptor's task, 124; vs. modern art forms, 277ff.
Policy-making, leadership in, 231ff.
Political doctrine, world survey (1939), 265ff.
Popular idol, creation of, by mass media, 114
Power, preservation of, through communication, 45; totalitarian monopoly of, 247; attention control and, 258; balancing of, 261f.
Power groups, use of mass media, 96
Pre-scientific orientation, disturbances due to, 68ff.
Press, changes in size and character, 201f.; self-discipline, 205f.; self-establishment of standards, 206f.; *see also* Freedom of the press; Newspapers
Prestige, conferral function of mass media, 101; effect of the communicator's status, 148; class structure of, 246; elite vs. non-elite, 256f.; *see also* Values
Priestley, J. B., 162; *Bright Day,* quoted, 134
Primitive societies, 10ff.
Printing, and Puritanism, 130

Projection, of individual experience, 71ff.
Propaganda, uses of, 18ff.; power of, 19; totalitarian use of, 19; control of, 24; industrial uses of, 96; for social objectives, 112ff.; democratic principles as basis of, 144f.; war, anthropological techniques in, 210; war uses of, 251; *see also* Mass communication
Prose, main characteristics of readable, 159
Psychiatrist, response to the patient's projection, 73
Public, apathy of, 248
Public administration, policy-oriented research, 233f.
Public exposure, in the enforcement of social norms, 102ff.; the Tweed Ring, 104
Public interest, radio and the, 182ff.; responsibility toward, 231
Public opinion, mobilization by radio and press, 191f.; leadership in molding of, 231ff.
Publishing, *see* Newspapers; Press, the; Printing
Puritanism, and printing, 130

Quiz Kids, 67

Radio, emotional reaction to, 13; influence of, 177; and the public interest, 182ff.; and public satisfaction, 185f.; listener responsibility for program standards, 187f.; and minority interests, 190f.; public apathy toward, 191; local station responsibility, 191; concentration of ownership, 202
Reactions, emotional, 11ff., 180; intellectual, 14, 46f.
Readability, 86f.; measurement of, 165f., 172
Reading, motives for, 172ff.
Reading habits, studies of, 249f.
Realism, in communication, 262ff.
Receptivity, conditions of, 150ff.
Redfield, Robert, *Tepoztlan,* 41n
Reform movements, social effects of, 99f.
Relay, link in, 48
Religious doctrines, 273ff.

Republic (Plato), 33

Research, by leadership groups, 232ff.

Responsibility, in the use of propaganda, 20ff.; individual, in the public interest, 182; of teachers, *re* radio, 192f.; of the press to the public, 204

Rhetoric, dialectical, 35f.

Richards, I. A., *Pocket Book of Basic English*, 65

—— and C. K. Ogden, 65

Rockwell, Norman, 135

Roethlisberger, F. T., and W. G. Dickson, *Management and the Worker*, 253n

Rogers, Ginger, 136

Roman Catholic Church, doctrines of civil authority, 273ff.

"Round Table on Germany after the War," 209n

Rousseau, 258n

Sapir, Edward, "Communication," quoted, 120

Saturday Evening Post, 166

Schaffner, Bertram, *Father Land*, 25n

Schizophrenic patients, language analysis of, 66

Secret service, *see* Espionage

Seldes, Gilbert, *The Seven Lively Arts*, 119

Semantics, 54, 160; and disturbances of speech, 63ff.; violations of principles of, 68; use of class names, 69f.; frequency count of words, 92

Sensitivity, communicator's need of, 148f.

Sentiment groups, 49f.

Sex behavior, Anglo-American misunderstandings *re*, 216ff.

Schismogenesis, 212ff.

"Science at Work," radio program, 214n

Short wave broadcasting, 207

Showmanship, *see* Staging

Skill, factors of, 47

Slang, 81

Slogan, 258f.

Smith, Bruce I., Harold D. Lasswell, and Ralph D. Casey, *Propaganda Communication, and Public Opinion*, 37n, 126, 249n

Smith, Kate, 113

Social conflict, 45ff.

Social control, media for acquiring, 96ff.

Social norms, enforcement of, 102ff.; deference of mass media to, 107

Social objectives, propaganda for, 112ff.; radio and, 178ff.; scientific concern with, 231ff.; leadership and policy-making, 231ff.

Speaker, the, effect of characteristics of, 61f.; consciousness of projection, 72f.; method of avoiding misinterpretation, 81; and knowledge of his audience, 84f., 149, 165

Speech, frustration, 53ff.; defects, 58ff., 65f.; effect of impaired transmission by nervous system, 75f.

Stagefright, 59f.

Staging, effective, 62

Standards, establishment of, in mass media, 206; American vs. British, 218f.

Status value, *see* Prestige

Stout, Rex, quoted, 172f.

Streamlining, 137

Stuttering, 58ff., 63

"Sucker" (term), 224ff.; American attitude toward, 224ff.

Sun Yat-sen, *San Min Chu I*, 276

Surveillance, *see* Espionage

"Sustaining programs," 186

Symbols, of values, use of, 20ff.; religious, use of, 22; irresponsibility in use of, 22ff.; of reference, 49f.; political, 265ff.

Taste, popular, 108f.; effect of mass media upon, 97; radio programs and, 188ff.; and art forms, 277ff.

Tavistock Institute, 233

Teachers, responsibility for mobilizing opinion *re* the radio, 192f.

Teachers College, 159

Technical terms, care in the use of, 150

Technology, and writing, 155ff.; effect on art forms, 277ff.

Television, 153

Tensions, verbalization of, 64f.

Textbooks, appropriateness to grade level, 85

Tobriand Islands, 102
True Romances, 165f.
Tweed Ring, 104

Understanding, *see* Misunderstanding; variations in, 79ff.
Understatement vs. boasting, 214f.
Unionization, effect of, 151
United States, attitude toward propaganda in, 19ff.; doctrines recognized in, 44; effects of mass communication, 96ff.; taste in art, 119ff.; radio audience in, 177ff.; parent-child relationship contrasted with British, 213ff.; American attitude toward inferiority, 224f.; wealth and income distribution, 246
—— Bureau of Indian Affairs, 233f.
—— Department of Agriculture, 234
—— Congress: Communications Act (1943), 182f.; Senate: 178f.; Temporary National Economic Committee, 246
USSR, 44, 107; use of mass propaganda, 116; "real production," 246

Validity, as a criterion for communication, 28ff.
Values, as symbols, 20, 43ff.; deficiencies of, in pre-scientific orientation, 68ff.; social and moral, 243ff.; distribution, 245f.; fostered by attention-functions, 251f.
Van Gogh, 123
Verbal output, restricted, 54ff.
Vocabulary, deficiency, 65f.; difficulty of, and misunderstanding, 86; tests of word knowledge, 88f.; *see also* Words

Voice defects, 58ff.

War, propaganda and, 210, 250; doctrinal symbols and, 259f.
War Savings campaign, 158
Warner, W. Lloyd, and Paul S. Lunt, "The Social Life of a Modern Community," 245n
Washington *Star,* 227
Wheeler, Burton, quoted, 227
Whyte, W. F., ed., *Industry and Society,* 233n
Winchell, Walter, 13
Word magic, reliance of business upon, 145f.
Words, communication by, 27f.; as symbols, misuse of, 47; faulty usage, 61; cultural reactions to, 71; tests of frequency of occurrence, 91f.; misunderstanding of, 150f.; choice of suitable, 160ff.; difficulty of, and usefulness, 165; implications of, in Anglo-American relationships, 227f.; doctrinal key words, 250; slogans, 258; as political symbols, 265ff.; *see also* Vocabulary
Workers, and management, relations, 252ff.
Writing, technology of, 155ff.; characteristics of good, 159; and readability, 165; identification of experiences, 160f.; a personal communication of the writer, 174f.

Yale Review, 165f.
Yale University Law School, 234
"Yankeetown," 245f.